The Gospel According to Matthew

VOLUME IV

The Gospel
According to Matthew

VOLUME IV
(Chapters 16—20)

by
Oliver B. Greene

The Gospel Hour, Inc., Oliver B. Greene, Director
Box 2024, Greenville, South Carolina 29602

Foreword

As we continue in our verse-by-verse study
of *The Gospel According to Matthew,* we will
cover chapters 16 through 20 in this volume. It
is in chapter 16 that Peter makes his bold confession of Jesus as "the Christ, the Son of the
living God," and the promise of the New Testament Church is given (vv. 16,18). In chapter 17
we encounter the scene of the Transfiguration.
Chapter 18 deals with the absolute necessity for
service and humility in the Christian life. In
chapter 19 our Lord ends His ministry in Galilee
and returns to Judaea, thus beginning His journey
back to Jerusalem—His last visit to His beloved
Holy City. In chapter 20, as He nears the city
and the time of His subsequent sacrifice of Himself
at Calvary, He consistently and lovingly teaches
His disciples of His approaching death and resurrection, preparing them for the event of His crucifixion as well as for the carrying on of His work
after His resurrection and ascension. Some of
the most beautiful and instructive parables of the

earthly ministry of our Lord Jesus Christ are found in the five chapters herein contained. To God be the glory for whatever this study accomplishes for Him.

—The Author

Contents

Chapter XVI

1. The Pharisees also with the Sadducees came, and tempting desired him that he would shew them a sign from heaven.

2. He answered and said unto them, When it is evening, ye say, It will be fair weather: for the sky is red.

3. And in the morning, It will be foul weather to day: for the sky is red and lowring. O ye hypocrites, ye can discern the face of the sky; but can ye not discern the signs of the times?

4. A wicked and adulterous generation seeketh after a sign; and there shall no sign be given unto it, but the sign of the prophet Jonas. And he left them, and departed.

5. And when his disciples were come to the other side, they had forgotten to take bread.

6. Then Jesus said unto them, Take heed and beware of the leaven of the Pharisees and of the Sadducees.

7. And they reasoned among themselves, saying, It is because we have taken no bread.

8. Which when Jesus perceived, he said unto them, O ye of little faith, why reason ye among yourselves, because ye have brought no bread?

9. Do ye not yet understand, neither remember the five loaves of the five thousand, and how many baskets ye took up?

1

10. Neither the seven loaves of the four thousand, and how many baskets ye took up?

11. How is it that ye do not understand that I spake it not to you concerning bread, that ye should beware of the leaven of the Pharisees and of the Sadducees?

12. Then understood they how that he bade them not beware of the leaven of bread, but of the doctrine of the Pharisees and of the Sadducees.

13. When Jesus came into the coasts of Caesarea Philippi, he asked his disciples, saying, Whom do men say that I the Son of man am?

14. And they said, Some say that thou art John the Baptist: some, Elias; and others, Jeremias, or one of the prophets.

15. He saith unto them, But whom say ye that I am?

16. And Simon Peter answered and said, Thou art the Christ, the Son of the living God.

17. And Jesus answered and said unto him, Blessed art thou, Simon Bar-jona: for flesh and blood hath not revealed it unto thee, but my Father which is in heaven.

18. And I say also unto thee, That thou art Peter, and upon this rock I will build my church; and the gates of hell shall not prevail against it.

19. And I will give unto thee the keys of the kingdom of heaven: and whatsoever thou shalt bind on earth shall be bound in heaven: and whatsoever thou shalt loose on earth shall be loosed in heaven.

20. Then charged he his disciples that they should tell no man that he was Jesus the Christ.

21. From that time forth began Jesus to shew unto his disciples, how that he must go unto Jerusalem, and suffer many things of the elders and chief priests and scribes, and be killed, and be raised again the third day.

22. Then Peter took him, and began to rebuke him, saying, Be it far from thee, Lord: this shall not be unto thee.

23. But he turned, and said unto Peter, Get thee behind me, Satan: thou art an offence unto me: for thou savourest not the things that be of God, but those that be of men.

24. Then said Jesus unto his disciples, If any man will come after me, let him deny himself, and take up his cross, and follow me.

25. For whosoever will save his life shall lose it: and whosoever will lose his life for my sake shall find it.

26. For what is a man profited, if he shall gain the whole world, and lose his own soul? or what shall a man give in exchange for his soul?

27. For the Son of man shall come in the glory of his Father with his angels; and then he shall reward every man according to his works.

28. Verily I say unto you, There be some standing here, which shall not taste of death, till they see the Son of man coming in his kingdom.

Jesus Rebukes the Pharisees and Sadducees for Their Spiritual Blindness

Verse 1: *"The Pharisees also with the Sadducees came, and tempting desired Him that He would shew them a sign from heaven."*

Jesus had wonderfully manifested the power of God among the people in the healing and the feeding of the great multitudes, but in spite of this the Pharisees and Sadducees appeared again in the presence of Jesus—not to *worship* Him, but to *tempt* Him by asking for a sign from heaven.

The Pharisees were the strictest sect among the Jews. Today, concerning rules, regulations,

3

dogmas, and traditions, they would be called "religious fanatics." They were ritualists, holding not only to the *letter* of the law, but also enforcing the traditional teachings of their forefathers. Jesus had severely censured the Pharisees as hypocrites and violators of God's Word and as blind guides of the people (Matt. 15:3-14).

The *scribes* were in accord with the Pharisees in that they were just as religiously ritualistic. They had the care of the written law and spent their time studying it. They also made the transcripts, expounded the law, and explained the law to the people who might encounter difficulties concerning legalities. The scribes also kept the records and on occasion they were referred to as "lawyers."

However, the *Sadducees* were just the opposite of the Pharisees, and the two groups hated each other. The Sadducees denied the supernatural, the spirit-world, and the resurrection from the dead. They are mentioned only once prior to this in the Gospel of Matthew. In Matthew 3:7 we are told that the Pharisees and Sadducees came to the baptism of John the Baptist; but John, being led and controlled by the Holy Spirit, recognized their hypocrisy and greeted them as a "generation of vipers."

In this first verse of chapter 16 we find the Pharisees and Sadducees temporarily united by common hostility to the Lord. Enemies often unite if their unity can destroy a common foe. Luke 23:12 tells us that Pilate and Herod, although "at enmity between themselves," joined forces in a common effort to condemn Jesus. So did the Pharisees and Sadducees agree *on one thing*— opposing Jesus.

True, these two religious groups hated each other royally, but they both possessed *a satanic hatred* for *Jesus.* His words had completely uncovered and laid bare the hypocrisy of the Pharisees. His deeds and mighty miracles had exposed the error of the Sadducees who denied the resurrection and the spirit-world. Therefore, while the Pharisees and Sadducees could not agree in doctrine and practice, they were in perfect harmony and accord concerning the rejection and destruction of the Lord Jesus Christ.

There are many today in the professing sphere of Christendom who have the same spirit as that of the Pharisees and Sadducees, "having a form of godliness, but denying the power thereof" (II Tim. 3:5). Sadduceeism typifies the liberal movement of our day—the new theology which puts super-naturalism out of the way. Today the "higher critics" deny the inspiration of the Bible, the virgin birth and the bodily resurrection of Christ.

Liberals first denied the *written* Word of God and brought about many new translations of the Scriptures. With the passing of time they became bolder and bolder until they now deny *the very existence* of the virgin-born Son of God — *the Word Incarnate:*

"*In the beginning was the Word,* and the Word was with God, and *the Word was God. . . .* And *the Word was made flesh, and dwelt among us,* (and we beheld His glory, the glory as of the only begotten of the Father,) full of grace and truth. . . . No man hath seen God at any time; the only begotten Son, which is in the bosom of the Father, He hath declared Him" (John 1:1, 14, 18).

In this present day there are opposing forces which have united in an effort to destroy the Person and the work of the Lord Jesus Christ. Religious movements which a few years ago fought each other are now uniting, and the day is not too far distant when there will be *ONE world church.* That church is now in the making, but the Rapture will occur before it becomes a reality in the fullest sense. The world church will be the most ritualistic and liberal union of religions ever to exist upon the face of this earth. It will include Protestant, Roman Catholic, and Jewish religions and will be founded upon the doctrine of "the Fatherhood of God and the brotherhood of man." This union will by-pass the cross of Christ and His blood atonement, and through education and reform it will bring men into the false kingdom of Satan.

The world church is definitely developing very rapidly throughout Christendom and will continue to grow as the end of this age approaches. We have various organizations, such as the National Council of the Churches of Christ and the World Council of Churches, and these organizations are meeting with their enemies of a few years ago and ironing out their differences. This ecclesiastical union will base its doctrines on the denial of the virgin birth, denial of the blood atonement, and denial of Christ's bodily resurrection, thereby ushering in the devil's "millennium." Immediately following the Rapture of the Church, the Antichrist will appear as a world leader, and will make promises that will bring in a great Utopia for a season, after which this earth will become a literal hell.

Concerning the second coming of Christ, Luke 18:8 asks, ". . . when the Son of man cometh, shall He find faith on the earth?" The reference here is not to individual or personal faith, but to general belief in the whole body of fundamental revealed truth. According to God's Word, *"As it was in the days of Noe (Noah),"* so shall it be in the days when the Son of man returns (Luke 17:26). Only eight people were saved in the hour when God destroyed the whole earth with a flood. "Likewise also as it was in the days of Lot . . ." (Luke 17:28). Only four people escaped from Sodom, and one of those four was turned into a pillar of salt! In II Timothy 3:13 Paul tells us that "evil men and seducers shall wax worse and worse, deceiving,

7

and being deceived"—and all of this will be in the name of "religion."

No person on earth desires peace any more than I do. I wish it were possible for every soldier to lay down his gun and go home to his loved ones. I wish it were possible that not another gun would ever be fired in battle to kill men. But as long as the devil is unchained and out of the pit there will be "wars and rumours of wars," and "when they shall say, Peace and safety; then sudden destruction cometh upon them, as travail upon a woman with child; and they shall not escape" (I Thess. 5:3).

There may be many sincere people in the peace movements of this hour, but they are fighting a losing battle. *Fanatical* peace movements are energized by Satan, for he knows if he can get people to believe in a counterfeit peace, then his program can be carried out much more easily. World peace will never come until Jesus, *the Prince of Peace,* sits on the throne of David in Jerusalem, and the knowledge of the Lord covers this earth as the waters now cover the sea (Isa. 11:9). Then— and only then—will men beat their swords into plowshares, their spears into pruning hooks, and study war no more (Isa. 2:4). Real and lasting peace will never occur *until Jesus comes to reign on earth.*

In our study here in Matthew chapter 16, the Pharisees and Sadducees came to Jesus, tempting

Him (or testing Him, hoping He would not be able to stand the test), asking Him to *"shew them a sign from heaven."* In Matthew 12:38 the Pharisees and scribes came to Jesus and asked to see a sign *from HIM:*

"Then certain of the scribes and of the Pharisees answered, saying, Master, we would see *a sign from THEE."* These religious rulers did not want just an *ordinary* sign. They wanted a *super* sign from heaven. Jesus had already performed many signs among these people, and *Jesus Himself* (God manifested in flesh) *was the GREATEST sign of all!* These ignorant and sinful men desired a "sign," when they were standing in the presence of Almighty God in flesh.

Suppose Jesus, very God in flesh, had exercised His power. Suppose He had uttered a word, opened the heavens and laid open to the vision of these men the unspeakable glory of the Father's throne and the angels. Would these deliberately stubborn religionists then have believed in their hearts that Jesus was truly the Son of God?

When the rich man of Luke 16:19-31 died and opened his eyes in hell, he begged, "Father Abraham, have mercy on me, and send Lazarus, that he may dip the tip of his finger in water and cool my tongue; for I am tormented in this flame." When he found that this was impossible, he then asked Abraham, "I pray thee therefore, father, that thou wouldest send him to my father's house:

9

for I have five brethren; that he may testify unto them, lest they also come into this place of torment." But Abraham answered him, "They have Moses and the prophets; let them hear them." The rich man replied, "Nay, father Abraham: but if one went unto them from the dead, they will repent." Then Abraham said, "If they hear not Moses and the prophets, *neither will they be persuaded, though one rose from the dead.*"

Jesus knew that these people who challenged Him would not believe, even if He *showed* them a great sign from heaven; therefore, He did not grant their request. Our Lord does not waste His power on men who are so completely energized by the devil that they have a closed mind. A person must *think* right about the Word of God before God can do business with him; for to deny the supernatural is to close the door in God's face, and there is no way for God to reveal Himself to a person guilty of such denial.

God makes Himself known through His Word. Jesus had spoken many wonderful words of life and had performed many outstanding miracles; but up to this point the religious leaders had not believed on Him and He knew they *would not* believe, regardless of anything He might do in an effort to impress them. If He had granted a sign from heaven, no doubt the Pharisees would have blasphemed and the Sadducees would have mocked.

The Pharisees and Sadducees said they wanted

a sign out of heaven. Atheists and infidels still demand a sign out of heaven. But Jesus did not come into this world to satisfy the requests of those who were children of the devil and hardened in their hearts. He came "to seek and to save" the lost (Luke 19:10); He came "to give His life a ransom for many" (Matt. 20:28).

Today, in some pulpits, there are men who have this same spirit of unbelief. I read in a published sermon not long ago where one minister said that when Elijah met the prophets of Baal on Mount Carmel and called down fire from heaven (I Kings 18:17-38), what really happened was that a stroke of lightning came down from heaven and licked up the sacrifice. The miracle of the crossing of the Red Sea, as recorded in Exodus 14:13-22, is explained away by saying that there was nothing supernatural about the parting of the waters, but that it was only a natural phenomenon.

Those who explain away the miracles of Jesus will one day stand before God, and their judgment will be much more severe than the judgment meted out to poor heathen people who live in the jungles and have never heard the name of Jesus Christ!

Verses 2 and 3: *"He answered and said unto them, When it is evening, ye say, It will be fair weather: for the sky is red. And in the morning, It will be foul weather to day: for the sky is red*

11

and lowring. O ye hypocrites, ye can discern the face of the sky; but can ye not discern the signs of the times?"

The Jews in general have always closely observed the signs of nature. Concerning the Jewish people, history gives this interesting note:

"In the going out of the last day of the feast of tabernacles, all observed the rising of the smoke. If the smoke bended northward, the poor rejoiced but the rich were troubled because there would be much rain the following year and the fruits would be corrupted; if it bended southward, the poor grieved and the rich rejoiced, for there would be fewer rains that year, and the fruit would be sound; if eastward, all rejoiced; if westward, all were troubled."

The religionists who came to Jesus seeking a sign from heaven could look at the sky and determine what kind of weather to expect. Therefore Jesus called them *"hypocrites"* because they could discern the signs of nature, but not the spiritual signs all around them. They could see the red sky—and interpret its meaning; but they could not see a blind man whose eyes were opened, or a multitude of hungry people fed, or a leper who was cleansed from his leprosy, *and realize that God in flesh was in the very midst of them.*

The Jews watched very closely the changes in nature, but the *"signs of the times"* they did not discern. If they had not been spiritually blind, they would have known that a great change of spiritual seasons had occurred—a much greater change than the change in nature from morning until evening. If they had not been spiritually blind, they would have seen in the miracles of Jesus that He was not just a man, nor was He just an extraordinary teacher. They would have seen that He was "that Prophet" spoken of by Moses (John 6:14; Deut. 18:15-19). If they had not been spiritually blind, they would have seen the evidence pointing to the fast approaching judgment that was about to fall upon them.

But they closed their eyes to the evidence all around them, evidence that should have plainly told them that Jesus was God in flesh. They were apostate even though they knew that their fathers had suffered when they rejected Jehovah and followed God's enemies instead. The people were blinded by the god of this age and their hearts and minds were closed to the evidence to be seen all around them in the miracles of Jesus and the words that He spoke. They were walking in their fathers' footsteps. Their Messiah had come, but they refused to recognize and receive Him.

What about this day and hour in which we live? Is Christendom any less blind than those who challenged Jesus? I know there are many genuine believers and God-fearing ministers today. There are many local churches that are doing a real job of spreading the Gospel and winning souls; but

Christendom *as a whole* is just as blinded by the devil as were those poor Jews two thousand years ago.

Make a survey of the outstanding schools of theology in America today. Find out what the preachers of tomorrow are studying. You will find that they study the records of the past—tradition, church history, antiquity, and many other such things. But they close their eyes to the signs of the times as related to the Scripture they are supposed to be studying. The vast majority of the ministers who come off the "assembly line" of religion today are liberals who deny the literal appearing of Jesus in the clouds in the air, the Rapture of the Church, and other wonderful scriptural truths. They refuse to see that "evil men and seducers" are waxing worse and worse. Such ministers possess a strange, unscriptural, satanically inspired optimism; and because of this, Christendom willfully closes its eyes to the signs of the approaching judgment of God upon this earth. Like the religious leaders in the days when Christ walked among men, these liberal ministers refuse to discern the signs of the times. Their spiritual blindness is as great as the blindness of the Pharisees and Sadducees—perhaps even greater.

But thanks be unto God, not all are willfully ignorant and spiritually blind. There are many ministers who see the approaching storm of judgment, and they faithfully sound the warning. They

14

also see the glorious Rapture of the Church and the return of Jesus to earth at the appointed hour in the fullness of time, to bring peace on earth. You may rest assured that as long as Jesus tarries and the true Church is here on earth, true born again believers and true ministers will be here, preaching and teaching these fundamental truths concerning the Rapture, the Millennium, and that glorious, eternal age of peace and prosperity without the presence of sin and the devil.

We are well aware that the majority of churches today are liberal, denying the signs of the times and the power of God; but we can thank God for the minority who are true to the cardinal truths of Christianity and the fundamentals of the faith.

Verse 4: *"A wicked and adulterous generation seeketh after a sign; and there shall no sign be given unto it, but the sign of the prophet Jonas. And He left them, and departed."*

Notice the cutting words Jesus used to describe the "sign-seekers": "A *WICKED* and *ADULTER-OUS* generation seeketh after a sign." This tells us why the Pharisees and the Sadducees could not discern the signs of the times. In the spiritual sense they were "wicked and adulterous," unfaithful to God and to His covenant.

A word to sign-seekers *today:* If you refuse to believe God, if you refuse to accept His Word by faith, just remember that this is the Dispensation of Grace and Hebrews 11:6 declares, ". . . *without FAITH* it is impossible to please (God)." His Word declares:

We are *saved* by grace through FAITH (Eph. 2:8).

"The just shall *live* by faith" (Rom. 1:17).

And *"whatsoever is NOT OF FAITH is SIN"* (Rom. 14:23).

"A wicked and adulterous generation . . . *there shall no sign be given it."* These cutting words of Jesus were directed to the Pharisees and Sadducees, but they also apply to those who demand a sign today, those who must *"see* something" or *"feel* something" before they will believe God. According to Jesus, such people are not righteous. They are wicked. Romans 4:3 tells us, ". . . *ABRAHAM believed God, and it was counted unto him for RIGHTEOUSNESS."* Abraham did not ask for "signs" or "feelings." God spoke, *and Abraham BELIEVED* simply because God is God. In Hebrews 11:1 we read this definition of faith: "Now faith is *the substance* of things hoped for, *the evidence* of things not seen."

So Jesus declared of the unbelieving, wicked and adulterous generation, *". . . there shall no sign be given unto it—but THE SIGN OF THE PROPHET JONAS."* The Prophet Jonah was a type of the Lord Jesus Christ in His death, burial, and resurrection. In Matthew 12:40 Jesus explained, "For as Jonas was three days and three nights in the whale's belly, *so shall the Son of man be three days and three nights in the heart of the earth."*

Jonah spent three days and three nights in the belly of the whale, and then he was cast out upon the shore. This presents a picture of the death, burial, and resurrection of Jesus. Many hours have been spent in discussing whether or not Jonah died in the belly of the whale. Personally, I believe that he *did* die, but it really does not matter whether he died or remained alive. In either case, it was a tremendous miracle.

From our Lord's reply to those men, pointing them to "the sign of the prophet Jonas," it is evident that they were familiar with the Old Testament Scriptures and the account of Jonah and the whale. Therefore His meaning should have been clear to them.

"And He left them and departed." You will notice again that Jesus does not waste words on those who have closed their eyes and sealed the door of their hearts against Him. His words here are significant, and His action is symbolic. In other words, the Jewish leaders had definitely *rejected Him,* and He turned and walked *away from them.*

Verse 5: *"And when His disciples were come to the other side, they had forgotten to take bread."*

In this verse, and those that follow, we see the unbelief and slowness of heart of the disciples who walked and talked with Jesus day by day. They saw His miracles, they heard His wonderful words of power and life—yet they were slow to believe. They had witnessed the feeding of the five thousand (Matt. 14:15-21). They were present at the feeding of the four thousand (Matt. 15:32-38). But in spite of having witnessed those great miracles they are here disturbed because they had forgotten to take along bread. Mark 8:14 tells us, "... neither had they in the ship ... more than *one loaf.*"

Jesus Interprets the Symbol of Leaven— A Type of Evil

Verse 6: *"Then Jesus said unto them, Take heed and beware of the leaven of the Pharisees and of the Sadducees."*

This warning was given soon after Jesus declared that the sign-seeking religionists were "a wicked and adulterous generation" (v. 4). He had turned His back on them and left them alone. The disciples then joined Him, and it was not by accident or chance that Jesus gave them the warning we find here in verse 6.

The disciples had been reared to respect the religious leaders. They had been taught many of the practices in the ritualism of their religious rulers. Therefore it is significant that Jesus took this opportunity to issue a warning against the doctrine and influence of the Pharisees and Sadducees. It is also significant that He sounded this warning just before He unfolded the truth concerning the Church which was to be built (v. 18), the Church of which He would be the head (Eph. 1:22, 23; Col. 1:18) and the foundation (I Cor. 3:11).

"Take heed and beware of the leaven of the Pharisees and of the Sadducees." At no time has this warning been so needed as in these very days in which we live. The "leaven" of the Pharisees, Sadducees, and scribes is certainly working today. God help us to beware of the damaging, pernicious work of that leaven. We must be extremely careful which church and minister we support with our presence, our prayers, and our gifts. We must be alert and discerning concerning what we listen to and what we read. The modern Pharisees are working overtime to corrupt and destroy true Christianity—but thanks be unto God, the gates of hell cannot prevail against the Church of the Lord God Almighty (Matt. 16:18).

Verse 7: *"And they reasoned among themselves, saying, It is because we have taken no bread."*

Does it not seem strange that the disciples would immediately begin to talk and to reason "among themselves" about the statement Jesus had just made? They had listened to every word He had said to the Pharisees and Sadducees. They had heard Him call them hypocrites, wicked and adulterous, and earlier they had heard Him give

19

the parable of the leaven (Matt. 13:33). Yet they were astonished when Jesus said to them, *"BE-WARE of the leaven* of the Pharisees and of the Sadducees,"* and they began to converse among themselves in an effort to figure out what He meant.

"It is because we have taken no bread." This not only implies a lack of spiritual insight on the part of the disciples; it also shows lack of faith and failure to trust in the Lord Jesus Christ.

Verse 8: *"Which when Jesus perceived, He said unto them, O ye of little faith, why reason ye among yourselves, because ye have brought no bread?"*

"O ye of little faith!" This mild rebuke from Jesus should have humbled the hearts of the disciples and moved them to recognition of, and sincere repentance for, their unbelief. To the Syrophenician woman, a heathen, a Gentile (a "dog" in the eyes of the Jews), Jesus had said, *"O woman, GREAT IS THY FAITH:* be it unto thee even as thou wilt."* (Read Matthew 15:21-28.) Yet these elect ones, chosen of God to walk and talk with the Lord Jesus Christ in His earthly ministry, must be rebuked by Him because of their *"LITTLE faith."*

". . . why reason ye among yourselves, because ye have brought no bread?" It is clear that the disciples did not understand what Jesus meant

when He warned them, "Beware of the leaven of the Pharisees and of the Sadducees." They took His words literally, supposing He had observed their lack of bread and was warning them not to *buy* bread made with the leaven used by the Pharisees and the Sadducees. Their unbelief and lack of understanding was displayed by their reasoning among themselves concerning the warning Jesus had given them. Instead of being concerned with their Messiah and spiritual things, they were concerned about food for their next *physical* meal!

Verse 9: *"Do ye not yet understand, neither remember the five loaves of the five thousand, and how many baskets ye took up?"*

"Do ye not yet UNDERSTAND, neither REMEMBER?" Could they have forgotten so soon? Only a short time before, Jesus had taken a little boy's lunch—five loaves and two fishes (Matt. 14:15-21)—and from that meager supply had fed five thousand hungry men (not counting women and children). Did the disciples not remember that the "leftovers" from that meal had filled twelve baskets? They had evidently forgotten both the *miracle* and the *lesson* the miracle had taught of the all-sufficiency of Christ, the Bread of Life. They thought He was concerning Himself about *KINDS of bread.*

Verse 10: *"Neither the seven loaves of the four thousand, and how many baskets ye took up?"*

"Neither the seven loaves of the four thousand . . . ?" Twice these disciples had seen Jesus feed the multitudes from whatever small number of loaves and fishes were at His command, with several baskets full of scraps left over after the thousands of hungry people were completely satisfied. But now they were concerned about food for just a handful of men! They were in the presence of the same Teacher, the same Lord who had fed five thousand men, not counting women and children, and who, on another occasion, had fed four thousand just as effectively, and they were fretting about their own temporal needs.

Verse 11: *"How is it that ye do not understand that I spake it not to you concerning bread, that ye should beware of the leaven of the Pharisees and of the Sadducees?"*

We might note here that in Mark's account of this incident, we find an even stronger rebuke of the unbelief of the disciples. In Mark 8:16-18 we read: "And they reasoned among themselves, saying, It is because we have no bread. And when Jesus knew it, He saith unto them, *Why reason ye, because ye have no bread? Perceive ye not yet, neither understand? Have ye your heart yet hardened? Having eyes, see ye not? and having ears, hear ye not? and do ye not remember?"*

"How is it that ye do not understand . . . ?" It is not unreasonable that the Lord was here express-

ing surprise, amazement, or even disappointment. Was it possible that these men had not seen beyond the *physical* satisfaction of the loaves and fishes, recognizing the lesson taught through the miracles and the *Power* that *produced* the miracles? Certainly He was omniscient and He knew the hearts of these men as He knows the hearts of all men (John 2:24, 25); but we must remember that He was also human, and *as man* He felt as we feel when we are disappointed or amazed.

"*. . . I spake it not to you concerning BREAD, that ye should beware of the leaven of the Pharisees and of the Sadducees.*" So Jesus told the disciples in plain words that He was not talking about the actual leaven in physical bread, but that He was speaking of the *doctrine* of the Pharisees and the Sadducees, the false and hypocritical teachings which the devil would use to lure true Christians into the religion practiced by the Jewish leaders.

Verse 12: "*Then understood they how that He bade them not beware of the leaven of bread, but of the doctrine of the Pharisees and of the Sadducees.*"

"*Then UNDERSTOOD they . . . .*" Jesus explained that the "leaven" of which He spoke typified the doctrine of the Pharisees and the Sadducees. Then the disciples understood that He was warning them against those religionists who were following tradition and dogma instead of concentrating on the words of the prophets in the Old Testament Scriptures. The Pharisees and Sadducees were teaching ideas concerning religious truth, Deity in general, and *in particular* concerning the Messianic reign. Such teaching as they were expounding was misleading and would have a corrupting influence on the disciples.

It is true that the Jews were looking for and *expecting* their Messiah, but they expected Him to be conformed to their own mistaken ideas of what kind of person He would be. They were looking for a powerful ruler who would outlaw Roman rule and deliver the Jews from slavery under Rome. They were not willing to accept the humble Nazarene as the Messiah promised them in the Old Testament. In spite of prophecies in the Old Testament concerning and describing Jesus, the religious rulers simply could not—or would not—believe that this Man of humble birth and compassionate manner was the One for whom they waited, and that He would deliver them *from the slavery of SIN*—spiritual slavery. Therefore this warning against the hypocritical religion of the Pharisees and Sadducees was in preparation for the great, approaching instruction about our Lord's true mission, as set forth in verses 18 through 21 of this chapter.

Peter's Great Confession

The remaining verses of this chapter constitute

one of the most important sections of the Gospel of Matthew. Herein we find revealed some of the most vital and solemn doctrines of Christianity. I approach these verses with fear and trembling. I feel as though I should remove the shoes from my feet for I realize that I stand on holy ground. My prayer is that God will give me the wisdom to rightly divide this extremely important section of the Word of God and make plain the doctrines here revealed.

I think we should note in passing that while Mark 8:27-30, Luke 9:18-21, and John 6:68, 69 all record Peter's confession that Jesus was indeed the Son of God, *Matthew* is the only Gospel writer who records the Lord's *full answer* to that confession, including the revelation that He would build a Church. In the account given in Mark and Luke there is no mention of the Church. In the Gospel of John we read, "Then Simon Peter answered Him, Lord, to whom shall we go? Thou hast the words of eternal life. *And we believe and are sure that THOU ART THAT CHRIST, THE SON OF THE LIVING GOD"* (John 6:68, 69). But again, there is no mention of the Church. Only Matthew records that promise.

Verse 13: *"When Jesus came into the coasts of Caesarea Philippi, He asked His disciples, saying, Whom do men say that I the Son of man am?"*

"When Jesus came into the coasts of Caesarea

25

Philippi . . . ." To me, it is extremely significant that this episode took place in Caesarea Philippi — *Gentile* territory. It seems to bear out the Scripture in John 1:11: "He came unto His own, *and His own RECEIVED HIM NOT.*" Yes, Jesus came to the Jews, but when they rejected Him He invited *any man — ALL men —* to come and drink of the water of life (John 7:37, 38). Here in a Gentile country, Jesus announced the future Church which would be made up of all who believe — Jew, Gentile, rich, poor, learned, unlearned, bond or free.

At the first great Church council held in Jerusalem, James made this announcement:

"Men and brethren, hearken unto me: Simeon hath declared how God at the first did visit *the GENTILES, to take out of them a people for His name.* And to this agree the words of the prophets; as it is written, After this I will return, and will build again the tabernacle of David, which is fallen down; and I will build again the ruins thereof, and I will set it up: *that the residue of men might seek after the Lord, and all the Gentiles, upon whom my name is called, saith the Lord, who doeth all these things.* Known unto God are all His works from the beginning of the world" (Acts 15:13-18).

Dispensationally this is the most important passage in the New Testament because it clearly gives *the Divine purpose* for this age — and for the beginning of the next. We will discuss this later when we study the Church in greater depth.

". . . He asked His disciples, saying, Whom do men say that I the Son of man am?" Jesus did not ask this question for His own information. He knew what men were saying and thinking about Him. Nor do I believe that His question included the proud, hypocritical, adulterous Pharisees. It is my belief that He was referring to the multitude who followed Him day by day, listening to His words and seeing His mighty miracles. (At a later time, Jesus did ask the Pharisees a similar question: *"What think ye of Christ? WHOSE SON IS HE?"* —Matt. 22:42.)

Notice that Jesus here referred to Himself as *"the Son of man,"* a title which He used of Himself about eighty times in His earthly ministry as recorded in Scripture. This was His racial name *as the representative MAN* in the sense it is used in I Corinthians 15:45-47. ("The Son of David" was His Jewish name. "The Son of God" was His divine name.) Jesus used the name "Son of man," implying that His mission on earth transcended in scope and result all merely Jewish limitations. (Please study Matthew 11:19; 12:40; 20:18; 24:37-44; and Luke 12:40; 19:10.)

When Nathanael confessed Jesus as "King of Israel," Jesus replied, ". . . Thou shalt see greater things . . . ye shall see heaven open, and the angels of God ascending and descending *upon THE SON OF MAN"* (John 1:47-51).

When Christ's messengers were cast out by the Jews, the thoughts of Jesus went forward to the time when the Son of man shall come—not to Israel only, but to the entire human race. (Please study Matthew 10:5, 6, 23.)

It is in the name *"Son of man"* that universal judgment is committed unto Jesus. (Study John 5:22-27.)

"Son of man" is also a name indicating that in Him is fulfilled the Old Testament prophecies concerning blessing *through a coming MAN* who would be the seed of woman. (Please study Genesis 1:26; 3:15; 12:3; Psalms 8:4; 80:17; Isaiah 7:14; 9:6, 7; chapter 11; 32:2; Zechariah 13:7.)

Verse 14: *"And they said, Some say that thou art John the Baptist; some, Elias; and others, Jeremias, or one of the prophets."*

The answer the disciples gave Jesus echoed the different voices in Israel and proved only too well that they did not recognize their Messiah. To them He was John the Baptist risen from the dead —or Elijah, Jeremiah, Zechariah, or one of the other prophets. They were not sure. They had mixed feelings about His identity. But while the people did not agree on who Jesus was, most of them recognized that He was not just an ordinary teacher or preacher.

Israel was God's elect nation, God's earthly people, but their unbelief which became more and more evident pointed to the setting aside of that nation for a time. We see this in the words of Jesus in Matthew 23:37-39:

"O Jerusalem, Jerusalem, thou that killest the prophets, and stonest them which are sent unto thee, how often would I have gathered thy children together, even as a hen gathereth her chickens under her wings, and ye would not! Behold, your house is left unto you desolate. For I say unto you, Ye shall not see me henceforth, till ye shall say, Blessed is He that cometh in the name of the Lord."

We see the same unbelief as the end of this Church Age approaches. There is an ever increasing denial of the deity of Jesus Christ and the verbal inspiration of the Bible. The sad thing is that these denials come from that which claims the name of Christ—*Christendom*. In II Corinthians 11:13-15 Paul warned against such false teaching. He declared:

"For such are *false apostles*, deceitful workers, transforming themselves into the apostles of Christ. And no marvel; for Satan himself is transformed into an angel of light. Therefore it is no great thing if his ministers also be transformed as the ministers of righteousness; whose end shall be according to their works."

Peter also tells us that many will be led astray by these false prophets:

"There were false prophets also among the

people, *even as there shall be false teachers among you, who privily shall bring in damnable heresies, even DENYING the Lord that bought them* and bring upon themselves swift destruction. *And many shall follow their pernicious ways;* by reason of whom the way of truth shall be evil spoken of. And through covetousness shall they with feigned words make merchandise of you: whose judgment now of a long time lingereth not, and their damnation slumbereth not" (II Pet. 2:1-3).

Paul instructed Timothy, *"Preach the WORD;* be instant in season, out of season; reprove, rebuke, exhort with all longsuffering and doctrine. *For the time will come when they will not endure sound doctrine;* but after their own lusts shall they heap to themselves teachers, having itching ears; *and they shall turn away their ears from the truth,* and shall be turned unto fables" (II Tim. 4:2-4).

Verses 15 and 16: *"He saith unto them, But whom say ye that I am? And Simon Peter answered and said, Thou art the Christ, the Son of the living God."*

". . . Simon Peter answered . . . ." The question was addressed to *all* of the disciples; but here, as on many other occasions, Peter was spokesman for the group. Not only was he the representative of the *disciples,* but in this case he was also *the mouthpiece of Almighty God* as he revealed this great truth concerning the Christ.

". . . Thou art THE CHRIST, the Son of the living God." This confession from Peter included much more than the prophetic statements recorded in the Old Testament Scriptures concerning the deity of the Messiah. It was not merely a confession of faith in the *fulfillment* of those prophecies concerning the Person of the Messiah. Peter's confession announced his *personal faith in Christ,* the Son of the living God. Even though Peter did not comprehend the Lord's crucifixion and resurrection at that time, *by faith* he accepted Jesus as his Messiah and Saviour. God the Father had revealed to Peter the truth that in Jesus was eternal life, and Peter confessed what had been revealed to his heart.

But the confession went *beyond Calvary and the grave* and declared the resurrection of the Son of God, even though at that time Peter did not grasp the full meaning of the words he spoke. When we confess Jesus as the Son of the living God, we confess Him *in ALL that He accomplished,* even though we may not fully understand it. The just (the born again) live *by FAITH,* not by understanding.

In John 5:25, 26 Jesus declared, "Verily, verily, I say unto you, The hour is coming, and now is, when the dead shall hear the voice of the Son of God: and they that hear shall live. *For as the FATHER hath life in Himself; so hath He given TO THE SON to have life in HIMSELF."*

Later, as revealed in Romans 1:3, 4, God proved that Jesus was His Son, "which was made of the seed of David according to the flesh; *and declared to be the Son of God with power, according to the spirit of holiness, BY THE RESURRECTION FROM THE DEAD.*" It was not possible for death to hold Jesus because He was the Son of the living God.

Peter's confession here includes all upon which personal saving faith in the Son of God rests. When the Holy Spirit spoke to Peter as he penned down the first epistle that bears his name, he wrote of *a LIVING HOPE "by the resurrection of Jesus Christ from the dead"* (I Pet. 1:3).

In his second epistle, Peter assures us that he *personally witnessed* proof that Jesus was truly the Son of God:

"Moreover I will endeavour that ye may be able after my decease to have these things always in remembrance. For we have not followed cunningly devised fables, when we made known unto you the power and coming of our Lord Jesus Christ, *but were EYEWITNESSES of His majesty.* For He received from God the Father honour and glory, when there came such a voice to Him from the excellent glory, *THIS IS MY BELOVED SON, in whom I am well pleased.* And this voice which came from heaven we heard, when we were with Him in the holy mount.

"We have also *a more sure word of prophecy;*

whereunto ye do well that ye take heed, as unto
a light that shineth in a dark place, until the
day dawn, and the day star arise in your hearts:
knowing this first, that *NO PROPHECY of the
Scripture is of any PRIVATE INTERPRETATION.
For the prophecy came not in old time by the will
of MAN: but holy men of God spake as they were
MOVED BY THE HOLY GHOST"* (II Pet. 1:15-21).

The Great Revelation Given to Peter—
The First Mention of the Church

Verse 17: *"And Jesus answered and said unto
him, Blessed art thou, Simon Bar-jona: for flesh
and blood hath not revealed it unto thee, but
my Father which is in heaven."*

"Blessed art thou, Simon Bar-jona." Notice
Jesus announced the *blessedness* of Peter—a blessedness which is given *to each sinner* who believes
in Christ and is saved.   Peter was no different
from all other sinners who have been saved by
grace in this blessedness bestowed by God.
*". . . for flesh and blood hath not revealed it
unto thee, but MY FATHER which is in heaven."*
None but the Father knows the Son (Matt. 11:27).
Peter's confession was not his own insofar as his
mind and spirit were capable of knowing the
truth—that is, his confession was not *of human
origin.*   It was through *the Father's revelation,*
something altogether new.

Verse 18: *"And I say also unto thee, That thou art Peter, and upon this rock I will build my Church; and the gates of hell shall not prevail against it."*

"I SAY also unto thee . . . ." Jesus spoke in His own right by divine authority in making a new revelation concerning His Church.

". . . Thou art Peter, and upon this rock I will build my Church; and the gates of hell shall not prevail against it." The Greek word here translated *"Peter"* is *petros*, meaning *a little stone*. *"Rock"* is from the word *petra* and denotes *a huge rock* or solid foundation. Thus we see that the Church is not built upon *Peter*. It is built upon *Christ the ROCK*.

Here the word *ecclesia* is used for the first time in the Bible. In the Greek, *ecclesia* means *"the called out."* The *true Church* is made up of "called-out ones"—i. e., those who by faith have received Jesus as Saviour and have been translated into the Kingdom of God's dear Son (Col. 1:13). When Jesus announced, *"Upon this rock I will build my Church,"* He indicated what He was going to do with all who, like Peter, exercised faith in Christ. His Church is made up of all who confess with the heart that Jesus is the Son of God.

Since the passage we are now studying contains the word *ecclesia* (church) for the first time in Scripture, and the Church is spoken of as *future*

(Christ said *"I WILL build my Church"*), I see no reason for the confusion which presently exists concerning the birthday of the Church of the living God. When Jesus spoke these words to His disciples, the Church had not yet come into existence.

It is unscriptural to speak of "the *Old Testament* Church." There was no such institution in the Old Testament era. There are many who declare that *Israel* was the Church in the Old Testament era, using as proof the record in Acts 7:38 where we read of *"the church in the wilderness."* However, this term means simply *a congregation,* an *assembly of people* in the wilderness. *Israel was a congregation,* an assembly of called-out people, but that congregation (or assembly) *was not* the New Testament Church of which Christ speaks here in Matthew 16:18.

The confusion existing today in Christendom concerning the Church has been brought about by wrongly dividing the Word of truth. We cannot take the promises God made to His earthly people, Israel, and apply them to the New Testament Church in an attempt to force the fulfillment of those promises in this present Age of Grace. *Israel and the Church are NOT one and the same.*

There are many *types* in the Old Testament which indicate that a Church would be called into existence, and we now *understand* those types, since God has revealed the mystery of the New Testament Church. The Old Testament prophets saw *Christ's FIRST coming* and His glorious *SEC-OND coming;* but they did not see *between* those two advents the Dispensation of the Church, which dispensation has already lasted almost two thousand years.

"... *I will build MY Church* . . . ." In this announcement the emphasis is on the possessive pronoun "MY." Jesus announced that *HE would call out* an assembly of people for Himself. The formation of this assembly began on the Day of Pentecost. (It could not begin until after the completion of the work Jesus came to do. He must suffer, die, rise again from the dead, and be received up into glory. The Holy Spirit came on the Day of Pentecost, and it was on that glorious occasion that the Church was born.)

The Church

Even though the Gospel according to Matthew is "the Kingdom book," I feel that it will be profitable to take time here to look a little deeper into the truths of the New Testament Church, because in this hour the devil is making his last great drive to undermine the fundamentals of the faith and pervert the truth concerning the Church.

As already pointed out, the word "church" comes from the Greek word *ecclesia,* meaning "called out." Doctrinally, the New Testament Church is a body made up of born again believers *called out* by the power of God, called unto faith

36

in the crucified, buried, risen Lord. Through the miracle of the new birth, a person is born of the Spirit, receives the nature of the risen Christ in the inner man, and is indwelt by the Holy Spirit. He becomes a member of the body of Christ. (All believers are made members *one of another* and are united, by the Holy Spirit, to the risen Christ.) Thus we sit together with Christ in heavenly places (Eph. 2:6). We are hid with Christ in God (Col. 3:3). *THIS is the New Testament Church.*

I repeat, the Church did not exist during the Old Testament economy. The Church Age (this Dispensation of Grace) was a mystery "hid in God." Paul clearly states this in Ephesians 3:1-5, 9, 10:

"For this cause I Paul, the prisoner of Jesus Christ for you Gentiles, if ye have heard of the dispensation of the grace of God which is given me to you-ward: how that by revelation He made known unto me *the mystery;* (as I wrote afore in few words, whereby, when ye read, ye may understand my knowledge in the mystery of Christ) *which IN OTHER AGES was not made known unto the sons of men, as it is now revealed unto His holy apostles and prophets by the Spirit....* And to make all men see what is *the fellowship of the MYSTERY, which from the beginning of the world hath been hid in God,* who created all things by Jesus Christ: to the intent that now unto the principalities and powers in heavenly places might be known by the Church the manifold wisdom of God."

The saints of the Old Testament era were not in the Church of which Jesus spoke here in Matthew 16:18. They were *quickened* by the Spirit of God, but they were not united to the risen Man in heaven as believers are today. In the days of the patriarchs, the Christ who died for us and rose again had not yet been manifested.

The Church had no existence while Jesus remained upon the earth. In our present chapter Jesus spoke of the Church as yet future. The mission of Christ was to "the lost sheep of the house of Israel," as plainly spoken by Christ in Matthew 15:24: "He answered and said, I am not sent but *unto the lost sheep of the house of Israel.*"

When Jesus sent His disciples forth, He said to them, "Go not into the way of the Gentiles, and into any city of the Samaritans enter ye not: but go rather *to the lost sheep of the house of Israel*" (Matt. 10:5, 6). Even the *enemies* of Christ realized that He had come to the Jewish nation. As He hung on the cross they "set up over His head His accusation written, THIS IS JESUS *THE KING OF THE JEWS*" (Matt. 27:37).

Paul also refers to this truth in Romans 15:8: "Now I say that *Jesus Christ was a minister of the circumcision* for the truth of God, to confirm the promises made *unto the fathers.*"

Chapter 16:18

The Beginning of the Church

It has been suggested that the Church had its beginning just after the resurrection when Jesus breathed on the disciples and said to them, "Receive ye the Holy Ghost" (John 20:22). However, as I have already stated, I believe the Church was born on the Day of Pentecost, because it was on that day that the Holy Spirit came and made Himself manifest in the earth, witnessing that Jesus had risen from the dead and had ascended to the Father.

In Acts 1:3-9 we learn that Jesus "shewed Himself alive after His passion by many infallible proofs, *being seen of them forty days, and speaking of the things pertaining to the Kingdom of God:* and, being assembled together with them, commanded them that they should not depart from Jerusalem, but wait for the promise of the Father, which, saith He, ye have heard of me. For John truly baptized with water; but *ye shall be baptized with the Holy Ghost not many days hence.*

"When they therefore were come together, they asked of Him, saying, Lord, wilt thou at this time restore again the Kingdom to Israel? And He said unto them, It is not for you to know the times or the seasons, which the Father hath put in His own power. *But YE SHALL RECEIVE POWER after that the Holy Ghost is come upon you:* and ye shall be witnesses unto me both in Jerusalem, and in all Judaea, and in Samaria, and unto the uttermost part of the earth.

"And when He had spoken these things, while they beheld, He was taken up; and a cloud received Him out of their sight."

In Luke 24:49 Jesus commanded the disciples, "...Tarry ye in the city of Jerusalem, *until ye be ENDUED WITH POWER from on high.*" They did as Jesus commanded. They remained in Jerusalem for the coming of the Holy Spirit.

The events on the Day of Pentecost are recorded in Acts chapter 2:

"And when the Day of Pentecost was fully come, they were all with one accord in one place. And suddenly there came a sound from heaven as of a rushing mighty wind, and it filled all the house where they were sitting. And there appeared unto them cloven tongues like as of fire, and it sat upon each of them. And they were all filled with the Holy Ghost, and began to speak with other tongues, as the Spirit gave them utterance.

"And there were dwelling at Jerusalem Jews, devout men, out of every nation under heaven. Now when this was noised abroad, the multitude came together, and were confounded, because that every man heard them speak in his own language. And they were all amazed and marvelled, saying one to another, Behold, are not all these which speak Galilaeans? And how hear we every man in our own tongue, wherein we were born? Parthians, and Medes, and Elamites, and the dwellers in Mesopotamia, and in Judaea, and Cappadocia, in Pontus, and Asia, Phrygia, and Pamphylia, in Egypt, and in the parts of Libya about Cyrene, and strangers of Rome, Jews and proselytes, Cretes and Arabians, we do hear them speak in our tongues the wonderful works of God. And they were all amazed, and were in doubt, saying one to another, What meaneth this? Others mocking said, These men are full of new wine.

"But Peter, standing up with the eleven, lifted up his voice, and said unto them, Ye men of Judaea, and all ye that dwell at Jerusalem, be this known unto you, and hearken to my words: for these are not drunken, as ye suppose, seeing it is but the third hour of the day. But this is that which was spoken by the prophet Joel; And it shall come to pass in the last days, saith God, I will pour out of my Spirit upon all flesh: and your sons and your daughters shall prophesy, and your young men shall see visions, and your old men shall dream dreams: and on my servants and on my handmaidens I will pour out in those days of my Spirit; and they shall prophesy: and I will shew wonders in heaven above, and signs in the earth beneath; blood, and fire, and vapour of smoke: the sun shall be turned into darkness, and the moon into blood, before that great and notable day of the Lord come: and it shall come to pass, that whosoever shall call on the name of the Lord shall be saved.

"Ye men of Israel, hear these words; Jesus of Nazareth, a Man approved of God among you by miracles and wonders and signs, which God did by Him in the midst of you, as ye yourselves also know: Him, being delivered by the determinate counsel and foreknowledge of God, ye have taken, and by wicked hands have crucified and slain: whom God hath raised up, having loosed the pains of death: because it was not possible that He should be holden of it.

"For David speaketh concerning Him, I foresaw the Lord always before my face, for He is on my right hand, that I should not be moved: therefore did my heart rejoice, and my tongue was glad; moreover also my flesh shall rest in hope: because thou wilt not leave my soul in hell, neither wilt thou suffer thine Holy One to see corruption. Thou hast made known to me the ways of life; thou shalt make me full of joy with thy countenance.

"Men and brethren, let me freely speak unto you of the patriarch David, that he is both dead and buried, and his sepulchre is with us unto this day. Therefore being a prophet, and knowing that God had sworn with an oath to him, that of the fruit of his loins, according to the flesh, He would raise up Christ to sit on his throne; he seeing this before spake of the resurrection of

Christ, that His soul was not left in hell, neither His flesh did see corruption.

"This Jesus hath God raised up, whereof we all are witnesses. Therefore being by the right hand of God exalted, and having received of the Father the promise of the Holy Ghost, He hath shed forth this, which ye now see and hear. For David is not ascended into the heavens: but he saith himself, The Lord said unto my Lord, Sit thou on my right hand, until I make thy foes thy footstool. Therefore let all the house of Israel know assuredly, that God hath made that same Jesus, whom ye have crucified, both Lord and Christ.

"Now when they heard this, they were pricked in their heart, and said unto Peter and to the rest of the apostles, Men and brethren, what shall we do? Then Peter said unto them, Repent, and be baptized every one of you in the name of Jesus Christ for the remission of sins, and ye shall receive the gift of the Holy Ghost. For the promise is unto you, and to your children, and to all that are afar off, even as many as the Lord our God shall call. And with many other words did he testify and exhort, saying, Save yourselves from this untoward generation.

"Then they that gladly received his word were baptized: and the same day there were added unto them about three thousand souls" (Acts 2:1-41).

Peter's sermon at Pentecost can be read in five minutes, but it produced more genuine results than some religious leaders produce in a lifetime. It brought a deep conviction of sin and men were stirred to the depths of their being. These were genuine conversions, true confessions of Christ; they were not spasmodic, high-pressure reactions brought about by the psychological pull of a crowd. People who heard the Word *received it gladly* and were baptized.

There was true Christian communion, too, for those who were saved "continued stedfastly in the apostles' doctrine and fellowship, and in breaking of bread, and in prayers. And fear came upon every soul: and many wonders and signs were done by the apostles. And all that believed *were TOGETHER*, and had all things common, and sold their possessions and goods, and parted them to all men, as every man had need. And they, continuing daily *with ONE ACCORD* in the temple, and breaking bread from house to house, did eat their meat with gladness and *singleness of heart*" (Acts 2:42-46).

The sermon Peter preached that day had a singular motive— *the unfolding of the Person of the Lord Jesus Christ.* His sermon was scripturally based, including almost word-for-word quotations from Joel 2:28-32, Psalm 16:8-11, and Psalm 110:1. In addition to his quotations taken from those Old Testament Scriptures, he made many *references* to Scripture, and his entire sermon was seasoned with scriptural statements. Thus we see

that the Holy Spirit manifests His power and
presence where the Word of God is preached in
all of its purity and simplicity.

We might sum up Peter's sermon by saying
that he glorified God, exalted Christ, and honored
the Holy Spirit.   Any preacher who will follow
this example can expect great results from God.
The greatest need in pulpits today is more Gospel,
more Scripture, more glory and praise to Christ,
more submission to the Holy Spirit—and less recognition of programs and denominational machinery!
Jesus said, *"And I, if I be LIFTED UP from the
earth, will draw all men unto me"* (John 12:32).
He was speaking of His death on the cross, but
a secondary interpretation of this statement is
that *if we EXALT CHRIST, He will draw men
to salvation.*

The Church was born at Pentecost, in an upper
room, with about one hundred and twenty souls
present.   After Peter's sermon, three thousand
were added to the Church and united with the
other believers.

Acts chapter 2 closes with these words: *"... And
the LORD added to the Church daily such as
should be saved"* (Acts 2:47).   The *church clerk*
does not add us to the Church.   *Water baptism*
does not add us to the Church.   *Good works* do
not add us to the Church.   *GOD ALMIGHTY adds
us to the Church WHEN WE ARE SAVED.*

When the miracle of the new birth occurs, we

are born of the Spirit, united to the body of Christ, sealed, indwelt, and led by the Spirit — and one glorious day He will raise us bodily from the dead. (Please study John 3:1-7; Romans 8:9, 11, 14, 16; I Corinthians 12:12, 13; and Ephesians 4:30.)

The Foundation of the Church

The full revelation concerning the Church was not given in Matthew 16, nor was it given on the Day of Pentecost. If Peter were the "rock" upon which the Church is built, we could surely expect that when he preached on the Day of Pentecost he would have referred to *himself* and to the *Church;* but no such references were made in Peter's message that day. When the Lord God was ready to reveal the mystery of the Church, He entrusted this great revelation to the Apostle Paul rather than Peter. Paul was called to minister to the Gentiles, as he plainly declared in Romans 11:13, 14: "For I speak to you Gentiles, inasmuch as *I am the apostle of the Gentiles,* I magnify mine office: if by any means I may provoke to emulation them which are my flesh, and might save some of them."

Through the epistles given to us by the Apostle Paul, we have the full revelation of the Church, the revelation to which Paul refers in Ephesians 3:1-12:

"For this cause I Paul, *the prisoner of Jesus Christ for you Gentiles,* if ye have heard of the dispensation of the grace of God which is given me to you-ward: how that *by revelation He made known unto me the mystery;* (as I wrote afore in few words, whereby, when ye read, ye may understand my knowledge in the mystery of Christ) *which in other ages was not made known unto the sons of men,* as it is now revealed unto His holy apostles and prophets by the Spirit; that the Gentiles should be fellowheirs, and of the same body, and partakers of His promise in Christ by the Gospel: whereof I was made a minister, according to the gift of the grace of God given unto me by the effectual working of His power.

"Unto me, who am less than the least of all saints, is this grace given, *that I should preach among the Gentiles the unsearchable riches of Christ;* and to make all men see what is the fellowship of the mystery, which from the beginning of the world hath been hid in God, who created all things by Jesus Christ: to the intent that now unto the principalities and powers in heavenly places might be known by the Church the manifold wisdom of God, according to the eternal purpose which He purposed in Christ Jesus our Lord: in whom we have boldness and access with confidence by the faith of Him."

Since the mystery of the Church was revealed to the Apostle Paul rather than to Peter, we are left with the question of what Jesus really meant when He said, "Thou art Peter, *and upon this rock*

I will build my Church." He certainly did not mean that *Peter* was the one upon whom the Church would be built.

As already pointed out, the Greek word for "Peter" is *petros,* which means a little stone, a part of a rock, or a pebble. When the Lord spoke of the "rock" upon which He would build His Church, He did not use *petros.* He used *PETRA,* which means a *ROCK.* It is *petra* (the big *rock*), from which *petros* (the little stone) is hewn. *PE-TRA* is the rock upon which the Church is built, and *that ROCK is the Lord Jesus Christ Himself.*

The word *petra* was used by Jesus for the first time in the Sermon on the Mount, when He spoke of the wise man who built his house upon *petra,* a rock (Matt. 7:24,25). When the rains came and the storms beat upon the house, it did not fall because it was built upon *petra.* The Rock upon which the Church is built is *"CHRIST, the Son of the living God,"* as confessed by Peter in verse 16 of our present chapter.

Then we might ask why the Holy Spirit, in recording this message through Matthew, used both *petros* and *petra,* since the similarity of those two words has caused much confusion and false teaching. The use of both *petros* and *petra* brings out the precious truth that Christ is the foundation upon which the Church is built, and every born again believer is building *upon that foundation.* Paul points this out in I Corinthians 3:9-11:

"For we are labourers together with God: ye are God's husbandry, ye are God's building. According to the grace of God which is given unto me, as a wise masterbuilder, I have laid the foundation, and another buildeth thereon. But let every man take heed how he buildeth thereupon. *For other foundation can no man lay than that is laid, which is Jesus Christ."*

In his first epistle, Peter gives much light on the *Rock* and the little *stones:*

". . . the Lord is gracious. To whom coming, as unto a living stone, disallowed indeed of men, but chosen of God, and precious, ye also, *as lively stones,* are built up a spiritual house, an holy priesthood, to offer up spiritual sacrifices, acceptable to God by Jesus Christ. Wherefore also it is contained in the Scripture, *Behold, I lay in Sion a chief CORNER STONE, elect, precious:* and he that believeth on Him shall not be confounded. Unto you therefore which believe He is precious: but unto them which be disobedient, the stone which the builders disallowed, the same is made the head of the corner" (I Pet. 2:3-7).

In these verses, Peter himself made it perfectly clear that Christ is the Rock upon which the Church is built. Peter, like every other true believer, is but *a living stone built upon Christ the Rock.*

Who Is a Member of the Church?

Paul answers this question in I Corinthians

12:12-31.   He clearly tells us who is a member of the New Testament Church, and what happens when one *becomes* a member of that body:

"For as the body is one, and hath many members, and all the members of that one body, being many, are one body: *so also is Christ.* For by one Spirit are we all baptized into one body, whether we be Jews or Gentiles, whether we be bond or free; and have been all made to drink into one Spirit.   For the body is not one member, but many.

"If the foot shall say, Because I am not the hand, I am not of the body; is it therefore not of the body?   And if the ear shall say, Because I am not the eye, I am not of the body; is it therefore not of the body?   If the whole body were an eye, where were the hearing?   If the whole were hearing, where were the smelling?   But now hath God set the members every one of them in the body, as it hath pleased Him.   And if they were all one member, where were the body?   But now are they many members, yet but one body. And the eye cannot say unto the hand, I have no need of thee: nor again the head to the feet, I have no need of you.

"Nay, much more those members of the body, which seem to be more feeble, are necessary: and those members of the body, which we think to be less honourable, upon these we bestow more abundant honour;   and our uncomely parts have more

50

abundant comeliness. For our comely parts have no need: but God hath tempered the body together, having given more abundant honour to that part which lacked: that there should be no schism in the body; but that the members should have the same care one for another. And whether one member suffer, all the members suffer with it; or one member be honoured, all the members rejoice with it.

"Now *ye are the body of Christ, and members in particular.* And God hath set some in the church, first apostles, secondarily prophets, thirdly teachers, after that miracles, then gifts of healings, helps, governments, diversities of tongues. Are all apostles? are all prophets? are all teachers? are all workers of miracles? Have all the gifts of healing? do all speak with tongues? do all interpret? But covet earnestly the best gifts: and yet shew I unto you a more excellent way."

In this passage, Paul plainly teaches that all born again believers are members of the Church of the living God. All believers are baptized into the body of Christ at the very moment of the new birth. There are no scriptural grounds to suggest that a person can be a child of God apart from the baptism of the Holy Spirit, *"for BY ONE SPIRIT are we ALL baptized INTO ONE BODY"* (v. 13).

The Word of God clearly teaches, "One Lord, one faith, one baptism, one God and Father of all,

51

who is *above* all, and *through* all, *and IN YOU ALL"* (Eph. 4:5, 6).

In Romans 8:9 Paul declares, "Ye are not in the flesh, but in the Spirit, if so be that the Spirit of God dwell in you. Now *if any man HAVE NOT the Spirit of Christ, he is NONE OF HIS."* Later in that same chapter we read, "As many as are *led by the Spirit of God,* they are *the SONS of God"* (Rom. 8:14).

In Ephesians 4:30 we are commanded, "Grieve not *the Holy Spirit of God, whereby ye are sealed* unto the day of redemption."

In the light of the revealed truth of God's Word, it is foolish to suppose that any person can become a member of the New Testament Church, the body of Christ, apart from possessing the blessed Holy Spirit.

Jesus said, "Verily, verily, I say unto thee, Except a man be born of water *AND OF THE SPIRIT, he cannot enter into the Kingdom of God. That which is born of the flesh is FLESH; and that which is born of the Spirit is SPIRIT"* (John 3:5, 6).

In the passage just previously quoted from I Corinthians chapter 12, Paul compares the New Testament Church to the human body, in that there is *one body* but *many members.* Although some members may seem to be more important than others, in the final analysis each and every member is important, providing perfect balance, and when one member suffers, the whole body suffers. Paul uses this illustration to show that the Church of God is not divided, but is *one body.*

I thank God for people of all denominations who believe in the virgin birth, the blood atonement, the verbal inspiration of the Scriptures, and other cardinal truths of fundamental Christianity. We may not all agree on all details of doctrine, but if we agree on the major, we can disagree on the minor and still work and pray together to win souls. *All born again people,* regardless of denomination, are members of the true Church, the body of Christ.

The Divine History of the First Days of the Church on Earth

In most Bibles, the Book of Acts is called "The Acts of the Apostles." Actually, it is the record of *the acts of the HOLY SPIRIT in the first days of the New Testament Church.* In Acts 2, Peter opens the door of Christian opportunity to Israel on the Day of Pentecost, and the message of the first ten chapters of Acts is directed primarily to the Jews. In Acts chapter 10 we read of Peter's second use of "the keys of the Kingdom" (Matt. 16:19), where the Gospel is given to the Gentiles and where we find the record of Peter's tremendous sermon on that occasion. (Read Acts 10:34-43.)

In the eleventh chapter of Acts the Church passes out of the confines of Judaism and broadens to peoples of all races; and in Acts chapter 13 the Church receives Gentiles as members.

In Acts 15:13-18 we find the clearest blueprint of God's plan for the ages that is found anywhere in the entire Bible. If you read these verses carefully you will find, first, that God would visit the Gentiles and take out of them a people for His name. This part of His divine plan has been going on for almost two thousand years. That does not mean that Jews are not being saved during this dispensation, but in the Church of God there is neither Jew nor Gentile. *ALL are one in Christ:* "There is neither Jew nor Greek, there is neither bond nor free, there is neither male nor female: *for ye are all one in Christ Jesus*" (Gal. 3:28).

Primarily, however, the New Testament Church is made up of Gentiles, and when the Gentile bride of Christ is complete, the Church will be called out of this earth to meet Jesus in the air (I Thess. 4:13-18). This present age is called the Church Age, the Dispensation of Grace, or the Christian era.

There are those who close their eyes to dispensational truth, thereby closing their eyes to a full understanding of the Word of God. It is absolutely impossible to understand the Bible if we do not recognize dispensational truth and rightly divide the Word, comparing Scripture with Scripture and spiritual things with spiritual.

Paul—Called of God and Anointed
As the Minister to the Gentiles

I pointed out that Paul personally declared, "I am the apostle of the Gentiles" (Rom. 11:13). Doctrinally speaking, the New Testament Church was fully revealed to the Apostle Paul *alone*. God *called* him, and *God anointed him* as a specifically chosen vessel to carry the Gospel message to the Gentiles. God further honored Paul by giving to him fourteen of the New Testament epistles.

In Ephesians 3:1-12 (quoted earlier) we learned that God revealed to Paul the mystery of the body of Christ (the New Testament Church), a mystery hidden through preceding ages but made known to Paul—and, through Paul, made known to all who will believe the Gospel.

Paul had the assurance that his wisdom concerning the Church came to him *by revelation, direct from God*—not from other apostles or from any human source. Although he considered himself the least of all saints, God gave him the privilege of making known the unsearchable riches of Christ and the mystery which was hidden from the beginning of the world. To Paul, God gave a revelation not given to any other person at any time.

There Is Neither Jew Nor Gentile
in the Church

In the Old Testament economy, God called and

elected the nation Israel as His chosen people. Likewise, the Gospel was given first to the Jews, according to Romans 1:16. Paul said, "I am not ashamed of the Gospel of Christ: for it is the power of God unto salvation to every one that believeth; *to the Jew first,* and also to the Greek." But now, both Jew and Gentile belong to one body in Christ. This is clearly seen in Ephesians 2:11-22:

"Wherefore remember, that ye being in time past Gentiles in the flesh, who are called Uncircumcision by that which is called the Circumcision in the flesh made by hands; that at that time ye were without Christ, being aliens from the commonwealth of Israel, and strangers from the covenants of promise, having no hope, and without God in the world: but now in Christ Jesus ye who sometimes were far off are made nigh by the blood of Christ.

"For He is our peace, who hath *made both one, and hath broken down the middle wall of partition between us;* having abolished in His flesh the enmity, even the law of commandments contained in ordinances; for to make in Himself of twain one new man, so making peace; and that He might *reconcile both unto God in one body* by the cross, having slain the enmity thereby; and came and preached peace to you which were afar off, and to them that were nigh. *For through Him we BOTH have access by one Spirit unto the Father.*

"Now therefore ye are no more strangers and foreigners, but *fellowcitizens with the saints, and of the household of God;* and are built upon the foundation of the apostles and prophets, Jesus Christ Himself being the Chief Corner Stone; in whom all the building fitly *framed together* groweth unto an holy temple in the Lord: in whom ye also are *builded together* for an habitation of God through the Spirit."

The Church Is the Body of Christ

In Ephesians 1:22, 23, Paul explains that the Church is the body of Christ and that God "hath put all things under His (Christ's) feet, and gave Him (Christ) *to be the head over all things to the CHURCH, which is HIS BODY,* the fulness of Him that filleth all in all."

In Colossians 1:23, 24 Paul speaks of "the Gospel, which ye have heard, and which was preached to every creature which is under heaven; whereof I Paul am made a minister; who now rejoice in my sufferings for you, and fill up that which is behind of the afflictions of Christ in my flesh *FOR HIS BODY'S SAKE, which is THE CHURCH.*"

Every born again, blood-washed, redeemed child of God is a *member* of the body of Christ (I Cor. 12:27). "So *we,* being *many,* are *ONE BODY in Christ,* and every one members *one of another*" (Rom. 12:5).

Ephesians 5:22-33 is one of the most enlightening

passages in the Word of God concerning what the Church is and its relationship to us and to Christ:

"Wives, submit yourselves unto your own husbands, as unto the Lord. For the husband is the head of the wife, even as *Christ is the head of the Church: and He is the Saviour of the body.* Therefore as the Church is subject unto Christ, so let the wives be to their own husbands in every thing. Husbands, love your wives, even as Christ also loved the Church, and gave Himself for it; that He might sanctify and cleanse it with the washing of water by the Word, that He might present it to Himself a glorious Church, not having spot, or wrinkle, or any such thing; but that it should be holy and without blemish.

"So ought men to love their wives as their own bodies. He that loveth his wife loveth himself. For no man ever yet hated his own flesh; but nourisheth and cherisheth it, even as the Lord the Church: *for we are members of His body, of His flesh, and of His bones.* For this cause shall a man leave his father and mother, and shall be joined unto his wife, and they two shall be one flesh. This is a great mystery: but I speak concerning Christ and the Church. Nevertheless let every one of you in particular so love his wife even as himself; and the wife see that she reverence her husband."

In this marvelous passage the Holy Spirit compares Christ and His Church to husband and wife.

In verses 23 and 24 we are told that the husband is the head of the wife, *even as CHRIST is the head of the CHURCH.* And as the Church is subject unto Christ, so should the wife be subject unto her husband.

In verse 30 Paul clearly states that believers are members of the body of Christ, *of His flesh and of His bones.* The Holy Spirit baptizes believers into the body of Christ, and thus we become part of the *INVISIBLE body* made up of all born again believers since Pentecost.

The New Testament Church
Is the Bride of Christ

According to the Scriptures, *the Church is the BRIDE of Christ,* and one glorious day there will be *a wedding in the sky.* God revealed this wonderful truth to John the Beloved on the Isle of Patmos:

"Let us be glad and rejoice, and give honour to Him: *for the marriage of the Lamb is come, and His wife hath made herself ready.* And to her was granted that she should be arrayed in fine linen, clean and white: for the fine linen is the righteousness of saints. And he saith unto me, Write, Blessed are they which are called unto *the marriage supper of the Lamb.* And he saith unto me, These are the true sayings of God" (Rev. 19:7-9).

We read in Revelation 21:9: "And there came

unto me one of the seven angels which had the seven vials full of the seven last plagues, and talked with me, saying, Come hither, I will shew thee *the bride, the Lamb's wife.*"

Look again, if you will, at Paul's testimony concerning Christ and His relationship to the Church:

"Husbands, love your wives, *even as Christ also loved THE CHURCH, and gave Himself for it;* that He might sanctify and cleanse it with the washing of water by the Word, that He might present it to Himself *a glorious Church, not having spot, or wrinkle, or any such thing; but that it should be holy and WITHOUT BLEMISH*" (Eph. 5:25-27).

Yes, one day Christ will present the Church to Himself—a *glorious* Church without "spot or wrinkle," flawlessly perfect! That will be the day when the Church (the bride) and Christ (the Bridegroom) will be married, and there will be a great marriage supper in the sky. Then the bride will return with Christ to this earth, to reign with Him for one thousand glorious, golden years—the years of the Millennium. Certainly if we accept the Scriptures, we need not stretch our imagination to see the truth of this statement.

The Ministry of the Church on Earth Today

Many church members are confused concerning the mission of the Church on earth. The ministry

of the Church is a gift from the ascended Lord
and Saviour Jesus Christ. The following verses
will bear out this truth, and will point out the
ministry of the Church in this day and hour:

"There is one body, and one Spirit, even as ye
are called in one hope of your calling; one Lord,
one faith, one baptism, one God and Father of all,
who is above all, and through all, and in you all.
But unto every one of us is given grace according
to the measure of the gift of Christ. Wherefore
He saith, When He ascended up on high, He led
captivity captive, and gave gifts unto men. (Now
that He ascended, what is it but that He also
descended first into the lower parts of the earth?
He that descended is the same also that ascended
up far above all heavens, that He might fill all
things.)

"And He gave some, apostles; and some, proph-
ets; and some, evangelists; and some, pastors and
teachers; for the perfecting of the saints, for the
work of the ministry, for the edifying of the body
of Christ: till we all come in the unity of the
faith, and of the knowledge of the Son of God,
unto a perfect man, unto the measure of the stature
of the fulness of Christ: that we henceforth be no
more children, tossed to and fro, and carried about
with every wind of doctrine, by the sleight of men,
and cunning craftiness, whereby they lie in wait
to deceive; but speaking the truth in love, may
grow up into Him in all things, which is the head,

even Christ: from whom the whole body fitly joined together and compacted by that which every joint supplieth, according to the effectual working in the measure of every part, maketh increase of the body unto the edifying of itself in love" (Eph. 4:4-16).

In these verses we see that Jesus, as head of the Church, *gave gifts unto men.* In verse 11 we find a definite statement concerning the *different offices* (or ministries) which Jesus gave to believers until the time when the Church will be complete and will be caught up out of the earth to meet Jesus in the clouds in the air.

In I Corinthians 12:27, 28, we find similar words relative to the various offices and ministries in the Church:

"Now ye are *the body of Christ,* and members in particular. And God hath set some in the church, first *apostles,* secondarily *prophets,* thirdly *teachers,* after that *miracles,* then *gifts of healings, helps, governments, diversities of tongues.*"

Please note that in these Scriptures there is no mention of the office of a high priest. The office of priesthood is not needed in the New Testament Church because *Jesus Christ is OUR High Priest:* "*. . . we have a great High Priest, that is passed into the heavens, Jesus the Son of God . . .*" (Heb. 4:14). He is now seated at the right hand of God, "now to appear in the presence of God for us" (Heb. 9:24). It is true that there were priests in the Old Testament era, priests so ordained of God; "and they truly were many priests, because they were not suffer'ed to continue by reason of death" (Heb. 7:23). When a priest *died* his priesthood ceased and a new priest was of necessity appointed. But *Jesus,* our High Priest, is "a priest *for ever*" (Heb. 5:6), and "because He continueth ever, hath *an unchangeable priesthood*" (Heb. 7:24).

In Hebrews 10:11-14 we read: "Every priest standeth daily ministering and offering oftentimes the same sacrifices, which can never take away sins: *but THIS MAN, after He had offered ONE SACRIFICE FOR SINS FOR EVER, sat down on the right hand of God;* from henceforth expecting till His enemies be made His footstool. For *by one offering* He hath perfected for ever them that are sanctified."

Christ made *one offering,* once for all. He offered His own precious, sinless blood, thereby purchasing redemption for the believer and for the Church. God *accepted* His Son's sacrifice. So the Lord Jesus Christ, *"by His own blood ... entered in ONCE into the holy place, having obtained ETERNAL REDEMPTION for us"* (Heb. 9:12). No sacrifice for sin is required in the future because *Jesus satisfied God's holiness,* God's *righteousness,* and God's *law* concerning sin. Therefore *OUR High Priest* does not appear with blood and sacrifices as the Old Testament priests did. With His one perfect offering He paid sin's debt *forever,* and today He is our "Advocate with the Father" (I John 2:1), the "one Mediator between God and men" (I Tim. 2:5). In the Church today God has appointed various ministries, but He has made no mention of a high priest.

I Peter 2:9 tells us that *every believer* is a priest: "... ye are *a chosen generation, a ROYAL PRIEST-HOOD, an holy nation, a peculiar people;* that ye should shew forth the praises of Him who hath called you out of darkness into His marvellous light." If you will read the verses immediately preceding and following this verse, you will discover that these words were spoken of born again believers. We find this same truth in Revelation 1:5, 6, where John tells us that Jesus "loved us, and washed us from our sins in His own blood, *and hath made us kings and PRIESTS unto God and His Father . . . .*"

Under the Old Testament economy the priest *revealed MAN to GOD;* but in this Day of Grace the minister of the Gospel *reveals GOD'S LOVE to man.* In I Corinthians 1:21 we read, "For after that in the wisdom of God the world by wisdom knew not God, it pleased God by the foolishness of preaching to save them that believe."

God's minister is to preach the Gospel—and the Bible definition of the Gospel is found in I Corinthians 15:1-4:

"Moreover, brethren, I declare unto you *the GOSPEL* which I preached unto you, which also ye have received, and wherein ye stand; by which also ye are saved, if ye keep in memory what I preached unto you, unless ye have believed in vain. For I delivered unto you first of all that which I also received, how that *Christ DIED for our sins according to the Scriptures; and that He was BURIED, and that He ROSE AGAIN the third day according to the Scriptures.*"

Yes, there is a vast difference between the *Gospel ministry* of this Church Age and the Old Testament *priesthood.* The priesthood on earth witnessed that man was separated from God; but the ministry in this Day of Grace witnesses that God has entered into communion with man by the miracle of the new birth through the power of the Holy Spirit. (Please study John 5:24; 6:44; and I Peter 1:23.)

Under this Dispensation of Grace, there is no distinction in class because, as I have already pointed out, *every born again believer is a spiritual priest:*

"Ye also, as lively (living) stones, are built up a spiritual house, *an holy priesthood,* to offer up spiritual sacrifices, acceptable to God by Jesus Christ" (I Pet. 2:5).

This "spiritual house" is not a temple made with hands, like Solomon's temple, where evil separated man from the holy of holies. *Each believer* is a part of this building, a *spiritual* house. Every believer is a holy priest—but we do not offer the blood of doves or lambs. *We offer "SPIR-ITUAL sacrifices, acceptable to God BY JESUS CHRIST."* The only way we can please God or hope to meet Him in peace is *in Christ* (Eph. 1:6).

The priesthood of men on earth today is unscriptural. It is definitely against the teaching of the New Testament, and any attempt to set up priests in the New Testament Church is rebuked in Scripture: "For if He (Jesus) were on earth, *He should NOT be a priest,* seeing that there are priests that offer gifts according to the law" (Heb. 8:4). If Jesus were on earth today He would not be a priest. Furthermore, He would recognize priesthood *only in ISRAEL,* and even then He would recognize it only in the tribe of Levi and the family of Aaron!

Israel is *not* the Church, nor is the Church a continuation of *Israel.* The English-speaking people are *not* the ten lost tribes of Israel. To take the promises God made to Israel and give them to the Church is nothing short of spiritual robbery. It is true that Israel is blinded for a season, but God has not cast them away forever (Rom. chapter 11). The time will come when a nation will be saved in a day (Isa. 66:8) and God will turn again to His chosen people, Israel. There was a priesthood in Israel, but there has never been a priesthood in the Church other than the *spiritual* priesthood made up of all born again believers.

Since Christ's priesthood is in heaven alone

(and only for those represented as seated "in heavenly places in Christ Jesus" — Eph. 2:6), the acceptance by the Church of priesthood on earth would nullify and set aside the priesthood of Christ. The Church's acceptance of priesthood on earth would put her *under law* and outside of *grace.* Priesthood in the Church today would contradict Scripture and would deny that the blood of Jesus Christ is sufficient to cleanse from all sin. (Read I John 1:7.) Priesthood in the Church would deny that we are complete in Jesus, who is declared to be "the head of all principality and power" (Col. 2:10).

In the Church, every believer *as a royal priest* is invited to enter boldly into the holy of holies:

"Having therefore, brethren, *boldness to enter into the HOLIEST by the blood of Jesus,* by a new and living way, which He hath consecrated for us, through the veil, that is to say, His flesh; and having an High Priest over the house of God; let us draw near with a true heart in full assurance of faith, having our hearts sprinkled from an evil conscience, and our bodies washed with pure water. Let us hold fast the profession of our faith without wavering; (for He is faithful that promised)" (Heb. 10:19-23).

In this wonderful Dispensation of Grace, it is senseless, inexcusable ignorance for any man to be set up as a priest representing God on earth: *"For there is ONE GOD, and ONE MEDIATOR between God and men, THE MAN CHRIST JE-SUS''* (I Tim. 2:5).

We are instructed to confess our sins to Jesus (I John 1:9; 2:1, 2). He is our Intercessor and He alone can forgive sins. No man can approach God on our behalf except to *pray* for us that we will be stronger Christians with greater dedication to God. We must *confess our own sins,* and the confession must be made in the name of *Jesus,* for His sake, honor, and glory.

In the true Church there is no distinction between the clergy and the laity. Peter exhorts ministers as follows: "Feed the flock of God which is among you, taking the oversight thereof, not by constraint, but willingly; not for filthy lucre, but of a ready mind; neither as being *lords* over God's heritage, but being *ensamples to the flock''* (I Pet. 5:2, 3). No member of the New Testament Church should make any distinction which would indicate his official superiority over other members of his congregation. There are no "superiors" and "inferiors" in the Church. We are *all ONE* in the Lord Jesus Christ. Each and every believer is a royal priest, and each and every believer is invited to enter boldly into the holy of holies through *"a new and living way''* opened by the shed blood of God's dear Son, our own High Priest.

Among the gifts set forth as given to the Church by the Lord Jesus, *elders* and *bishops* are not mentioned. (See Ephesians 4:7-11.) These were appointed by the local churches where they served:

"When they had *ordained them elders in every church*, and had prayed with fasting, they commended them to the Lord, on whom they believed" (Acts 14:23).

Paul gave instructions to Titus concerning this matter: "For this cause left I thee in Crete, that thou shouldest set in order the things that are wanting, and *ordain elders in every city*, as I had appointed thee" (Tit. 1:5).

Then in I Peter 5:1, 2 we read: *"The elders which are among you* I exhort, who am also an elder, and a witness of the sufferings of Christ, and also a partaker of the glory that shall be revealed: feed the flock of God which is among you, taking the oversight thereof, not by constraint, but willingly; not for filthy lucre, but of a ready mind."

From these passages we see that the ministry of an elder or bishop is to *feed the flock of God and watch over them*.   Elders and bishops are not to be dictators. They are to keep a protecting eye over the Church.

The Pastor

A true Bible pastor is *called* of God, *ordained* of God, and *sent* by God as an undershepherd of the Lord Jesus Christ who is the Chief Shepherd: "When *the Chief Shepherd* shall appear, ye shall receive a crown of glory that fadeth not away" (I Pet. 5:4).

In the true sense of the word, *"pastor"* signifies a shepherd as illustrated in Jeremiah 3:15: "I will give you pastors according to mine heart, which shall feed you with knowledge and understanding."

The duty of the pastor is to feed the flock—not with physical bread and meat which satisfies the flesh, but with knowledge and understanding that come only through the preaching of the pure Word of God. Woe be unto the minister who neglects this high calling!

In order for the pastor to feed the flock, *HE must first be fed.* The apostles ordained deacons to take care of the secondary matters of the church so that the ministers might give themselves continually to prayer and the ministry of the Word. (Please study Acts 6:1-7.)

There is no theological school in existence that can "manufacture" a true pastor. According to the Scriptures, true pastors are called of God, and they *learn* at the feet of Jesus before an open Bible. I hope I will not be misunderstood on this subject. *Certainly I believe in SCHOOLS.* I believe that a minister should prepare himself for the ministry, educationally speaking. But *true spiritual understanding* comes from the *Lord.* Paul instructed young Timothy to *STUDY to show himself approved unto God,* "a *workman* that needeth not to be ashamed," but the instruction also included *"rightly dividing the WORD"* (II Tim. 2:15).

Being "approved of *God*" does not necessarily mean being approved by a denomination, but the *wisdom* and *knowledge* needed for rightly dividing the Word must come from God.

I believe some pastors go out too soon, without proper preparation; but I also believe some men who are studying for the ministry stay *too long* in educational institutions and fail to reach the field at the appointed time. There is a time to *prepare,* and there is a time to *go.* In II Samuel 5:18-25, David defeated the Philistines in battle because he obeyed God and waited until the appointed time to go up against the enemy. With his army he waited in the grove of mulberry trees until he heard "the sound of a going in the tops of the mulberry trees." Then, confident that God went before him, he went out as the Lord had commanded him and won a great victory. God's man needs to prepare—but he should also listen for "the sound of a going," that he may know when his study has been *approved of God.*

Instructing the leaders in the church at Ephesus, Paul admonished: "Take heed therefore unto *yourselves,* and to *all the flock,* over the which the Holy Ghost hath made you *overseers, to FEED the Church of God, which He hath purchased with HIS OWN BLOOD*" (Acts 20:28).

In the Gospel of John, chapter 21, Jesus gave an excellent lesson in service. In that passage we find that after Jesus was crucified, Peter decided

71

to return to his nets and go fishing. Some of the other disciples went with him. They toiled at their nets all night but caught nothing. When the morning came, Jesus stood on the shore and called to them, "Children, have ye any meat?" They answered, "No." Jesus then said to them, "Cast the net on the right side of the ship, and ye shall find." They obeyed Him, *"and now they were not able to draw it for the multitude of fishes"* (v. 6).

When the disciples brought their boat to shore, they saw fish roasting over a fire, and they also saw bread. Then "Jesus saith unto them, *Come and dine.* And none of the disciples durst ask Him, Who art thou? knowing that it was the Lord" (v. 12). Thus Jesus showed them that He who had *called* them was also able to *provide* for them. He had called these men to be soulwinners, *"fishers of men"* (Matt. 4:19), and it was certainly unprofitable for them to spend their time fishing all night without catching any fish.

So when they had eaten, Jesus asked Peter, "Do you love me?" Peter answered, "Yes, Lord, I love you." Jesus then asked him a second and a third time, "Do you love me?" and each time Peter gave an affirmative answer. In the process of this lesson, Jesus said to Peter, *"Feed my lambs. . . . Feed my sheep"* (vv. 15-17). The most important business of a pastor is to feed the lambs and the sheep of the flock of God.

God is bestowing great honor upon any man

who is called of Him to be a pastor or overseer of God's flock; but the *responsibility* of that calling is as great as the *honor* it bestows. Pity the pastor who allows his flock to go unfed and un-protected, exposed to the dangers of the wolves and hounds of hell who seek to destroy the lambs and sheep at the slightest opportunity!

When God calls a man to pastor a church, He does not leave that man unattended and uncared-for. *"Even so hath the Lord ordained that they which PREACH the Gospel should LIVE of the Gospel"* (I Cor. 9:14). To the Philippian church Paul wrote, "My God shall supply *all your need* according to His riches in glory by Christ Jesus" (Phil. 4:19). Jesus Himself promised, "Seek ye first the Kingdom of God, and His righteousness— *and ALL THESE THINGS shall be added unto you"* (Matt. 6:33). God has never called a preacher He would not take care of if that preacher put Christ first in all things.

To the Church God also gave *evangelists.* The evangelist differs from the pastor in that he delivers the Gospel to stir the people and open the door of God's grace to those who will hear and enter. He invites the hungry to come and eat of the bread of life. He invites the thirsty to come and drink of the water of life. But unlike a pastor, when a series of services is completed, the evangelist moves on to assist another pastor in another church.

The Church also has *teachers* who set forth the

doctrines and related truths of the Word of God. Their responsibility is to build up believers in the faith, pointing them to full surrender and a deeper spiritual life.

The *deacons* in the Church are appointed to take care of the secondary (or business) matters of the Church, thus giving the pastor more time for prayer, study, and ministering of the Word (Acts 6:3, 4).

The Church also sends out *missionaries,* according to the commandment of God, unto the ends of the earth.

Upon Which Day Should the Church Assemble to Worship?

It is the will of God in His program for believers to assemble in a group and worship together. His Word has so instructed us:

"Let us consider one another to provoke unto love and to good works: *not forsaking the assembling of ourselves together,* as the manner of some is; but exhorting one another: and so much the more, as ye see the day approaching" (Heb. 10:24, 25). Believers are to exhort and encourage one another, and we are also told to bear one another's burdens "and so fulfil the law of Christ" (Gal. 6:2).

In Acts 20:7 we read, "And upon *the first day of the week,* when the disciples came together to break bread, Paul preached unto them . . . and continued his speech until midnight."

Paul wrote to the Corinthian church, "Concerning the collection for the saints, as I have given order to the churches of Galatia, even so do ye. Upon *the first day of the week* let every one of you lay by him in store, as God hath prospered him, that there be no gatherings when I come" (I Cor. 16:1, 2).

There are many other passages in the New Testament that bear out the fact that it is God's will and to His glory that the saints meet together in groups, and worship the Lord Jesus Christ on *the first day of the week.* Of course we should worship God *EVERY* day, but *Sunday, the first day of the week,* is a special day of *worship, fellowship, communion,* and *giving to the work of the Lord.*

The question is often asked, "If Christians are to worship on *Sunday,* why did Paul and the other apostles go into the synagogues to preach on the Jewish *Sabbath* (Saturday)?" We must remember that the apostles were preaching during the transition period, the beginning of the Church Age, when Judaism was fading away and Christianity was taking its place. The *Jews* met in the synagogue on the Sabbath. Therefore the Sabbath was the opportune *time* and the synagogue was the opportune *place* for the apostles to deliver the message of the grace of God to the Jews.

The unbelieving Jews worshipped on the Sabbath, and the apostles availed themselves of that excellent opportunity to give them the Gospel; but the New Testament Church met on the first day of the week, a fact which is established by Scripture. *Christianity is NOT the keeping of DAYS, feasts and rituals;* but Sunday, the first day of the week, is the day on which Jesus rose from the dead (Matt. 28:1-6; Mark 16:1-8; Luke 24:1-12; John 20:1-20), and I believe with all my heart that Sunday is the day God has ordained for His Church to meet together to worship Him.

In this brief discourse on the New Testament Church I have not *begun* to fully discuss all phases of that subject. I have given you only a bare outline. We have seen that the Church of the living God is not a building made of brick, mortar, and stained glass windows. The Church is *a living organism* of which Jesus is the head and the foundation. The *local* church (the local assembly) is ordained of God, and I believe that every born again believer should be a part of a local assembly where the pastor preaches the true Word of God; but *the TRUE Church is INVISIBLE.*

We have also noted that in the true Church, God has ordained pastors, evangelists, and teachers to preach and teach the Word, to feed the flock of God and lead them in the paths of right living and Christian conduct, but the Church does not have *priests*, as Israel did under the law. The only priesthood acceptable with God in this Church Age is the royal priesthood of believers.

We have learned that the mission of the Church on earth today is not to convert the world and bring in the Kingdom, but to carry the message of salvation to every creature. Thus, through the preaching of the Gospel the Holy Spirit is calling out a Gentile bride for the Lord Jesus Christ.

The Church has been in existence since the Day of Pentecost, almost two thousand years ago, and will continue in existence on earth until the bride is complete. The Church will then be taken out of this earth—caught up to meet Jesus in the clouds in the air. Christians will be rewarded for their stewardship and will rejoice at the marriage supper of the Lamb. Then we, the Church, the bride of Christ, will return to this earth to reign with Christ for one thousand years.

We might note here that the Church will not enter or go through any part of the Great Tribulation period, the time when Antichrist will be in power here on earth. When the trumpet sounds, "the dead in Christ shall rise first. Then we (believers) which are alive and remain shall be caught up together with them in the clouds, to meet the Lord in the air; *and so shall we ever be with the Lord*" (I Thess. 4:16, 17).

What about the Church *after* the Millennium? The Church is called the pearl of great price, the bride of Christ, a peculiar people, the holy nation of God. The Church is the most glorious trophy of God's grace. Paul described the future of the Church in these words:

"God, who is rich in mercy, for His great love wherewith He loved us, even when we were dead in sins, hath quickened us together with Christ, (by grace ye are saved;) and hath raised us up together, and made us *sit together in heavenly places in Christ Jesus: that IN THE AGES TO COME He might shew THE EXCEEDING RICH-ES OF HIS GRACE in His kindness toward us through Christ Jesus"* (Eph. 2:4-7).

On the Isle of Patmos, John saw what Paul described in these verses, and John verified this glorious truth that the Church, the bride of Christ, will be put on display in the Pearly White City to show the exceeding riches of God's marvelous grace. John wrote of the revelation given to him:

"I saw a new heaven and a new earth: for the first heaven and the first earth were passed away; and there was no more sea. And I John saw the Holy City, new Jerusalem, coming down from God out of heaven, prepared as a bride adorned for her husband. . . . And there came unto me one of the seven angels which had the seven vials full of the seven last plagues, and talked with me, saying, Come hither, I WILL SHEW THEE THE BRIDE, THE LAMB'S WIFE. And he carried me away in the spirit to a great and high mountain, and shewed me that great city, the holy Jerusalem, descending out of heaven from

God, having the glory of God: and her light was like unto a stone most precious, even like a jasper stone, clear as crystal; and had a wall great and high, and had twelve gates, and at the gates twelve angels, and names written thereon, which are the names of the twelve tribes of the children of Israel: . . . And the twelve gates were twelve pearls; every several gate was of one pearl: and the street of the city was pure gold, as it were transparent glass.

"And I saw no temple therein: for the Lord God Almighty and the Lamb are the temple of it. And the city had no need of the sun, neither of the moon, to shine in it: for the glory of God did lighten it, and the Lamb is the light thereof. And the nations of them which are saved shall walk in the light of it: and the kings of the earth do bring their glory and honour into it. And the gates of it shall not be shut at all by day: for there shall be no night there. And they shall bring the glory and honour of the nations into it. And there shall in no wise enter into it any thing that defileth, neither whatsoever worketh abomination, or maketh a lie: but they which are written in the Lamb's book of life" (Rev. 21:1, 2, 9-12, and 21-27).

It is wonderful to be a Christian even in this present day and age. It is wonderful beyond words to have the heavenly peace and joy that *nothing on this earth* can bring. But for the true believer, the best is in the future, when we will receive a glorified body like unto the body of the risen Christ, and we will be with Him throughout the unending ages of eternity. We will occupy the Pearly White City, *the place Jesus has gone to prepare for us.* (Please read John 14:1-6.)

Are you a born again believer? Or are you just a member of a local church? If you do not know beyond any shadow of doubt that you are born again, saved by God's grace and covered by the blood of Jesus, united to the body of Christ by the Holy Spirit, then *I beg you to give your heart to Jesus NOW.* Receive Him by faith and be prepared to experience all of these glorious things that are in store for the members of the true Church.

Verse 19: *"And I will give unto thee the keys of the Kingdom of Heaven: and whatsoever thou shalt bind on earth shall be bound in heaven: and whatsoever thou shalt loose on earth shall be loosed in heaven."*

"I will give unto thee the keys of the Kingdom of Heaven." This statement has been grossly misunderstood, misinterpreted, and misapplied. Some of the most abominable doctrines extant today have been built upon Christ's words to Peter in this verse. However, if we look into the Word of God with an open mind, comparing Scripture with Scripture and spiritual things with spiritual, we

80

will understand what Jesus meant when He made this promise. It is when we turn aside from the Word and embrace *man's ideas* that we end up in confusion.

Jesus knew that not many days hence He would be arrested, condemned, crucified—and insofar as His bodily presence was concerned, He would be absent from the earth for a long time. It was therefore needful that the King, before departing the earth, should make known who could enter the Kingdom—and under what conditions they must enter.

We must remember that the New Testament had not been written at that time. The Old Testament Scriptures had been written, but not one book of the New Testament had been penned before Jesus was crucified, buried, risen, and ascended back to the Father. It was imperative that He leave representatives on earth, and on this particular occasion He chose *Peter* to speak for Him concerning the Kingdom. There can be no doubt that Jesus spoke directly to Peter, for He addressed him individually, using *singular pronouns*—"I will give *unto THEE* . . . whatsoever *THOU* shalt bind . . . whatsoever *THOU* shalt loose."

Also, if we carefully study the Word and trace Peter's movements after Jesus ascended back to the Father, we will find that *Peter alone* opened the doors to the Kingdom of Heaven to various groups.

81

First, on the Day of Pentecost, Peter opened the doors of the Kingdom to Israel when he said, "for the promise is unto you, and to your children, and to all that are afar off, even as many as the Lord our God shall call" (Acts 2:39). Other disciples also preached at Pentecost, but Peter was the chief spokesman.

The *second* time Peter used the keys was when, in the house of Cornelius, he opened the doors of the Kingdom to the vast Gentile world. (You can read the entire account in Acts chapter 10.) Cornelius was "a devout man," a praying man. He feared and worshipped God according to all the light and understanding he had, but Acts 11:14 plainly tells us that he was not born again. The angel of God commanded Cornelius to send men to Joppa where they were to call for Simon Peter.

Meanwhile, in Joppa, Peter was praying; and God gave him a great vision which would prepare his heart for the mission to the house of Cornelius, a Gentile. Peter saw in the vision a great sheet, "knit at the four corners . . . wherein were all manner of fourfooted beasts of the earth, and wild beasts, and creeping things, and fowls of the air." Peter was hungry, but when God told him to "kill, and eat," Peter replied that he had never eaten anything that could be declared common or unclean. Then the voice from heaven rebuked Peter: *"What God hath cleansed, that call not thou common."* Three times this was done, and while Peter wondered what the vision meant, the men from the house of Cornelius came, and the Holy Spirit instructed Peter to go with them. Thus by the vision God showed Peter that the "unclean" Gentiles were no longer unclean, for God had given the cleansing blood of the Lamb—blood that would cleanse Gentiles as well as Jews. Peter immediately went to the house of Cornelius and preached the Gospel to those who had assembled there. They received the Word, the Holy Spirit fell upon them, and they were saved:

"And they of the circumcision (Jews) were astonished, as many as came with Peter, because that on the Gentiles also was poured out the gift of the Holy Ghost. For they heard them speak with tongues, and magnify God. Then answered Peter, Can any man forbid water, that these should not be baptized, which have received the Holy Ghost as well as we? And he commanded them to be baptized in the name of the Lord. Then prayed they him to tarry certain days" (Acts 10:45-48).

As you study the Scriptures you will see that never again was there any use of the keys of the Kingdom. The doors were now open to all, and all who would might enter in.

". . . *whatsoever thou shalt bind on earth shall be bound in heaven; and whatsoever thou shalt loose on earth shall be loosed in heaven.*" Some religionists have attempted to put Peter on a pedestal, declaring that he had authority and power which has been passed on down to men today; but Peter himself made no assumption of any such authority. (Please study Acts 15:7-11.) He claimed no more for himself than that he was "an apostle of Jesus Christ" (I Pet. 1:1) and an elder by office (I Pet. 5:1).

This last part of our present verse has nothing to do with forgiving sins or saving souls. Furthermore, the power of "binding" and "loosing" was not given exclusively to Peter, but was shared by the other apostles (Matt. 18:1-18). That it did not involve the determination of the eternal destiny of the soul is proved in Revelation 1:18 where the risen, glorified Christ declared, "I am He that liveth, and was dead; and, behold, I am alive for evermore, Amen; *and have the keys of hell and of death.*"

The keys of death and hell are held by the Lord Jesus Christ alone. Remember His words in John 10:9: *"I am THE Door.* By me if any man enter in, he shall be saved . . . ." All who attempt to enter heaven by any way other than by THE DOOR, "the same is a thief and a robber" (John 10:1). In John 14:6 Jesus also declared, *"I am the WAY,* the truth, and the life: *NO MAN cometh unto the Father, BUT BY ME."*

The doctrine that Peter could forgive sins—or that he could *refuse* to forgive sins—is pure heresy! When Jesus said to Peter, "I will give unto thee the keys of the Kingdom of Heaven," He meant that He would make Peter the instrument to open the door of faith to the whole world—to Jews and Gentiles alike. But the power to "bind" and "loose" was also given to the other apostles along with Peter.

"*. . . WHATSOEVER thou shalt bind . . . WHATSOEVER thou shalt loose . . .*" does not refer to *persons.* It says "*WHATsoever,*" not "*WHOsoever.*" Therefore it refers to *things* and not to living souls. It has to do with various ceremonies and rites in the Church. The expressions "to bind" and "to loose" were used by the Jews quite often. The meaning was to *prohibit* on one hand, and to *permit* on the other. To "bind" meant to *forbid* whatever it was. To "loose" meant to *allow* whatever was in question. The Jewish customs were many, and those customs were to be forbidden in the Church. In giving the apostles the power to bind or loose, Jesus meant that whatsoever they, as the Holy Ghost led them, should forbid in the Church here on earth, the same would be honored by divine authority in heaven. By like token, whatsoever they, led by the Spirit, permitted or commanded in the Church on earth, the same would have divine authority and permission in heaven.

I repeat—the Church at that time did not have the epistles as we have them today. They did not have all truth as we have it today. In John 16:12-15 Jesus explained to the disciples, "I have yet many things to say unto you, but ye cannot bear them now. Howbeit *when He, the SPIRIT OF TRUTH, is come, He will guide you into all truth:* for He shall not speak of Himself; but whatsoever He shall hear, that shall He speak: and *He will shew you things to come.* He shall glorify me: for He shall receive of mine, and shall shew it unto you. All things that the Father hath are mine: therefore said I, that *He shall take of mine, and shall shew it unto you."* Jesus gave to the apostles this power to "bind" or to "loose," but it was not handed down to any other minister or teacher after those apostles.

As the apostles organized local assemblies in the various communities where they carried the good news of salvation, they were to be guided, first by the teachings of Christ, and then by the Holy Spirit; and when one is guided by the words of Jesus and the leadership of the Holy Spirit, he will not make rules or regulations according to man's ideas. There are customs and teachings—both major and minor—in various denominations today, and some of these customs and teachings are *deadly to the Spirit.* Others, while not deadly to the Spirit, greatly hinder the work of the Lord in the Church and community.

The apostles who organized the first local assemblies were the only persons to direct young converts in matters pertaining to what they should, or should not, do in the Church in order to honor the Lord Jesus Christ. We see an example of this in Acts 15:20 where the Gentile converts were commanded to "abstain from pollutions of idols, and from fornication, and from things strangled, and from blood."

The rules and regulations laid down by the apostles in the Book of Acts and in the epistles constitute the *only* rules and regulations which are binding upon Christians. These are the only rites and ceremonies to be observed in the order of the New Testament Church. It was from abuse of such Scriptures as Matthew 16:19, 18:18, and John 20:23 that many erroneous teachings sprang up shortly after the death of the apostles. In some religions, even today, it is taught that man can forgive sins, and that the authority given to Peter has been passed on down to men today. It is Gospel truth that the minister, the evangelist, and Bible teacher called of God may teach the *conditions* of forgiveness; but no man has the inspired power to discern the spiritual condition of a person's heart. No man on earth today has the power to determine whether a person is saved or lost, and no man has the authority to forgive sins. *ONLY JESUS can forgive sins.*

Verse 20: *"Then charged He His disciples that they should tell no man that He was Jesus the Christ."*

"Then charged He His disciples . . . ." The

87

meaning here is that Jesus *commanded* the disciples, or charged them in a very strict manner, as concerning a matter of extreme importance. He was not yet ready to arouse any more Jewish malice against Himself and further endanger His life by letting the disciples declare at that particular moment that He was truly the Messiah of God, Saviour of sinners, very God in flesh. Therefore He commanded them *to "tell no man that He was Jesus the Christ."*

Christ Foretells His Death and Resurrection

Verse 21: *"From that time forth began Jesus to shew unto His disciples, how that He must go unto Jerusalem, and suffer many things of the elders and chief priests and scribes, and be killed, and be raised again the third day."*

"From that time forth began Jesus to shew unto His disciples . . . ." In this verse Jesus mentions Calvary for the first time. Here He gives the disciples the first intimation that He would die on a Roman cross. He had been very careful to first convince them that He was Messiah, the One promised to Israel; and when Peter confessed, "Thou art the Christ, the Son of the living God," Jesus knew that these men now recognized that He was the true Messiah. He then began to prepare their hearts and minds for the events that were shortly to follow.

You see, if Jesus had made His coming persecution and crucifixion known to each of the disciples as He called them to discipleship, it is doubtful that any of them would have followed Him. They were expecting the Messiah, a powerful King, a victorious Leader, and it was necessary that they be convinced that Jesus was truly the Christ of God before He could teach them of the proper character, mission, and ministry of the Messiah. He here *begins* His instructions, but repeats those instructions again and again as His ministry continues. (Please notice Matthew 17: 9-23; 20:18, 19; 26:2, 12, 31; and John 12:23.)

Here begins a new epoch in the ministry of Jesus here on earth, an epoch that lasted probably from six to nine months before He was arrested, condemned, and crucified. This was a new teaching to the disciples—but let us not assume that *Jesus Himself* did not know of His approaching death until this time. Jesus knew when He left the Father's bosom exactly why He was coming into the world. (Study John 2:19; 3:14; Matthew 9:15; 10:38; and 12:40.)

Jesus began to explain to the disciples *"how that He MUST go unto Jerusalem . . . ."* Notice the words used here. Jesus *"must"* go—that is, it was a divine necessity that He go into Jerusalem at that time in order to carry out His mission and accomplish the work the Father had given Him to do. (Read Matthew 26:54 and Luke 24:26.)

At that particular moment, Jesus was as far from Jerusalem as it was possible for Him to be and still remain in Palestine. At Jerusalem the opposition to Him was extremely bitter. Those who had assailed Him most fiercely in Galilee came from Jerusalem (Mark 3:22; Matt. 15:1). He had not openly attended the preceding Passover because the Jews at Jerusalem were determined to kill Him (John 7:1). But from this time forward the thought of going to Jerusalem and facing all that awaited Him there was the outstanding thought in His mind. What He was to accomplish in Jerusalem and what would befall Him there *could not happen EXCEPT in Jerusalem.*

Luke tells us that "He went through the cities and villages, teaching, and *journeying toward Jerusalem. . . .* The same day there came certain of the Pharisees, saying unto Him, Get thee out, and depart hence: for Herod will kill thee. And He said unto them, Go ye, and tell that fox, Behold, I cast out devils, and I do cures to day and to morrow, and the third day I shall be perfected. Nevertheless I must walk to day, and to morrow, and the day following: *for it cannot be that a prophet perish out of Jerusalem"* (Luke 13:22, 31-33).

". . . and suffer many things of the elders and chief priests and scribes . . . ." The elders, the chief priests, and the scribes were the Lord's most fierce and deadly enemies. Those three classes

90

constituted the Sanhedrin, the ruling body of the Jews.

"... *and be killed, and be raised again the third day.*" Can you imagine how the announcement of His forthcoming death affected the disciples of Jesus? They could not imagine that He, their Lord, the promised Messiah, would be killed. They were so upset about His death, I doubt that they even *heard* His final statement that He would rise again!

The fact that Jesus would "be raised again the third day" had been obscurely given to His enemies (John 2:19; Matt. 12:40), but until now He had not given it directly to the disciples. He gave it to them here in simple but distinct words, and He repeated the statement on two subsequent occasions (Matt. 17:23; 20:19).

In Matthew 17:9 Jesus declared the fact of His resurrection without mentioning the three days. In Mark 8:31, 32 we read: "And He began to teach them, that the Son of man must suffer many things, and be rejected of the elders, and of the chief priests, and scribes, and be killed, and after three days rise again. *And He spake that saying OPENLY,*" as opposed to the previous obscure expressions.

The disciples believed in a resurrection at the last day. (Read John 11:24.) But they knew that was not the meaning of what Jesus was saying here, for how then could He do the work of the

Messiah that was to be done on earth? They knew that other persons had been raised from the dead. Jesus Himself had raised the daughter of Jairus (Matt. 9:18-26) and the son of the widow of Nain (Luke 7:11-17). But the disciples could not understand that Jesus their Lord, their Messiah, would die, be placed in a tomb, and then shortly—after three days—would come forth from that tomb alive. Perhaps they thought He was speaking figuratively. That they did not believe He would be raised again *bodily* is proved by the fact that after Jesus was crucified and had been placed in Joseph's tomb, Peter and the other disciples returned to their nets and went fishing, indicating that their high hopes for the Kingdom were dead. Had they believed that Jesus would return from the dead they would certainly have lingered at the sepulchre for the allotted three days to pass.

Luke 24:13-35 tells us that the *risen Christ* was not recognized when He joined the two men who were journeying to Emmaus. He walked and talked with them in the way, discussing His own death — "but their eyes were holden that they should not know Him. And He said unto them, What manner of communications are these that ye have one to another, as ye walk, *and are sad?* And the one of them . . . answering said unto Him, Art thou only a stranger in Jerusalem, and hast not known the things which are come to pass there in these days? . . . Concerning Jesus of Nazareth, which was a Prophet mighty in deed and word before God and all the people: and how the chief priests and our rulers delivered Him to be condemned to death, and have crucified Him. *But we trusted that it had been He which should have redeemed Israel: and beside all this, to day is the third day since these things were done.* Yea, and certain women also of our company *made us astonished,* which were early at the sepulchre; and when they found not His body, they came, saying, that they had also seen a vision of angels, *which said that He was alive."*

When they reached Emmaus, the men invited Jesus to have the evening meal with them, and "as He sat at meat with them, He took bread, and blessed it, and brake, and gave to them. And their eyes were opened, and they knew Him; and He vanished out of their sight." Later that same day, Jesus told His disciples, "These are the words which I spake unto you, while I was yet with you, *that all things must be fulfilled, which were written in the law of Moses, and in the prophets, and in the psalms, concerning me"* (v. 44).

Jesus had said to Peter (in verse 18 of Matthew chapter 16), "Upon this rock *I WILL build* my Church," but the beginning of the building of the Church could not be possible until the redemptive work of the Lord Jesus Christ was finished.

Verse 22: *"Then Peter took Him, and began to*

rebuke Him, saying, Be it far from thee, Lord: this shall not be unto thee."

". . . Peter took Him, and began to rebuke Him." This same disciple, only a little while ago, had made the God-revealed confession, "Thou art *the Christ*, the Son of the living God." Now he has become a mouthpiece for the adversary, the arch-enemy of the Lamb of God. Peter spoke here in the impulsiveness of the flesh. It was the *natural* man speaking, not the spiritual man. Peter was a Jew, and with his fellow disciples he strongly believed that Jesus would destroy the enemies of the Jews, set up a glorious Kingdom, and that the disciples would reign with Him and have a very prominent place in the Kingdom.

The implication here is that Peter drew Jesus aside to make his rebuke personal and private. Possibly he did not want to embarrass Jesus before the other disciples. So he took Him aside *"and began to rebuke Him."* The word *"rebuke"* here signifies *wrong*—that is, Peter did not agree with what Jesus had just said. He did not appreciate the *"must"* in verse 21 as denoting the absolute and divine necessity of the death of Jesus in Jerusalem. Peter was saying, "That is not necessary. There is no reason for it."

Peter believed that Jesus was Messiah, but according to all the Messianic prophecies in the Old Testament he also understood that Messiah would be a great King and would re-establish the glory of Israel in the Kingdom on earth. Certainly, in Peter's thinking, "the Christ, the Son of the living God" would not be put to death in the Holy City Jerusalem.

"Be it far from thee, Lord: this shall not be unto thee." This is practically the same as saying, *"God forbid!"* Literally, Peter was saying, "God will have mercy on thee. God will not allow this to happen to thee!" Peter was so sure in his heart that such a thing should not happen, and—for the moment at least—he was persuaded that Jesus would follow his protestations and not go to Jerusalem and expose Himself to His enemies.

Verse 23: *"But He turned, and said unto Peter, Get thee behind me, Satan: thou art an offence unto me: for thou savourest not the things that be of God, but those that be of men."*

"Get thee behind me, Satan." This expresses the same revulsion and horror with which Jesus spoke directly to Satan when, on the Mount of Temptation, He commanded, "Get thee hence, Satan" (Matt. 4:10). Peter loved his Lord, but he was impulsive. He had a zeal, but it was zeal without knowledge. In refusing to accept the fact of Calvary, he was playing the tempter's part, repeating the temptation Satan had used in his attempt to get Jesus to by-pass Calvary. (Please read Matthew 4:3-11.)

"Thou art an offence unto me." The meaning

95

here is that Peter was a stumblingblock, an obstacle, something which would hinder Jesus from going forward to complete the work He had come into the world to do. Satan *knew* why Jesus was on earth, and he did everything in his diabolical power to forestall and circumvent that mission. He knew that the death of Jesus on the cross, the path of humiliation and obedience unto death, would lead to his defeat. He knew that when Jesus said "It is finished," Satan's power over death would be broken and his defeat assured. Therefore, the devil made a very subtle attempt to use the Apostle Peter to hinder the Lord in His walk toward Calvary.

"Thou savourest not the things that be of God . . . ." In other words, "You are not thinking of, attending to, or minding the things of God, *but those that be of men."* Peter was carried away by the traditional human view of the way Messiah would set up His Kingdom. He had no idea of the full import of the words he had spoken so rashly.

Verse 24: *"Then said Jesus unto His disciples, If any man will come after me, let him deny himself, and take up his cross, and follow me."*

These words were spoken to the disciples of Jesus—*saved* men, not unbelievers. Therefore it is plain that we are not asked to deny self and take up a cross in order to be born again. We are born again by faith in the finished work of the Lamb of God. We are born again through the incorruptible seed, the Word of God (I Pet. 1:23). "Giving up... denying self... taking up a cross"—these things will not *save*. Salvation is *the gift of God,* freely given. But one who is truly born again *will* deny self and take up his cross if he desires to follow Jesus.

In this present verse Jesus incorporated, briefly, the great truths of the spiritual association of the believer with our Lord. In the epistles, the Holy Spirit brings out fully what Jesus states here in few words. In the Gospel of John we read, "Verily, verily, I say unto you, Except a corn of wheat fall into the ground and die, it abideth alone: but if it die, it bringeth forth much fruit. He that loveth his life shall lose it; and he that hateth his life in this world shall keep it unto life eternal. If any man serve me, let him follow me; and where I am, there shall also my servant be: if any man serve me, him will my Father honour" (John 12: 24-26).

There is a vast difference between the Lord Jesus Christ and the believer—e. g., *ONLY Jesus* could drink the bitter cup, the cup He saw in the Garden when He cried out, "If it be possible, let this cup pass from me"—and then added, "Nevertheless, not as I will, but as thou wilt" (Matt. 26:39). He alone could fill the requirement of Almighty God. He alone could walk the path that is our path today because He walked it for us.

Isaiah 26:3 declares, "Thou wilt keep him in perfect peace, whose mind is stayed on thee . . . ." In this Dispensation of Grace the believer is to keep his eyes on Jesus, walk in His footsteps, and allow Him to lead us in the paths of righteousness for His name's sake.

In Joshua chapter 3 we find an interesting account of God's people crossing over Jordan. The ark of the covenant led the way, and the people followed, keeping a space of two thousand cubits between the ark of the covenant and the people. Thus the ark opened the way over Jordan, and the people, following the ark, passed dry-shod through Jordan into Jericho. This sets forth a beautiful type for us: *Jesus made the way,* and we are to follow Him: "For even hereunto were ye called: because Christ also suffered for us, *leaving us an example, that ye should follow His steps*" (I Pet. 2:21). If we follow as He leads, one day we will be like Him:

"Behold, what manner of love the Father hath bestowed upon us, that we should be called the sons of God: therefore the world knoweth us not, because it knew Him not. Beloved, now are we the sons of God, and it doth not yet appear what we shall be: *but we know that, when He shall appear, we shall be LIKE HIM; for we shall see Him as He is.* And *every man that hath this hope in Him PURIFIETH himself, even as He is pure*" (I John 3:1-3).

God forbid that I should judge any man, but Jesus declared, "Wherefore by their fruits ye shall know them" (Matt. 7:20). As you look at professed Christians in your community, in your church, and in the place where you work, how many do you know who *deny themselves* to serve God? There is little self-denial in the world today. Many believers do not follow Jesus step by step, they do not walk in the path He marked out for us. Yes, it is entirely possible to be a born again believer and still not follow Jesus step by step. There are many such believers today. Their souls are saved, their spirits will dwell eternally in that beautiful city—but they will have no reward because they are selfish, self-centered, and unconcerned about the things of Christ. They will be saved *"so as by fire"* (I Cor. 3:15).

To deny self, as here spoken of by Jesus, means renouncing oneself in the same manner the Jews renounced (or denied) Jesus the Messiah. In Acts 3:14 Peter said to the Jews, "Ye *denied* the Holy One and the Just, and desired a murderer to be granted unto you."

When a believer denies self, he will not allow self and selfish desires to rule him or dictate his aims in life. A believer who denies himself determines in his heart and mind not to live according to his own inclinations and desires, but to be so completely controlled by the Holy Spirit that whatever he says or does is said or done to the glory

99

of God. The Apostle Paul so instructs us in I Corinthians 10:31:

"Whether therefore ye EAT, or DRINK, or WHATSOEVER ye do, do ALL to the glory of God."

The Christian who is willing to deny himself must resolve to live not after the things of this life such as pleasure, fame, and fortune. We are commanded, "Love not the world, neither the things that are in the world. If any man love the world, the love of the Father is not in him. For all that is in the world, the lust of the flesh, and the lust of the eyes, and the pride of life, is not of the Father, but is of the world. And the world passeth away, and the lust thereof: but he that doeth the will of God abideth for ever" (I John 2:15-17).

Sometimes it is necessary for a Christian to deny himself for the sake of a weaker brother in Christ. There may be things in which you or I could take part—not evil, lust, or ungodliness, but various and sundry things in our society— and our participation would not affect our own Christian life. But if, to a weaker brother, our participation in those things would seem wrong, then we would bring harm to his spiritual life and cause his weak faith to become even weaker. Paul was so careful and considerate of weaker Christians that he declared, "Wherefore, if meat make my brother to offend, I will eat no flesh while the world standeth, lest I make my brother to offend" (I Cor. 8:13). Paul knew that it was not a sin for him to eat meat that had been offered to idols; but some of the new converts felt that it was wrong to partake of such meat. Therefore Paul would deny himself rather than offend a weaker Christian who had not the knowledge Paul had. To sin against a weak brother by offending his conscience is to sin against Christ (I Cor. 8:12).

Paul explains, "For none of us liveth to himself, and no man dieth to himself. For whether we live, we live unto the Lord; and whether we die, we die unto the Lord: whether we live therefore, or die, we are the Lord's. For to this end Christ both died, and rose, and revived, that He might be Lord both of the dead and living. . . . If thy brother be grieved with thy meat, now walkest thou not charitably. Destroy not him with thy meat, for whom Christ died. Let not then your good be evil spoken of" (Rom. 14:7-9, 15, 16).

"Take up his cross" is not to be understood to mean that we should choose a cross, or find a cross of our choosing and then take that cross. Notice Jesus said *"HIS cross."* That is, *the individual's* cross, not the same cross Jesus bore when He went up the hill to be crucified. You may rest assured that when a believer practices self-denial and is fully surrendered to the leadership of the Holy Spirit, the cross for that believer

will appear! Let us take up the cross willingly, and follow Jesus.

Verse 25: *"For whosoever will save his life shall lose it: and whosoever will lose his life for my sake shall find it."*

Please notice that verses 25, 26, and 27 open with the preposition *"for."* The fact that each of these verses begins with *"for"* points to that which precedes with a truth or a motive. In our present verse, the Lord passes *from BODILY life to SPIRITUAL life*—from the temporal to the eternal. He also passes from the vital principle of the body (the natural life) to the immortal principle (that which has to do with the spiritual life). Therefore we understand that Jesus is saying here, "Whosoever desires to save his temporal, fleshly, bodily life shall lose his spiritual, eternal life."

In Galatians 6:8 Paul explains that if we sow to the flesh, corruption is the result; but if we sow to the Spirit, life everlasting is the result. "The carnal mind is enmity against God" and therefore cannot be subject to the realm (or law) of God (Rom. 8:7). It must follow, then, that if a man has a mind *to SAVE his temporal life* and follow the desires and inclinations of the flesh, he will certainly *LOSE his spiritual life* because he cannot serve two masters (Matt. 6:24).

". . . whosoever will lose his life FOR MY SAKE

102

shall find it." In Mark 8:35 we read, ". . . whosoever shall lose his life *for MY SAKE and the GOSPEL'S*, the same shall *save* it."

Verse 26: *"For what is a man profited, if he shall gain the whole world, and lose his own soul? or what shall a man give in exchange for his soul?"*

To *"gain the whole world"* means to possess *(own)* the world with all of its riches, honors, pleasures, privileges—all that the world affords or could afford. By contrast, to lose one's soul means to be cast into the lake of fire, to be shut out from the Pearly White City, to dwell in outer darkness separated forever from God.

". . . what is a man profited, if he shall . . . lose his own soul? . . . what shall a man give in exchange for his soul?" Two things are implied by the Lord Jesus in these two questions: (1) Those who put riches and position ahead of serving the Lord will *lose their soul.* (2) If a man loses his soul, there is nothing that can be given *in exchange* for the soul that is lost. There is no redemption or pardon in hell. There is no chance for one to be saved beyond the grave.

Many men today are striving to possess more and more of this world's treasures and riches. They are not willing to forsake personal ambition in order to serve Jesus. They are not willing to trust the Holy Spirit to lead them in paths of righteousness and leave material things in the hands of God.

Do not misunderstand me—*riches do not damn the soul.* But if a person is married to riches, if riches have become his god, the riches become a stumblingblock, a barrier, between man and God. Proverbs 11:28 says, *"He that TRUSTETH in his riches shall FALL...."* Paul told Timothy, "They that will be rich fall into temptation and a snare, and into many foolish and hurtful lusts, which drown men in destruction and perdition. For *the love of money is the root of all evil:* which while some coveted after, they have erred from the faith, and pierced themselves through with many sorrows" (I Tim. 6:9, 10).

God blesses some Christians with material things, and those material things are in turn used to the glory of God in promoting the spread of the Gospel. But such a Christian does not make money his idol. The possession of material things will not damn the soul if those things are kept in proper perspective. It is when worldly possessions become an obsession and contribute to lack of faith in God that riches become deadly. *Unbelief* is the sin that damns the soul: "He that believeth on (Jesus) is not condemned: but *he that believeth NOT is condemned already, BECAUSE he hath not believed in the name of the only begotten Son of God"* (John 3:18).

The Greek word here translated *"lose"* means

forfeit. The verb is derived from the noun rendered *"loss"* as opposed to *"gain."* We find this in I Corinthians 3:15 where Paul speaks of *loss of reward,* and in Philippians 3:8 where Paul testifies, *". . . I count all things but loss* for the excellency of the knowledge of Christ Jesus my Lord: for whom I have suffered *the loss of all things,* and do count them but dung, *that I may win Christ."*

Thus, if a man gains the world with all its treasures but has not faith in Jesus, when that man comes to the end of life *he must pay the forfeit (or fine)* for serving the world and ignoring Christ—and the fine paid will be *the condemnation of his soul!*

In view of this divine fact, what, indeed, *"shall a man give IN EXCHANGE for his soul?"* What can man produce that will buy back the soul that is lost? All the world could not suffice. *One soul* in the eyes of Almighty God is of more value than all the wealth of all the world. The Greek here denotes that which, by exchange, takes the place of something else. Jesus paid our ransom. He suffered and died that we might have eternal life. He *"bare OUR sins in His own body on the tree,* that we, being dead to sins, should live unto righteousness . . ."* (I Pet. 2:24). *He took OUR place,* and if we fail to put our faith in Jesus and in His finished work, *"there remaineth no more sacrifice for sins"* (Heb. 10:26). There is none other who can redeem the soul. Peter declares, *"Neither* *is there salvation in any other: for there is none other name under heaven given among men, whereby we must be saved"* (Acts 4:12).

If a man should *gain* the whole world, he could not buy the freedom of one soul in hell! God's Word declares: "They that trust in their wealth, and boast themselves in the multitude of their riches; *none of them can by any means redeem his brother, nor give to God a ransom for him"* (Psalm 49:6, 7). The life Jesus lived, the sufferings He endured, the sacrifice He made through the blood He shed—these are of more value in the eyes of God than all the rubies, diamonds, gold, and silver, the multi-billions in wealth which the world might have to offer.

Is it any wonder that the blood of Jesus is called "precious"? Without the shedding of blood is no remission of sin, no redemption (Heb. 9:22). All things on earth combined could not redeem one soul:

"Forasmuch as ye know that *ye were not redeemed with corruptible things, as silver and gold,* from your vain conversation received by tradition from your fathers; *but with the PRECIOUS BLOOD OF CHRIST,* as of a lamb without blemish and without spot: who verily was foreordained before the foundation of the world, but was manifest in these last times for you" (I Pet. 1:18-20).

"If we walk in the light, as He is in the light, we have fellowship one with another, *and the blood of Jesus Christ His Son cleanseth us FROM ALL SIN"* (I John 1:7).

Verse 27: *"For the Son of man shall come in the glory of His Father with His angels; and then He shall reward every man according to his works."*

"For the Son of man shall come . . . ." Jesus here was not using a figure of speech. That great event will actually occur. One day the Son of man shall come, just as He promised. He said He would go and prepare a place for His own, and that He would return. (Read John 14:1-3.) In Acts 1:11 we are assured that *"this SAME JESUS . . . shall so come in like manner"* as He ascended into heaven.

Jesus will return to this earth, but His second coming will not be as a Babe in a manger. He will come *"in the glory of His Father with His angels"*—the glory the Son had with the Father "before the world was" (John 17:5). Jesus voluntarily left His glory and came to earth on a singular mission—to pay sin's debt by His death on the cross. He "made Himself of no reputation, and took upon Him the form of a servant, and was made in the likeness of men: and being found in fashion as a man, He humbled Himself, and became obedient unto death, even the death of the cross" (Phil. 2:7, 8). But when He comes again He will come in glory, not in humiliation.

Not only will He come in *glory.* He will come

107

"with His angels." (Please notice Matthew 13:41; 24:31; and 25:31.) Luke 9:26 speaks of Christ's coming "in His own glory, and in His Father's (glory), and of the holy angels," thus implying that the encompassing glory of the host of angels will enhance the glory of the Son of man. What a sight that will be—when we behold the glory of the Father, the glory of the Son, and the glory of the angels!

". . . and then shall He reward every man according to his works." This statement indicates that Jesus will be the final Judge, as set forth in Matthew 7:21-23, Matthew 25:31-34, and John 5:22. But He will not judge as man judges. He will judge in righteousness (Rev. 19:11), and He will reward men *according to their "works"*—that is, according to their actions, practices, and course in life. A righteous man works the works of righteousness. The unrighteous man works the works of unrighteousness. Sweet water cannot flow from a bitter fountain, nor can bitter water flow from a sweet fountain (James 3:11, 12).

The Righteous Judge will *"reward every man"*—yes, both saint and sinner—*according to that man's works* (or stewardship). Paul states: "For we (believers) must all appear before the judgment seat of Christ; that every one may receive the things done in his body, *according to that he hath done, whether it be good or bad"* (II Cor. 5:10).

In I Corinthians 3:11-15 Paul explains about the

rewards for the saints: "For other foundation can no man lay than that is laid, which is Jesus Christ. Now if any man build upon this foundation *gold, silver, precious stones, wood, hay, stubble; every man's work shall be made manifest:* for the day shall declare it, because *it shall be revealed by fire;* and the fire shall try every man's work *of what sort it is.* If any man's work abide which he hath built thereupon, he shall *receive a reward.* If any man's work shall be burned, *he shall suffer loss:* but he himself shall be saved; yet so as by fire."

Jesus will come in the Rapture, before the tribulation period, and will at that time call His saints up to meet Him in the air, and they will be judged. At the end of the tribulation period He will come in the Revelation, His feet will stand on the Mount of Olives (Zech. 14:4), and it is then that He will set up the millennial Kingdom. After the Millennium, sinners will be judged at the Great White Throne Judgment according to the degree of their wickedness:

"And I saw a great white throne, and Him that sat on it . . . . And I saw the dead, small and great, stand before God; and the books were opened: and another book was opened, which is the book of life: and *the dead were judged out of those things which were written in the books, according to their works.* And the sea gave up the dead which were in it; and death and hell delivered up the dead which were in them: and *they were judged every man according to their works"* (Rev. 20:11-13).

Verse 28: *"Verily I say unto you, There be some standing here, which shall not taste of death, till they see the Son of man coming in His Kingdom."*

Some ministers and teachers have suggested that Jesus was speaking here of the destruction of Jerusalem in 70 A. D. when Titus the Roman and his army leveled that city. Others suggest that Jesus was speaking of the New Testament Church. Personally, I cannot accept either of these interpretations. When Jerusalem was destroyed by the Romans, *Jesus did not appear.* I cannot accept the teaching that He was speaking of *the Church* because the Church is not the Kingdom. The Church is the body of Christ, His bride, but the Kingdom will be right here on earth.

Notice Jesus said, "There be *some* standing here *(not ALL, but SOME)* which shall not taste of death, till they see the Son of man coming in His Kingdom." I believe this statement referred to Peter, James, and John, and their experience on the Mount of Transfiguration when those three disciples witnessed the glory of Jesus as Moses and Elijah came down to talk with Him (Matt. 17:1-8). Peter speaks of this in II Peter 1:16: "We have not followed cunningly devised fables, when we made known unto you *the power and coming of our Lord Jesus Christ, but were eyewitnesses of His majesty."* We will take this up again in our next chapter when we discuss the verses which record the event of the transfiguration of Jesus.

Thank God for this glorious chapter we have just studied! I would like to point out and review two or three points for which I am doubly thankful, and which we covered in this chapter:

1. *The warning to be on guard against error* (vv. 6-12). Error is deceitful, cunning and sly. It works secretly—but effectually. We must be very careful about what we accept and believe as truth from those who profess to be preachers and teachers of the Word. The Word of God should be the standard by which we measure and compare all that is taught in our presence. False doctrine is always made as much like the true Gospel as the devil can possibly make it. Satan would like for us to embrace the doctrine that there is "a little *good* in *all* religions." He would have us *accept* the "good" in all religions, thus poisoning the mind and damning the soul! *There is only ONE WAY, one TRUTH, one LIFE, one NAME, one DOOR, one GATE. There are no detours and no side entrances to heaven.* We must be alert and vigilant at all times lest we support the enemies of Jesus, "for Satan himself is transformed into an angel of light. Therefore it is no great thing if his ministers also be transformed

111

as the ministers of righteousness; whose end shall be according to their works" (II Cor. 11:14, 15).

2. *The extreme importance of ascertaining definite views of Christ* (vv. 13, 15). "Whom do men say that I the Son of man am? . . . *Whom say YE that I am?*" We must accept what the Word of God reveals about Christ, not what men may teach about Him unless that teaching is backed up by "Thus saith the Lord."

3. *The teaching of the coming of the New Testament Church* (v. 18). Jesus *promised* to build His Church—and He kept His promise. The Church was born on the Day of Pentecost, and though the Church may suffer much, weep much, endure much persecution and at times appear weak and almost defeated, we are assured that even though rich and great rulers may set themselves against the Church, *the GATES OF HELL shall not prevail against it!*

Chapter XVII

1. And after six days Jesus taketh Peter, James, and John his brother, and bringeth them up into an high mountain apart,

2. And was transfigured before them: and his face did shine as the sun, and his raiment was white as the light.

3. And, behold, there appeared unto them Moses and Elias talking with him.

4. Then answered Peter, and said unto Jesus, Lord, it is good for us to be here: if thou wilt, let us make here three tabernacles; one for thee, and one for Moses, and one for Elias.

5. While he yet spake, behold, a bright cloud overshadowed them: and behold a voice out of the cloud, which said, This is my beloved Son, in whom I am well pleased; hear ye him.

6. And when the disciples heard it, they fell on their face, and were sore afraid.

7. And Jesus came and touched them, and said, Arise, and be not afraid.

8. And when they had lifted up their eyes, they saw no man, save Jesus only.

9. And as they came down from the mountain, Jesus charged them, saying, Tell the vision to no man, until the Son of man be risen again from the dead.

10. And his disciples asked him, saying, Why then say the scribes that Elias must first come?

11. And Jesus answered and said unto them, Elias truly shall first come, and restore all things.

12. But I say unto you, That Elias is come already, and they knew him not, but have done unto him whatsoever they listed. Likewise shall also the Son of man suffer of them.

13. Then the disciples understood that he spake unto them of John the Baptist.

14. And when they were come to the multitude, there came to him a certain man, kneeling down to him, and saying,

15. Lord, have mercy on my son: for he is lunatick, and sore vexed: for ofttimes he falleth into the fire, and oft into the water.

16. And I brought him to thy disciples, and they could not cure him.

17. Then Jesus answered and said, O faithless and perverse generation, how long shall I be with you? how long shall I suffer you? bring him hither to me.

18. And Jesus rebuked the devil; and he departed out of him: and the child was cured from that very hour.

19. Then came the disciples to Jesus apart, and said, Why could not we cast him out?

20. And Jesus said unto them, Because of your unbelief: for verily I say unto you, If ye have faith as a grain of mustard seed, ye shall say unto this mountain, Remove hence to yonder place; and it shall remove; and nothing shall be impossible unto you.

21. Howbeit this kind goeth not out but by prayer and fasting.

22. And while they abode in Galilee, Jesus said unto them, The Son of man shall be betrayed into the hands of men:

23. And they shall kill him, and the third day he shall be raised again. And they were exceeding sorry.

24. And when they were come to Capernaum, they that received tribute money came to Peter, and said, Doth not your master pay tribute?

25. He saith, Yes. And when he was come into the house, Jesus prevented him, saying, What thinkest thou, Simon? of whom do the kings of the earth take custom or tribute? of their own children, or of strangers?

26. Peter saith unto him, Of strangers. Jesus saith unto him, Then are the children free.

27. Notwithstanding, lest we should offend them, go thou to the sea, and cast an hook, and take up the fish that first cometh up; and when thou hast opened his mouth, thou shalt find a piece of money: that take, and give unto them for me and thee.

The Transfiguration—
A Picture of the Future Kingdom

Mark and Luke also record the events covered in this chapter of Matthew. It might be well to consider these other accounts in connection with Matthew's record of the Transfiguration. In *Mark 9:2-10* we read:

"And after six days Jesus taketh with Him Peter, and James, and John, and leadeth them up into an high mountain apart by themselves: and He was transfigured before them. And His raiment became shining, exceeding white as snow; so as no fuller on earth can white them. And there appeared unto them Elias with Moses: and they were talking with Jesus. And Peter answered and said to Jesus, Master, it is good for us to be here: and let us make three tabernacles; one for thee, and one for Moses, and one for Elias. For he wist not what to say; for they were sore afraid.

"And there was a cloud that overshadowed them: and a voice came out of the cloud, saying, This is my beloved Son: hear Him. And suddenly, when they had looked round about, they saw no man any more, save Jesus only with themselves. And as they came down from the mountain, He charged them that they should tell no man what things they had seen, till the Son of man were risen from the dead. And they kept that saying with themselves, questioning one with another what the rising from the dead should mean."

In *Luke 9:28-36* we find the same incident recorded:

"And it came to pass about an eight days after these sayings, He took Peter and John and James, and went up into a mountain to pray. And as He prayed, the fashion of His countenance was altered, and His raiment was white and glistering. And, behold, there talked with Him two men, which were Moses and Elias: who appeared in glory, and spake of His decease which He should accomplish at Jerusalem. But Peter and they that were with him were heavy with sleep: and when they were awake, they saw His glory, and the two men that stood with Him. And it came to pass, as they departed from Him, Peter said unto

Jesus, Master, it is good for us to be here: and let us make three tabernacles; one for thee, and one for Moses, and one for Elias: not knowing what he said.

"While he thus spake, there came a cloud, and overshadowed them: and they feared as they entered into the cloud. And there came a voice out of the cloud, saying, This is my beloved Son: hear Him. And when the voice was past, Jesus was found alone. And they kept it close, and told no man in those days any of those things which they had seen."

Because of the importance of the Transfiguration, I have given the account of that event from three of the Gospels. These verses are filled with such precious, positive, powerful teachings that I shudder in my spirit when I think of attempting to give an exposition of the transfiguration of the Lord Jesus Christ. I know it would be utterly impossible to touch on all the phases or all the lessons coming from these passages. In each of the accounts quoted we find special points pertaining to the Transfiguration, points made prominent in full accord with the meaning and the scope of that occurrence.

The Gospel of John does not give an account of the transfiguration of Jesus. John is the salvation book, and it was written specifically that we might believe on Jesus and be born again. The Gospel of John is the instrument to reveal Christ, the Son of the living God and the Author of eternal salvation; therefore the larger part of that Gospel speaks of believing, receiving, trusting, and feeding upon the living Word. In John 20:30, 31 the writer of that Gospel explains: "And many other signs truly did Jesus in the presence of His disciples, which are not written in this book: *but these are written, that ye might BELIEVE that Jesus is the Christ, the Son of God; and that believing ye might have LIFE through His name.*"

Then in John 21:25 we read: "And there are also many other things which Jesus did, the which, if they should be written every one, I suppose that even the world itself could not contain the books that should be written. Amen."

The Gospel of *Luke* presents the Lord Jesus as *the Son of man,* and the information Luke gives concerning the Transfiguration is in full accord with the message of the Gospel of Luke.

Mark presents Jesus as the *Servant,* while *Matthew* is the *Kingdom* book; and the Holy Spirit, the Narrator of the event, reports the occurrence in harmony with the purpose of each of these Gospels.

Verse 1: *"And after six days Jesus taketh Peter, James, and John his brother, and bringeth them up into an high mountain apart."*

"After six days . . . ." I am sure it will be noticed that Matthew and Mark say *"six* days"

118

and Luke says *"eight* days." This may seem to be a discrepancy in the Scriptures, but according to *People's Commentary,* "Luke's *'about an eight days after'* includes the day at the beginning and at the end of the time recorded, while Matthew and Mark exclude them." Since this is a verse-by-verse study in Matthew, we will use Matthew's "six days"—that is, six days after the conversation recorded at the close of chapter 16.

". . . Jesus taketh Peter, James, and John his brother . . . ." These three disciples were honored on more than one occasion. It was Peter, James, and John who went with Jesus into the Garden of Gethsemane (Mark 14:33). They seemed to have a more intimate fellowship with Jesus than the other disciples had. They were chosen to accompany the Lord at this time *"up into an high mountain apart."* This was no doubt referring to a secluded spot, apart from the other disciples.

The *"high mountain"* is not named. Various suggestions have been made by Bible teachers as to the name of the mountain, but that is not the important point in this passage. If the name of the mountain had been important, the Holy Spirit would have included the name in His account. The important thing is not the name of the mountain nor its location, but the event that took place there.

Luke's account tells us that Jesus took Peter, James, and John *"and went up into a mountain*

119

to PRAY." From the Scriptures we know that Jesus prayed often. Sometimes He prayed all night. He prayed on many occasions before making great decisions. He was God in flesh—but He was also man. But if *Jesus* needed to pray, *how much more do WE need to pray.* He set the example for us.

Verse 2: *"And was transfigured before them: and His face did shine as the sun, and His raiment was white as the light."*

The Greek word here translated *"transfigured"* means "to change the appearance or form," not the substance, person, or thing. Literally, the form of Jesus was *changed—"transfigured before them."* They *saw* it happen and they could bear witness that it *did* happen. His appearance was changed in their very presence. He was not changed in His innermost being—i. e., He was still *God in flesh.* He was still man and He was still God; but His *appearance* was changed, *transfigured in their presence.*

"And His face did shine as the sun." Only Matthew describes the transfigured face of Jesus in these words. Mark does not mention the transfiguration of the Lord's face, and Luke tells us that "as He prayed, *the fashion of His countenance was altered."* We are reminded that when *Moses* came down from the mountain after receiving the law, his face shone so brightly that the people

120

were afraid to come near him (Ex. 34:29, 30). In Hebrews 1:3 Paul speaks of Jesus as being *the brightness of God's glory.* Our verse in Matthew means the splendor or shining in the same manner that the sun shines when it is high noon and the sun is at its brightest.

"*. . . and His raiment was white as the light.*" Not only was the *face* of Jesus transfigured to equal the brightness of the noonday sun. His garments also were changed. Mark tells us, "His raiment became shining, exceeding white as snow; so as no fuller on earth can white them." Luke describes His raiment as being "white and glistering." "*Fuller,*" as used in the description in Mark, means one who bleaches cloth to make it white and who cleanses soiled garments. In that day, especially among the Greeks, the fuller had a distinct trade. The garments of Jesus, then, became whiter than any earthly endeavor could have made them.

This was no earthly light that illumined the Mount of Transfiguration. This was the light of the glory of God, celestial glory, which shone from within the transfigured Son of God. No wonder the disciples were astounded and afraid (v. 6).

Verse 3: *"And, behold, there appeared unto them Moses and Elias talking with Him."*

Moses and Elijah appeared with Jesus on the

121

Mount of Transfiguration and talked with Him. Luke tells us what they talked about: they *"spake of His decease* which He should accomplish at Jerusalem."

It is most significant that Moses and Elijah appeared with Jesus here. *Moses* was a distinguished prophet, an outstanding servant of God. It was to Moses that God gave the law, and the institutions of the law typified the Messiah. The holy days under the law were all *types,* and all pointed to the Lamb of God who would come to take away the sin of the world. Therefore it was proper that Moses should be present when those types and prophecies were about to be fulfilled in the Antitype, when the rites that existed under the law would be fulfilled and taken away.

Elijah was chief of prophets. He was no ordinary prophet. He was extraordinary in many ways, and he was taken to heaven without seeing death. (Please read II Kings 2:1-11.) God honored Elijah on many occasions, and in our present Scripture He honored that prophet by allowing him to be the model of the forerunner of the Messiah (Mal. 4:5; Matt. 11:14; Luke 1:17).

Luke 9:31 tells us that Moses and Elijah appeared "in glory." That is, they descended to the mountain exactly as they were in Paradise with the glory they possessed there. They brought their glory down to the mountaintop as they talked with Jesus about His coming death. I believe this was the greatest Bible conference ever held on earth!

Of course, to the spirits in Paradise the death of the Lamb of God was of great interest. It was by faith in the coming Messiah that they had been saved. All saved ones from Adam to Calvary were saved by looking forward to the shed blood of the Lamb of God. All offerings and rituals under the law pointed to a slain Lamb and the shed blood. We are saved today by *looking back* to Calvary—that is, we have faith in the Lamb who died on the cross. By contrast, the Old Testament saints looked *forward* to Calvary, and had faith in the Lamb who would come.

If the devil could have stopped Jesus from reaching Calvary and dying on the cross, the devil could claim every soul and damn every man, woman, and child ever to be born into this world! The blood Jesus shed on Calvary redeems the soul—in the Old Testament era, in this present Dispensation of Grace, and every soul that is yet to be born into the family of God. Since Moses was the one to whom God gave the law, and since Elijah was chief of prophets, it was proper and fitting that these two men should meet with Jesus on the mountaintop to discuss His death at Calvary.

Luke 9:32 tells us that Peter and the other two disciples "were heavy with sleep." It is possible that they slept through most of that great Bible class, but if so, they awakened in time for the benediction, in time to witness the Lord's transfiguration and the heavenly visitors.

Verse 4: *"Then answered Peter, and said unto Jesus, Lord, it is good for us to be here: if thou wilt, let us make here three tabernacles; one for thee, and one for Moses, and one for Elias."*

When Peter awakened and the glory of the Transfiguration met his eyes, he was no doubt filled with joy as well as bewilderment. Mark 9:6 tells us that the disciples were "sore afraid." To Peter, the scene before him was far more appealing than the thought of his Lord facing death in Jerusalem, and he cried out, *"Lord, it is good for us to be here!"* Then he at once offered a suggestion which, if followed, would at least *prolong* the visit of Moses and Elijah and forestall the journey into Jerusalem where Jesus would be arrested, tried, and sentenced to death.

Peter suggested, *"Let us make here three tabernacles . . . ."* In that day a tabernacle was simply a temporary dwelling place, a tent. (This has no reference to THE tabernacle used as a place of worship in the wilderness as the children of Israel traveled from Egypt to Canaan.) Tabernacles such as Peter referred to were constructed of goathides or similar material stretched over posts, much as we would put up a play tent for our children, or a tent such as we might take on a camping trip. Sometimes the tabernacles were made of branches, thus resembling a brush arbor. Whatever they were made of, they were only temporary dwelling places. But in Peter's mind even a temporary place of abode would keep this heavenly Bible class in session a bit longer. They would build a tabernacle for Jesus, one for Moses, and one for Elijah. Thus they could remain on the mountain and live in an atmosphere of glory, rejoicing, happiness and praise.

Verse 5: *"While he yet spake, behold, a bright cloud overshadowed them: and behold a voice out of the cloud, which said, This is my beloved Son, in whom I am well pleased; hear ye Him."*

Jesus had not come into the world to live on a mountaintop and escape the problems in the valley below. He came as a servant. He came to suffer and die, to give His life a ransom that others might live. And while Peter was still speaking, God sent a bright cloud which overshadowed the mountaintop with its heavenly visitors. Then a voice came out of the cloud:

"This is my beloved Son, in whom I am well pleased; hear ye Him." A cloud in the Old Testament era was the symbol of Divine presence. God went before the Israelites "by day in a pillar of a cloud, to lead them the way; and by night in a pillar of fire, to give them light; to go by day and night: He took not away the pillar of the

cloud by day, nor the pillar of fire by night, from before the people" (Ex. 13:21, 22).

God appeared to Moses on Mt. Sinai in a bright cloud: "And Moses went up into the mount, and a cloud covered the mount. And the glory of the Lord abode upon mount Sinai, and the cloud covered it six days: and the seventh day he called unto Moses out of the midst of the cloud. And the sight of the glory of the Lord was like devouring fire on the top of the mount in the eyes of the children of Israel. And Moses went into the midst of the cloud, and gat him up into the mount: and Moses was in the mount forty days and forty nights" (Ex. 24:15-18).

A cloud of shekinah glory filled Solomon's temple: "And it came to pass, when the priests were come out of the holy place, that the cloud filled the house of the Lord, so that the priests could not stand to minister because of the cloud: for the glory of the Lord had filled the house of the Lord" (I Kings 8:10, 11).

Peter, James, and John knew what the cloud meant when the mountaintop was overshadowed. Then a voice from the cloud gave testimony that God was well pleased with His beloved Son.

"Hear ye Him." The words of Jesus are the only words man needs today. His Word brings life, light, and eternal bliss. There was no reason for Moses and Elijah to remain on earth. They had finished their ministry, and God recalled them

immediately to Paradise. He wanted these disciples to realize that it was their duty to hear the words of Jesus and no other. The experience on the Mount of Transfiguration strengthened their faith. Not many days hence Jesus would die on Calvary, and these men must be bold in declaring the whole counsel of God without fear.

Verse 6: *"And when the disciples heard it, they fell on their face, and were sore afraid."*

I wonder if we can begin to imagine what these disciples experienced? They were accustomed to being in the presence of Jesus. They had recognized and accepted Him as the promised Messiah. But their minds staggered at the thought of His approaching death, and they had not been able to grasp the fact of His resurrection after three days in the tomb. Now, *"heavy with sleep,"* they were suddenly confronted with the transfigured Christ and the return of Moses and Elijah from glory! Before they could recover from their bewilderment at what they had seen and heard, the heavens opened and the glory of God in a bright cloud was manifested on the mountaintop. Then the voice of God spoke from the cloud, acknowledging Jesus as His beloved Son, expressing His divine pleasure in the Son, and commanding the disciples to hear whatever the Son had to say.

Any one of the events witnessed here by Peter, James, and John would have been enough to astonish them beyond words, and when the voice of God spoke from the cloud *they fell prostrate "and were SORE AFRAID."* They knew they were in the presence of Jehovah God—sinful men standing in the holy of holies.

Verse 7: *"And Jesus came and touched them, and said, Arise, and be not afraid."*

"Jesus came and touched them." How compassionate the Lord was toward these men! He understood that they were afraid. He also knew there was nothing to be afraid of. He touched them—a touch of reassurance and love, perhaps as the angel touched Daniel to comfort and strengthen that prophet (Dan. 8:18; 10:18).

"Arise, and be not afraid." As the three disciples lifted their faces and looked upon Jesus, they saw that the bright shining cloud was gone, and Moses and Elijah were also removed from the scene.

Verse 8: *"And when they had lifted up their eyes, they saw no man, save Jesus only."*

Jesus only! Jesus stood alone. He stands alone in the program of God from eternity through eternity. The Son of God, God in flesh, conceived of the Holy Ghost, born of the Virgin Mary, He came into this world and conquered the world, the flesh, the devil, death, hell, and the grave. Today He sits at the right hand of God the Father to make intercession for all who believe on His name. *Jesus only*—the one Mediator between God and man.   Jesus , for redemption, Jesus for victory, Jesus for reward.

The glorious scene on the Mount of Transfiguration is definitely a pattern of the return of Jesus to this earth, visibly, surrounded by His saints. It presents a perfect picture of the Kingdom to come: In the center, *Christ in glory*, His face like the sun; living saints caught up in the Rapture (here represented by Elijah), and the resurrected saints (represented here by Moses).   In that day we will see *Jesus ONLY* because He will be the center of all things.

Throughout the Old Testament prophecies, we read of the second coming of Jesus.   In fact, there is more in the Old Testament about His second coming than there is about His first advent.   For this reason, the transfiguration of the Lord was definitely a confirmation of these prophecies, a divine guarantee of the final and complete fulfillment of every Old Testament prophecy concerning the return of Jesus to this earth.

In the last verse of chapter 16 Jesus said, "There be some standing here which shall not taste of death, till they see the Son of man coming in His Kingdom."   The Transfiguration should silence forever any strange interpretation of those words. Some standing there that day *did not* taste death until they saw Jesus coming in His Kingdom.

Peter, James, and John beheld a pattern, a blueprint, of that event which is still future, but which will happen literally as declared in the Word of God.

Certainly the Apostle Peter was fully aware of what he had seen at the Mount of Transfiguration, because many years later he wrote of that event, explaining, "We have not followed cunningly devised fables, when we made known unto you the power and coming of our Lord Jesus Christ, *but were EYEWITNESSES of His majesty.* For He received from God the Father honour and glory, when there came such a voice to Him from the excellent glory, This is my beloved Son, in whom I am well pleased. *And this voice which came from heaven we heard, when we were with Him IN THE HOLY MOUNT"* (II Pet. 1:16-18).

It seems reasonable to me that the Transfiguration may have occurred at night. Several things indicate this. The disciples were heavy with sleep, and they slept through much of that glorious event. Also, Luke 9:37 tells us that Jesus returned to His other disciples *the next day.* And the shining of the Lord's face, the brightness of His garments, and the entire scene, would have been much more manifest at night than it would have been if it had happened at high noon.

The time of day in which the Transfiguration occurred is not of importance, but it does seem reasonable to me that it happened at night. Jesus

will return to this earth in the darkest hour of
human history, and I wonder if we have not about
reached that time! We are living in the darkest
hour in the history of mankind to date, and how
much darker it may get before the dawn, before
the Day Star arises, there is no way to guess.
However, events of this present day and hour
lead me to believe that the coming of Jesus must
be very near.

Verse 9: *"And as they came down from the
mountain, Jesus charged them, saying, Tell the
vision to no man, until the Son of man be risen
again from the dead."*

Here Jesus repeats His instructions of a week
before. In Matthew 16:20 He had instructed them
"that they should tell no man that He was Jesus
the Christ." But after the scene Peter, James,
and John had just witnessed on the mountaintop,
it was only natural that they would hastily tell
the other disciples of the new and wondrous confirmation of their faith that Jesus was indeed the
true Messiah. Therefore Jesus charged them that
*they were to tell the vision to no one, "until the
Son of man be risen again from the dead."* Mark
tells us that the three disciples "kept that saying
with themselves, questioning one with another
what the rising from the dead should mean" (Mark
9:10). They believed in a general resurrection of
the dead, but they could not understand that *Jesus*

would be put to death, buried, and then come forth alive again at the end of three days.

Why did Jesus command that Peter, James, and John say nothing to anyone about what they had witnessed on the mountain? If they gave an eyewitness account of what they had seen on the mountain, the mass of the people with their mistaken ideas about Messiah would have banded together and brought about a great crisis. You will recall that after the feeding of the five thousand the multitudes attempted to make Jesus King by force, but "He departed again into a mountain Himself alone" (John 6:14, 15). When the resurrection and ascension of Jesus had put an end to the thought of an earthly Kingdom at that time, and when the minds of the believers had been lifted to a right and just conception of their exalted Lord, then the account of the Transfiguration could be told.

Verse 10: *"And His disciples asked Him, saying, Why then say the scribes that Elias must first come?"*

The "disciples" mentioned here are Peter, James, and John. Evidently their experience on the Mount of Transfiguration had brought to mind the prophecy of Malachi 4:5: "Behold, I will send you Elijah the prophet before the coming of the great and dreadful day of the Lord." There was no doubt in their minds that Jesus was the Messiah.

Why, then, did the scribes and the religious leaders say that *Elijah* must first come? The scribes taught that Elijah would come before the Messiah and prepare the way for Him. This was their interpretation of Malachi's prophecy. So Peter, James, and John asked Jesus *why* the scribes declared that Elijah must come before the Messiah.

Verse 11: *"And Jesus answered and said unto them, Elias truly shall first come, and restore all things."*

Thus did Jesus assure them that there was nothing wrong with the prophecy of Malachi, and that prophecy would yet be fulfilled. Elijah *would come* as prophesied, and would "restore all things." Malachi 4:6 declares, "He shall turn the heart of the fathers to the children, and the heart of the children to their fathers," before that great day of the Lord shall come. This prophecy was fulfilled *in spirit* in John the Baptist. Elijah will come back again *literally,* but that has to do with the time when Jesus will come in the Revelation. In the Rapture Jesus will come for the Church, but in the Revelation He will be revealed to the nation Israel. It will be when He comes in power and great glory to set up the Kingdom that Elijah will come before Him and "restore all things."

Verse 12: *"But I say unto you, That Elias is come already, and they knew him not, but have*

*done unto him whatsoever they listed.   Likewise
shall also the Son of man suffer of them."*

"Elias is come already."   Jesus was speaking
here of John the Baptist who came *in the spirit* of
Elijah. We read in Matthew 11:14, "And if ye will
receive it, this is Elias, which was for to come."
John the Baptist, the forerunner of Jesus, came in
the spirit of Elijah, but Elijah himself will return
at the end of the age.

"They knew him not."   The pronoun "they" is
impersonal, speaking of the Jews in general, including the scribes and Pharisees. They did not
recognize the spirit of Elijah in John the Baptist,
and they did unto him *"whatsoever they listed"*—
meaning whatsoever they wished or chose to do.
The reference is of course to the way John the
Baptist was treated by the people in general—and
by Herod in particular. John was not Elijah appearing in his own person, but he was Elijah "in
spirit and power" (Luke 1:17). He was Elijah in
character and reforming influence (Matt. 3:1-6).

*"Likewise shall also the Son of man suffer of
them."*   The Son of man, the Lord Jesus Christ,
would suffer at the hands of the people—not necessarily the same persons who had mistreated John
and brought about his death, but the same generation.   Jesus came unto His own, *"and His own
received Him not"* (John 1:11). In His lament over
the Holy City, Jerusalem, He said:

"O Jerusalem, Jerusalem, thou that killest the

prophets, and stonest them which are sent unto
thee, how often would I have gathered thy children together, even as a hen gathereth her chickens
under her wings, *and ye would NOT!"* (Matt.
23:37).

Verse 13: *"Then the disciples understood that
He spake unto them of John the Baptist."*

The disciples then understood that Jesus was
speaking of John the Baptist who had come *in
the spirit and power* of Elijah.   John the Baptist
was the voice crying in the wilderness, "Repent
ye: for the Kingdom of Heaven is at hand. . . .
Prepare ye the way of the Lord, make His paths
straight" (Matt. 3:1-3).   The prophecy of the coming of Elijah will be *literally* fulfilled in the end
time.   The removal of the Church from the earth
will be followed by the last stage of the ending of
this age.   And during the time of the Great Tribulation Elijah will appear in person as one of the
two witnesses mentioned in Revelation 11:3-12.
He will appear in the land of Palestine, Israel's
land, and his ministry will be confined to the land
of Israel.   His message at that time will be, in
many ways, the message of John the Baptist. He
will call the nation to repentance and will cry out
that the King is coming.   He will preach the
message which will be received by the remnant
of Israel, and he will accomplish the mission
prophesied in Malachi 4:5, 6.

The Powerless Disciples — the Powerful Christ

Verses 14-16: *"And when they were come to the multitude, there came to Him a certain man, kneeling down to Him, and saying, Lord, have mercy on my son: for he is lunatick, and sore vexed: for ofttimes he falleth into the fire, and oft into the water. And I brought him to thy disciples, and they could not cure him."*

"When they were come to the multitude . . . ." This took place the day following the Transfiguration. The multitude spoken of here was very likely made up of persons who had attended on the ministry of Jesus, many of whom were true disciples following Him in sincerity and truth. However, we know there were unbelievers present also, because Mark 9:14 tells us that the scribes were there "questioning with them"—that is, questioning the other disciples. Mark tells us that Jesus rebuked the scribes for asking questions of His disciples while He was away: "And He asked the scribes, What question ye with them?" (Mark 9:16). But being guilty in their own conscience, they did not answer Him.

"When they were come to the multitude"—that is, when they reached the valley where the multitude was waiting—*"there came to Him a certain man kneeling down to Him . . . ."* Peter had wanted to build three tabernacles on the mountaintop and remain there, but Jesus, being om-

niscient, knew there were people in the valley who needed His help. Mountaintop experiences are great. It is wonderful to attend a great prayer meeting, a Spirit-filled testimonial meeting, or a great Bible class. Such experiences are food and strength to the soul of a believer. But if we *lived* on the mountaintop all of the time, the people in the valley would die for their need of Christ. They would never know the way of joy, peace, and eternal life. It is not God's will for us to remain on the mountaintop and live in heavenly ecstasy while multitudes die in the valley below.

"Lord have mercy on my son: for he is luna-tick, and sore vexed . . . ." Mark tells us that this man's son had *"a dumb spirit"* (Mark 9:17). In other words, he was a mute, unable to speak except when the demonic seizure came upon him— and of course it was the demons speaking then, crying out. Luke further enlightens us by telling us that this boy was the father's *only child* (Luke 9:38).

Small wonder then that this father came to Jesus, kneeling before Him and beseeching Him to have mercy on his son. The kneeling man denoted a heart of humility and reverence—not necessarily worship, but humble submission, in the interest of deliverance for his child.

The Greek word here translated *"lunatick"* does not appear anywhere else in the New Testament.

The symptoms described in Mark 9:18 and in Luke 9:39 indicate that the boy had epilepsy. He was also possessed of an evil spirit, a demon. He suffered intense agony, being greatly afflicted. Luke tells us that the spirit (or demon) *"hardly departeth from him"* (Luke 9:39), indicating that the spirit scarcely left the boy, or that it left him only for very short intervals.

". . . ofttimes he falleth into the fire, and oft into the water." Any father who is the right kind of father can sympathize with this man. He was helpless against the evil spirit that possessed his son; and through the years he had seen the boy, when the spirit tore him, fall into the fire and sometimes into the water. No wonder he brought him to Jesus. This was his last and only hope.

While Jesus had been on the mountaintop with Peter, James, and John, the man had brought his son to the disciples who remained with the multitude—but *"they could not cure him."* In Matthew 10:1-8, when Jesus sent out the twelve, He gave them power to cast out unclean spirits and to heal all manner of sickness and disease. He had even given them power to raise the dead. Evidently the disciples had cast out demons in earlier days during their mission and preaching tour in Galilee. Why then were they powerless in this instance?

Verse 17: *"Then Jesus answered and said, O faithless and perverse generation, how long shall*

I be with you? how long shall I suffer you? bring him hither to me."

"O FAITHLESS and PERVERSE generation!" Faith is the key that unlocks the powerhouse of heaven. Without faith it is impossible to please God (Heb. 11:6). The faith of these disciples was weak, therefore they could not cast out the demon from the afflicted boy.

"Perverse" means that which is twisted or turned from the proper direction. To apply the word to a generation of men means that those men hold doctrines different from that which they are intended to hold. They are "perverted," turned from the truth and wicked in their daily conduct. I believe Jesus applied this term to the Jews in general and not to the disciples alone.

"How long shall I be with you? How long shall I suffer you?" These words of Jesus were not so much words of impatience or complaint as they were words of reproof for the people being so slow to believe in Him as Messiah. Notwithstanding His miracles they had witnessed, they should have believed *simply because of His Word.* "Now faith is the substance of things hoped for, the evidence of things not seen" (Heb. 11:1). When we demand to *see* something, that is not faith. Faith believes *without* seeing. On many occasions the Lord rebuked His disciples for their unbelief.

"Bring him hither to me." If we look at Mark's account of this miracle we are told that the father

said to Jesus, "If thou canst do any thing, have compassion on us, and help us." Jesus replied, "If thou canst believe, all things are possible to him that believeth." Then the father cried out, in tears, *"Lord, I believe! Help thou mine unbelief"* (Mark 9:22-24). The healing of the son depended upon faith. Jesus had the power to heal, but the faith of the father and the faith of the disciples would make possible the healing. Jesus had power to heal but He would not exert that power except as the father exercised faith. When the man prayed, "Help thou mine unbelief," he was saying to Jesus, in effect, *"If my faith is faulty, YOU are the only One who can help me. Please GIVE me the kind of faith I must have in order that my child may be healed."*

Verse 18: *"And Jesus rebuked the devil; and he departed out of him: and the child was cured from that very hour."*

The word here translated *"rebuke"* means to reprove and command. Jesus reproved the demon—but He also *commanded* him. Mark 9:25 tells us that Jesus "rebuked the foul spirit, saying unto him, Thou dumb and deaf spirit, I charge (command) thee, come out of him, and enter no more into him."

When the demon came out of the boy, the child had a terrible convulsion. The spirit "cried, and rent him sore, and came out of him: and he was as one dead; insomuch that many said, *He is dead!* But Jesus took him by the hand, and lifted him up; and he arose" (Mark 9:26, 27). Luke adds, "Jesus rebuked the unclean spirit, *and healed the child, and delivered him again to his father. AND THEY WERE ALL AMAZED AT THE MIGHTY POWER OF GOD"* (Luke 9:42, 43 in part).

Verse 19:   *"Then came the disciples to Jesus apart, and said, Why could not we cast him out?"*

After the marvelous healing, Jesus and His disciples retired to a house near where the miracle was performed (Mark 9:28), and the disciples then asked Jesus privately why *they* could not cast out the demon.

Verse 20:   *"And Jesus said unto them, Because of your unbelief: for verily I say unto you, If ye have faith as a grain of mustard seed, ye shall say unto this mountain, Remove hence to yonder place; and it shall remove; and nothing shall be impossible unto you."*

How direct, simple, and understandable was the answer Jesus gave to His disciples: *"Because of your UNBELIEF."* The disciples lacked faith in that their minds and hearts were not yet fully surrendered to the spiritual. They were still putting too much dependence in the flesh and not enough in the Lord.

"If ye have faith as a grain of mustard seed ye shall say unto this mountain, Remove hence to yonder place; and it shall remove. And nothing shall be impossible unto you." In Matthew 13:32 Jesus explained that the mustard seed is the smallest of all seeds. Some Bible scholars believe that Jesus was saying, in essence, "If you disciples have the very *smallest* or *weakest* faith, if that small amount of faith is genuine, *you can do all things."* The disciples had been given the power to cast out demons, but their faith was so weak they were unable to do so. Unbelief had robbed them of their ability.

Ministers today have the same power possessed by men of God in times past, when they preached and mighty revivals broke out. Ministers have *the power of God*—but in many instances their ability is crippled because of unbelief. They major on the incidentals instead of majoring on spiritual things.

How little we are willing to believe God for! Unbelief is the root of all inability on the part of Christians to do things for Christ. *If we BELIEVE, all things are possible.* Those are the words of Jesus, and we dare not count them untrue. If the disciples failed because of the weakness of their faith, so do believers fail today for the same reason. There is no fault in the power of God. The fault lies in our own unbelief.

Please do not misunderstand me. I am not

suggesting that those disciples represented the true Church. That would be unscriptural. But we do find here *a lesson for the Church.* The principles underlying this incident have a deep spiritual application for us. Believers today live in the midst of a wicked, perverse, evil world. The whole world lies in the lap of the Wicked One. The devil is the god of this age, and the atmosphere above us is literally filled with demons. Complete victory and power over the world, the flesh, and the devil have been given to the true believer by Almighty God—and yet there are many Christians who are helpless and powerless in the face of world conditions. As we look around us we see weakness in the spiritual realm. Instead of exercising strong faith in our mighty God and demonstrating the power to overcome evil and cause righteousness to advance, many times we allow our faith to grow weak and we do very little for the cause of Christ. The *power* is there, but our faith is too weak to use it. Unbelief gives power to the world and the devil, whereas true faith in God can cause "the walls of Jericho" to crumble.

In Mark 11:23, 24 Jesus said: "Verily I say unto you, That whosoever shall say unto this mountain, Be thou removed, and be thou cast into the sea; *and shall not doubt in his heart, but shall BELIEVE that those things which he saith shall come to pass; HE SHALL HAVE WHATSOEVER*

HE SAITH. Therefore I say unto you, *What things soever ye desire, when ye pray, BELIEVE that ye receive them, and YE SHALL HAVE THEM."*

Faith can, and does, remove mountains — all kinds of mountains; but there is only one way for a believer to have this kind of faith.

Verse 21: *"Howbeit this kind goeth not out but by prayer and fasting."*

What does Jesus mean here? Does He mean that we are to abstain from food, and that we should pray twenty-four hours a day? No, this is not the meaning. *Fasting,* in the spiritual sense, means losing sight of self. It means self-denial. *Prayer* is communion with God, and when we are praying and communing with Him, we are not thinking of self or fulfilling selfish desires. Praying in the spirit means not only *communion* with God, but *total dependence on Him* with no confidence in the flesh. If we spend our time thinking of satisfying self, we will not have power with God; but if we put God first and do all that we do to His glory, nothing shall be impossible to us.

Jesus Again Foretells
His Death and Resurrection

Verses 22 and 23: *"And while they abode in Galilee, Jesus said unto them, The Son of man shall be betrayed into the hands of men: and they shall kill Him, and the third day He shall be raised again. And they were exceeding sorry."*

In Mark 9:30-32 we read this account of what Matthew recorded in the verses just quoted:

"And they departed thence, and passed through Galilee; and He would not that any man should know it. For He taught His disciples, and said unto them, The Son of man is delivered into the hands of men, and they shall kill Him; and after that He is killed, He shall rise the third day. But they understood not that saying, and were afraid to ask Him."

"While they abode in Galilee . . . ." Jesus and His disciples left the place where the demoniac boy was healed near the Mount of Transfiguration, and Mark tells us that they "passed through Galilee." They seemed to be gathering as a group, returning from different groups to a designated point in Galilee, *"and He would not that any man should know it."* Jesus did not want the masses to know exactly what was taking place. The verses just quoted from Mark indicate that Jesus wanted to pass on unnoticed, *"for He taught His disciples."* He was privately teaching His disciples concerning His approaching death. Also, it may have been that He sought to avoid the fanatical multitude who, after the feeding of the five thousand, attempted to make Him King after their own notion (John 6:15).

145

"The Son of man shall be betrayed into the hands of men." This is the first time Jesus has specifically stated that He would be delivered *into the hands of MEN.* In Matthew 16:21 He revealed to His disciples that He would go into Jerusalem and suffer many things of the elders, chief priests and scribes, but He did not say that He would be delivered into the hands of *men.*

". . . and they shall kill Him . . . ." The disciples could not imagine their Master suffering at the hands of ungodly men and finally being put to death. The first part of the announcement was so overpowering and unbelievable that apparently only that part of it actually penetrated their minds. If they heard the second part of the Lord's announcement they heard it only as an afterthought. As plainly as He told them of His coming death, He also told them, *"and the third day He shall rise again."*

"And they were exceeding sorry." At least they understood His *words* when He told them He was to die, though there was much involved that they did not understand. But His statement that He would rise from the dead in only three days somehow failed to cheer their hearts and lift them from their despondency. They were "exceeding sorry," and both Mark and Luke tell us that the disciples did not understand the saying and were afraid to ask Jesus any more about it— probably with that feeling which often restrains

persons from seeking more information which would only increase their distress.

The Miracle of the Tribute Money

Verse 24: *"And when they were come to Capernaum, they that received tribute money came to Peter, and said, Doth not your Master pay tribute?"*

The half-shekel tribute money was a religious payment, not a tax levied year by year. It was originally based on the law (Ex. 30:11-16) and every male past twenty years of age, rich and poor alike, was to give one-half shekel. This was to support the temple. Upon this, Joash based his demand for a special collection to repair the temple (II Chron. 24:6). Nehemiah and his followers made "ordinances"—not as being required by the Law of Moses, but as a voluntary agreement to pay, once a year, *one-third* of a shekel for the service of the temple (Neh. 10:32, 33). Part of this money provided sacrifices for the temple for those who were too poor to purchase animals to offer.

Bible antiquity tells us that the Jews in Palestine were expected to give their tribute money before the Passover. Those who lived *outside* Palestine were allowed until the Day of Pentecost— or even until the feast of tabernacles; and there was a special chest in the temple for contributions due the previous year, if they had not been paid at that time.

"... *they that received the tribute money*" were thus designated, by way of separating them from the publicans and tax collectors who were sent out *by the government* to collect taxes *for* the government. Josephus the historian tells us that in foreign countries the money was collected by leading Jews and kept in some fortified city until it could be safely delivered to Jerusalem.

The collectors of the half-shekel did not approach Jesus. They addressed Peter, and the question they asked him was ensnaring: *"Doth not your Master pay tribute?"* The question suggests, *"Surely your Master pays tribute!"* Only Matthew records the incident of this temple contribution *"when they were come to Capernaum."* Mark also tells us that they came to Capernaum (Mark 9:33), seemingly the Lord's last visit to that city which had been His abode for a long time (Matt. 4:13).

Verse 25: *"He saith, Yes. And when he was come into the house, Jesus prevented him, saying, What thinkest thou, Simon? Of whom do the kings of the earth take custom or tribute? Of their own children, or of strangers?"*

Peter was in such a hurry to clear up the matter and vindicate the Lord Jesus that he immediately said *"Yes."* He could have asked Jesus about the matter before he gave answer to the men,

148

or he could have referred the collectors to Jesus. But his impulsiveness and his desire to protect his Master caused him to answer "Yes." In other words, Peter was saying, "Certainly my Master pays tribute! Who would entertain the idea that He does not?"

"When he was come into the house, Jesus prevented him . . . ." No doubt Peter came immediately into the house, intending to tell Jesus what had happened and what he had said to the men who collected the tribute. But "Jesus prevented him"—i. e., Jesus knew exactly what had taken place outside, and He spoke first, before Peter could say anything.

"What thinkest thou, Simon?" Jesus was going to let Peter be the judge in this case. *"Of whom do the kings of the earth take custom or tribute? Of their own children, or of strangers?"* The answer was apparent. The family of the king was always *free* from taxes or tribute. The king's subjects, especially strangers (aliens) under his rule, paid taxes, but the blood royal were free from any tax. Should Jesus pay redemption money for Himself to God? He was God in flesh. Should He who was the King's Son come under the rule of ordinary people and pay tribute money to His Father? Peter was a believer, a child of God. Therefore neither he nor Jesus was under duty to pay tribute, but Peter had not seen the matter in that light.

Verse 26: *"Peter saith unto Him, Of strangers. Jesus saith unto him, Then are the children free."*

"Strangers" here does not refer to foreigners but to people who were not members of the royal family. Peter knew that taxes or tribute would not be required of the members of the king's family.

"Then are the children free." Jesus knew the money in question was taken up for the service of the temple, service to God; and since He was the only begotten Son of God, very God in flesh, for whom the money was taken up, the law could not require Him or His children to pay the tribute.

Verse 27: *"Notwithstanding, lest we should offend them, go thou to the sea, and cast an hook, and take up the fish that first cometh up; and when thou hast opened his mouth, thou shalt find a piece of money: that take, and give unto them for me and thee."*

". . . lest we should offend them . . . ." In other words, Jesus was saying, "Even though you and I are not obligated to pay tribute, we do not want the collectors of the tribute money to think that we despise the service of the temple." This would no doubt have provoked needless opposition. They would, therefore, pay tribute whether or not they were bound by custom or law to do so.

"Go thou to the sea . . . ." Capernaum was

located on the shore of the Sea of Galilee, so Peter would not have to go far. *". . . and cast an hook, and take up the fish that first cometh up . . . ."* This is the only time in the New Testament when a hook is said to be used in connection with fishing. When I visited in that area, the people who lived there told the missionary who guided our group that fish could not be caught with a hook in those waters. They must be taken with nets. The reason for this, we were told, is that there is so much natural food in the Sea of Galilee that the bait on a hook holds no allure for the fish. Yet Peter did not question the Lord's instruction to go down to the sea *and cast a hook.* After the many miracles he had witnessed in the presence of Jesus, it did not seem strange to him that he should follow such instructions.

"And when thou hast opened his mouth, thou shalt find a piece of money." There need be no attempt to explain away this miracle. I do not believe that Peter's method of fishing had anything to do with his catching a fish in exactly the way Jesus said he would. This was a miracle, and I find no difficulty in believing that it happened exactly as Jesus said it would.

". . . That take, and give unto them for me and thee." Jesus never performed a miracle for His own personal benefit, comfort, or gain. This miracle was in the interest of clearing His name

before the religionists who collected the tribute money. Perhaps Matthew recorded this event to show the Jewish people that on the one hand Jesus felt Himself entitled to the respect due Messiah, but on the other hand He was careful to keep the law in all respects so that He could not be accused of breaking the law in any way. The piece of money Peter found in the mouth of the fish would have been one shekel, sufficient to pay tribute for Jesus and himself.

Chapter XVIII

1. At the same time came the disciples unto Jesus, saying, Who is the greatest in the kingdom of heaven?

2. And Jesus called a little child unto him, and set him in the midst of them,

3. And said, Verily I say unto you, Except ye be converted, and become as little children, ye shall not enter into the kingdom of heaven.

4. Whosoever therefore shall humble himself as this little child, the same is greatest in the kingdom of heaven.

5. And whoso shall receive one such little child in my name receiveth me.

6. But whoso shall offend one of these little ones which believe in me, it were better for him that a millstone were hanged about his neck, and that he were drowned in the depth of the sea.

7. Woe unto the world because of offences! for it must needs be that offences come; but woe to that man by whom the offence cometh!

8. Wherefore if thy hand or thy foot offend thee, cut them off, and cast them from thee: it is better for thee to enter into life halt or maimed, rather than having two hands or two feet to be cast into everlasting fire.

9. And if thine eye offend thee, pluck it out, and cast it from thee: it is better for thee to enter into life with one eye, rather than having two eyes to be cast into hell fire.

10. Take heed that ye despise not one of these little ones; for I say unto you, That in heaven their angels do always behold the face of my Father which is in heaven.

11. For the Son of man is come to save that which was lost.

12. How think ye? if a man have an hundred sheep, and one of them be gone astray, doth he not leave the ninety and nine, and goeth into the mountains, and seeketh that which is gone astray?

13. And if so be that he find it, verily I say unto you, he rejoiceth more of that sheep, than of the ninety and nine which went not astray.

14. Even so it is not the will of your Father which is in heaven, that one of these little ones should perish.

15. Moreover if thy brother shall trespass against thee, go and tell him his fault between thee and him alone: if he shall hear thee, thou hast gained thy brother.

16. But if he will not hear thee, then take with thee one or two more, that in the mouth of two or three witnesses every word may be established.

17. And if he shall neglect to hear them, tell it unto the church: but if he neglect to hear the church, let him be unto thee as an heathen man and a publican.

18. Verily I say unto you, Whatsoever ye shall bind on earth shall be bound in heaven: and whatsoever ye shall loose on earth shall be loosed in heaven.

19. Again I say unto you, That if two of you shall agree on earth as touching any thing that they shall ask, it shall be done for them of my Father which is in heaven.

20. For where two or three are gathered together in my name, there am I in the midst of them.

21. Then came Peter to him, and said, Lord, how oft shall my brother sin against me, and I forgive him? till seven times?

Chapter 18

22. Jesus saith unto him, I say not unto thee, Until seven times: but, Until seventy times seven.

23. Therefore is the kingdom of heaven likened unto a certain king, which would take account of his servants.

24. And when he had begun to reckon, one was brought unto him, which owed him ten thousand talents.

25. But forasmuch as he had not to pay, his lord commanded him to be sold, and his wife, and children, and all that he had, and payment to be made.

26. The servant therefore fell down, and worshipped him, saying, Lord, have patience with me, and I will pay thee all.

27. Then the lord of that servant was moved with compassion, and loosed him, and forgave him the debt.

28. But the same servant went out, and found one of his fellowservants, which owed him an hundred pence: and he laid hands on him, and took him by the throat, saying, Pay me that thou owest.

29. And his fellowservant fell down at his feet, and besought him, saying, Have patience with me, and I will pay thee all.

30. And he would not: but went and cast him into prison, till he should pay the debt.

31. So when his fellowservants saw what was done, they were very sorry, and came and told unto their lord all that was done.

32. Then his lord, after that he had called him, said unto him, O thou wicked servant, I forgave thee all that debt, because thou desiredst me:

33. Shouldest not thou also have had compassion on thy fellowservant, even as I had pity on thee?

34. And his lord was wroth, and delivered him to the tormentors, till he should pay all that was due unto him.

35. So likewise shall my heavenly Father do also unto you, if ye from your hearts forgive not every one his brother their trespasses.

A Lesson In Humility:
Subjects of Messiah's Kingdom Must Be Childlike

Verse 1: *"At the same time came the disciples unto Jesus, saying, Who is the greatest in the Kingdom of Heaven?"*

"At the same time . . . ." The time must be when Jesus was in the house at Capernaum, possibly even at the time Peter was gone fishing to obtain the tribute money.

". . . came the disciples unto Jesus. . . ." Mark 9:33 tells us that when the disciples came into the house where Jesus was, He asked them, "What was it that ye disputed among yourselves by the way?" That is, as they had journeyed to Capernaum. Luke 9:46, 47 says that "there arose a reasoning among them" and Jesus perceived the thought of their hearts. Therefore it was not really necessary that they *ask* the question they had come to ask, because Jesus already knew they had been discussing it among themselves and He knew the thoughts of their hearts.

"Who is the greatest in the Kingdom of Heaven?" Jesus was here approaching the close of His ministry in Galilee. In the first verse of the next chapter, He leaves Galilee and returns to Judaea. The disciples, having been convinced that He was the true Messiah, the Christ of God, as Peter declared in chapter 16 verse 16, had now begun to wonder about, and discuss, the matter of which

of them should have the highest office in His
Kingdom.   Bear in mind that they still believed
that it would be a *secular* Kingdom. They did not
yet understand that it would be spiritual. Since
they expected a temporal Kingdom they naturally
expected that there would be offices and officials,
of both high and low degree. It also seems that
they expected to be appointed as *officials* in the
Kingdom.

"Greatest" here means literally one greater than
all others.   Strange as it may seem among this
chosen group of men, jealousy was evidently rais-
ing its head.   Even though Jesus had recently
explained to them that it was impossible to follow
Him except in self-denial (chapter 16, verse 24),
they were here intent on exalting themselves to a
place higher than that of their Christian brothers.
We are not told what prompted this concern among
the disciples. We know that *John* was spoken of
as the disciple "whom Jesus loved" (John 13:23;
21:20), and Christ had spoken directly and specifically to *Peter* concerning the building of the
Church (Matt. 16:18). But we are not told whether
or not it was from such incidents that the disciples
were led to wonder just who among them should
have the highest place in the Kingdom. Later, as
we study chapter 20, we will find that *James* and
John, with their mother as spokesman, requested
that *they* might have the two highest places in
the Kingdom.   How sad when the minds of men

run in the line of thought that seeks glorification and honor for themselves, instead of honoring the Lord Jesus Christ. This seems to have been a turning point in the unity of the disciple band and the beginning of the tension that stayed with them until the crucifixion.

Verse 2: *"And Jesus called a little child unto Him, and set him in the midst of them."*

The fact that Jesus *called* the child to Him tells us that the child was old enough to walk, yet, according to Mark 9:36, small enough for Jesus to hold in His arms. Luke 9:47 says that Jesus took the child "and set him by (or beside) Him." From these verses we know that this was not an infant nor was it a child of what we would consider the age of responsibility. In order to present the object lesson Jesus was about to teach, this would have been a child in the age of innocence.

Please note here that *Jesus called* and the child *came to Him.* He came without having to be begged or coaxed. We see part of the lesson in this immediate obedience. The sinner must come willingly to Jesus. The Lord does not force sinners to accept salvation. He invites, He calls—but the sinner must come willingly.

Verse 3: *"And said, Verily I say unto you, Except ye be converted, and become as little children, ye shall not enter into the Kingdom of Heaven."*

"VERILY I say unto you . . . ." Here we find Jesus using another "verily," indicating that something of extreme importance is about to be said.

". . . except ye be converted . . . ." To be converted is to turn about, to turn from one course of action to another. The disciples, then, must turn from their jealousy and self-seeking pride, and *"become as little children"* — embrace the character, trust, and faith of a little child. Otherwise they could not even *enter* the Kingdom and certainly they would not reign or rule there.

A small child is not faultless. We know they often get angry, and it is not uncommon for a little child to show jealousy, envy, or selfishness. But Jesus was speaking here of the character of a little child in general. A child is trusting. My boys are grown men now, but how well I remember when they were children. They had unshakeable confidence in me, their father. When they were little they believed that I was the greatest, strongest, wisest man on earth. They thought there was nothing I could not do, and when I made a promise they fully expected that promise to be kept. They had perfect faith in my ability to protect and provide for them.

Believers should have perfect faith and trust in the heavenly Father. His promises are sure, His protection and provision are guaranteed. We need not question anything He says in His Word nor anything He brings into our lives. Whatever He does for us is for our good and His glory. We are assured that *"ALL things work TOGETHER for good* to them that love God, to them who are the called according to His purpose" (Rom. 8:28).

A little child possesses the greatest of all virtues — *simplicity.* The child which Jesus set in the midst of His disciples was young and free from passions.

Another outstanding characteristic of a little child is *forgiveness.* How quickly the small child dispenses with anger, grief, unhappiness! Only a matter of moments after becoming angry or offended, the child is happy again, anger and grief seeming never to have been. Playmates may disagree to the point of violence, only to be playing joyfully together again in complete harmony a minute or so later. A little child does not carry a grudge or harbor ill will. Believers need to be of a forgiving spirit, free of ill will and resentment toward fellow Christians. Jesus is teaching here that we are to be children in humility of mind. We are to be *child-LIKE,* not *childish,* in our conduct toward others.

". . . ye shall not enter into the Kingdom of Heaven." How could anything be made plainer? In simple, straightforward words and by unmistakeable example Jesus instructed the ambitious disciples that their present attitude of self-seeking

160

must change to one of humility and faith comparable to that of a little child. They were debating about which of them would be appointed to the highest office in the coming Kingdom, and in no uncertain terms He let them know that self must be denied and humility and faith become the order of the day, or they would not even *enter* the Kingdom over which they were anxious to officiate or govern.

In John 3:3 Jesus declared, "Except a man be born again, he cannot see the Kingdom of God." Were the *disciples* not born again at this time? Were they destitute of saving grace and faith? They would provide the answer themselves—that is, if they turned from their worldly ambition and personal jealousy and showed forth childlike humility and trust in God, then they would bring forth fruits declaring that they were saved.

Of course we know that *Judas* never reached that point in his association with Jesus. Judas was never saved. In John 12:4-6 we read that when Mary anointed the feet of Jesus with precious ointment Judas complained. He asked, "Why was not this ointment sold for three hundred pence, and given to the poor?" Then the Scripture carefully explains, "This he said, *not that he cared for the poor; but because he was a THIEF, and had the bag, and bare what was put therein.*"

Further information concerning the spiritual state of Judas is found in John 6:70, 71 where Jesus said to His disciples, "Have not I chosen you twelve, *and one of you is a devil?*" He was speaking here "of Judas Iscariot the son of Simon: for he it was that should betray Him, being one of the twelve." Judas was a member of the disciple band, treasurer for the group, but he was never saved.

Verse 4: *"Whosoever therefore shall humble himself as this little child, the same is greatest in the Kingdom of Heaven."*

He who shall be most Christlike in humility and love in this life shall be most Christlike in power and glory in the Kingdom. That is the lesson Jesus is teaching here.

In Matthew 23:11, 12 Jesus said, "He that is greatest among you shall be your servant. And whosoever shall exalt himself shall be abased; and he that shall humble himself shall be exalted."

Matthew 20:26-28 reads, in the words of Jesus, ". . . whosoever will be great among you, let him be your minister; and whosoever will be chief among you, let him be your servant: *even as the SON OF MAN came not to be ministered unto, but to minister, and to give His life a ransom for many."*

Paul deals with the same subject in Philippians 2:5-8: "Let this mind be in you, which was also in Christ Jesus: who, being in the form of God, thought it not robbery to be equal with God:

162

but made Himself of no reputation, and took upon Him the form of a servant, and was made in the likeness of men: and being found in fashion as a man, *He humbled Himself, and became obedient unto death, even THE DEATH OF THE CROSS!"*

Christ's Little Ones

Verse 5: *"And whoso shall receive one such little child in my name receiveth me."*

In Mark's record we read, "Whosoever shall receive *one of such children* in my name, receiveth me: and whosoever shall receive me, receiveth not me, but Him that sent me" (Mark 9:37). Luke's Gospel expresses it thus: "Whosoever shall receive *this child* in my name receiveth me: and whosoever shall receive me receiveth Him that sent me: for he that is least among you all, the same shall be great" (Luke 9:48).

Matthew says "one such little child." Mark says "one of such children." Luke says "this child." However, these expressions do not necessarily refer to a literal *child*, but to the childlike believer—one who is humble, trusting in Jesus for salvation.

Humility is too often mistaken for weakness. You know as well as I do that there are many arrogant Christians—believers who, although believing on Christ for salvation, have not learned humility in service. They seem to give credit to themselves for their talents, and they have a tendency to overlook or ignore the humble, lowly believer who serves in simple faith.

The Psalmist exclaimed, "O Lord our Lord, how excellent is thy name in all the earth! . . . *What is MAN, that thou art mindful of him?*" (Psalm 8:1, 4). What indeed! Man has nothing that God has not given. Therefore the Christian who has been blessed with talent, super-intelligence, or perhaps a comfortable share of worldly goods, has no right whatsoever to look down upon or offend one of God's "little ones," the simple, humble believer who recognizes his own nothingness and rests wholly and obediently upon Jesus.

The disciples, at the time Jesus gave them this object lesson, were in a jealous mood among themselves, displaying not a humble spirit and lowly mind, but selfish ambition. Their attitude was far from what Jesus intended it to be. The Lord Himself was always kind and tender toward the man in the gutter—the beggar, the leper, the outcast and the downcast. He was an example to His followers and He was teaching them that they must follow in His footsteps.

There is also a lesson here concerning the "little ones" of Jesus who occupy a lowly station in life. There are many degrees of intelligence and personalities among God's children, as well as many different levels of financial and social status. No matter how simple and lowly the estate of a born again believer, that believer is not to be offended, neglected, or denied fellowship because of his social standing. It is easy to be attracted to the attractive. But those believers who are not personally or socially attractive are to be heartily and joyfully received as Christ's children if they have been saved by God's grace.

James teaches concerning this in the epistle that bears his name. In James 2:1-5 we read:

"My brethren, have not the faith of our Lord Jesus Christ, the Lord of glory, with respect of persons. For if there come unto your assembly a man with a gold ring, in goodly apparel, and there come in also a poor man in vile raiment; and ye have respect to him that weareth the gay clothing, and say unto him, Sit thou here in a good place; and say to the poor, Stand thou there, or sit here under my footstool: are ye not then partial in yourselves, and are become judges of evil thoughts? Hearken, my beloved brethren, *Hath not God chosen the poor of this world RICH IN FAITH, and heirs of the kingdom which He hath promised to them that love Him?*"

Notice we are always to receive these "little ones" *in the NAME OF JESUS.* By so doing, our verse declares, we *receive Jesus.* Mark and Luke both add that whosoever receives Jesus also receives the One who *sent* Jesus. We should count it an honor indeed to accept and receive God's "little ones"!

Verse 6: *"But whoso shall offend one of these little ones which believe in me, it were better for him that a millstone were hanged about his neck, and that he were drowned in the depth of the sea."*

To receive one of Christ's humble ones is to entertain the Lord Jesus Himself. By contrast, to offend, pervert, or molest the humble is to bring God's displeasure and judgment upon the person guilty of such. Those who believe on Jesus, no matter how small, simple, or humble, are under His special care, and woe unto anyone who makes them to stumble.

Jesus said "one of these little ones *which believe in me . . . ."* This proves that the reference is not to *infants* who are too young to know right from wrong. The reference is to childlike born again believers. Children do sometimes become born again believers, but only after they are old enough to understand and choose for themselves. Infants cannot choose for themselves, and the grace of God takes care of them until they reach the age of accountability.

"It were better for him that a millstone were hanged about his neck, and that he were drowned in the depths of the sea." Strong words, these, falling from the lips of the lowly, gentle, tenderhearted Jesus. But remember, it is Jesus, *Lord of glory,* who will one day judge "the quick and the dead" (II Tim. 4:1). When He judges *He will*

166

judge righteously. He is righteous and He cannot judge wrongly.

If we expand the words of Jesus here to their full meaning, He actually was declaring that those who offend, abuse or mistreat the humble child of God do not deserve to live. He tells us that such a person should have a millstone hanged about his neck, and that he should be carried out to sea and drowned. That is, take him out from shore, throw him overboard, and let him sink to the very depths of the sea with no possibility of his being rescued or getting out alive!

The *"millstone"* is itself an interesting subject here. In Matthew 24:41 Jesus speaks of *"two women . . . grinding at the mill."* The millstone there would be small, and would be turned by hand. But the Greek word denoting "millstone" in our present verse indicates a large millstone which would have to be turned by an animal—an ass or other beast of burden. With such a burden about a man's neck he would be doomed indeed if he were cast into the sea.

Verse 7: *"Woe unto the world because of offences! for it must needs be that offences come; but woe to that man by whom the offence cometh!"*

The true believer will find no comfort in the world. Those who are saved by God's grace, born into the family of God by the Holy Spirit,

167

are no longer citizens of this world, but citizens of heaven, "from whence also we look for the Saviour, the Lord Jesus Christ" (Phil. 3:20). It must follow, then, that we are, as I Peter 2:11 declares, "strangers and pilgrims" on earth.

In John 15:19 Jesus told His disciples, "If ye were of the world, the world would love his own: but *because ye are not of the world, but I have chosen you out of the world, therefore the world hateth you."*

". . . it must needs be that offences come . . . ." We know that offences will come our way. The Lord was persecuted and offended—but He overcame the world. He conquered that we might conquer. We might illustrate here by comparing this phrase with the words of a present-day physician who says, "It must be that this particular disease come. There is no way to keep it out of the community. But it is not a necessary consequence that people die. Those who will recognize the disease and take precautionary measures such as vaccination, innoculation, will not be destroyed by the disease even though it comes."

The same is true, in fashion, of the believer in this sad, unfriendly world. Offences will come, temptations will be upon us; but the Christian who takes precautionary measures can overcome: "There hath no temptation taken you but such as is common to man: but God is faithful, who will not suffer you to be tempted above that ye are able; but will with the temptation also make a way to escape, that ye may be able to bear it" (I Cor. 10:13).

The world will put many stumblingblocks in the way of the believer. But Jesus walked this way before us, and He overcame the world, the flesh, the devil, death, hell, and the grave that we might have victory in Him.

"... *but woe to that man by whom the offence cometh!*" Men who live humble, holy lives are least likely to make others stumble. The woe of God is therefore the sure heritage of the proud and haughty, the self-centered and ambitious, who cause offences to God's children.

Verse 8: *"Wherefore if thy hand or thy foot offend thee, cut them off, and cast them from thee: it is better for thee to enter into life halt or maimed, rather than having two hands or two feet to be cast into everlasting fire."*

Notice the pointed address in the second person singular: *"If THY hand or THY foot offend thee ...."* This speaks of worldly attachments—business, politics, worldly friendships, employment of any kind which one cannot pursue without participating in ungodliness, worldliness and sin. It matters not how dear or profitable may be whatsoever it is, it is best that a person lose all else than that he lose his eternal soul—man or woman!

In simple explanation, if one cannot use his

169

two hands to the glory of God, if he must use those hands to bring judgment upon himself or his fellowman, then he would be better off with one hand than with two. If a man cannot walk where God directs, if his feet consistently lead him outside of God's will where his walk cannot bring glory to God, then that man would be better off with only one foot!

Verse 9: *"And if thine eye offend thee, pluck it out, and cast it from thee: it is better for thee to enter into life with one eye, rather than having two eyes to be cast into hell fire."*

The Lord Jesus here repeats a passage which we studied earlier, in the Sermon on the Mount (Matt. 5:29, 30). Great truths need to be oft repeated and taught. Jesus made no apology for repetition.

Our Lord is teaching here how dangerous temptations are. The eye is perhaps man's most valuable faculty. Eyesight is to be treasured. But if one finds in himself that which would cause him to stumble in sin—even if it be the treasured vision—it is better to become like the halt and the maimed than to have all of his members and burn in hell. As Jesus asked in Matthew 16:26, *"For what is a man profited if he shall gain the whole world, and lose his own soul? or what shall a man give in exchange for his soul?"*

The main concern of any person should be to

enter into life eternal; and if this costs one of the hands, or feet, or eyes, then it is to his good and eternal profit that he let these go and have that which is eternal—salvation by faith in the shed blood of Jesus. A dear saint of God, though he may be lame, maimed, half-blind here on earth, is far better off than a sinner who is one hundred per cent whole, insofar as his physical faculties are concerned, but who never comes to know the Saviour. To have two hands, two feet, and two eyes will be of no advantage if one is cast for all eternity into the lake of fire and brimstone.

God wants our soul, spirit, and body! Writing to the Thessalonian believers, Paul said, "...I pray God your whole *spirit* and *soul* and *body* be preserved blameless unto the coming of our Lord Jesus Christ" (I Thess. 5:23). And in Romans 12:1 we read, "I beseech you therefore, brethren, by the mercies of God, that ye *present your bodies a living sacrifice, holy, acceptable unto God, which is your reasonable service.*"

Jesus' Solemn Warning of Hell

I declare that the simplest, most understandable—and yet the most *scorching*—sermon ever preached on hell is found in Mark's Gospel, and it was preached by the Lord Jesus Christ. Let me give it to you without comment. Please read it carefully:

"Whosoever shall offend one of these little ones

that believe in me, it is better for him that a millstone were hanged about his neck, and he were cast into the sea. And if thy hand offend thee, cut it off: it is better for thee to enter into life maimed, than having two hands to go into hell, into the fire that never shall be quenched: where their worm dieth not, and the fire is not quenched.

"And if thy foot offend thee, cut it off: it is better for thee to enter halt into life, than having two feet to be cast into hell, into the fire that never shall be quenched: where their worm dieth not, and the fire is not quenched. And if thine eye offend thee, pluck it out: it is better for thee to enter into the Kingdom of God with one eye, than having two eyes to be cast into hell fire: where their worm dieth not, and the fire is not quenched" (Mark 9:42-48).

Verse 10: *"Take heed that ye despise not one of these little ones; for I say unto you, That in heaven their angels do always behold the face of my Father which is in heaven."*

". . . despise not one of these little ones . . . ." I believe most Scripture has a *primary* and a *secondary* interpretation. Here Jesus is speaking primarily of babes in Christ (I Pet. 2:1-3), "little ones" young in the faith. But I also believe He is speaking of little ones in the natural life, as well as in the spiritual life. I believe every little

innocent child, before it reaches the age of accountability, has a guardian angel, and in times of
danger the guardian angel protects the little child.
I believe that if a child dies before it reaches the
age of accountability, God's grace takes care of
that child in redemption. *No little child, who
dies before it is old enough to be saved, is LOST.*
Paul says, ". . . now are they *holy*" (I Cor. 7:14).
A *holy* child, young or old, is a *saved* child.

". . . *despise not* . . . ." Some people despise
Christians and look down on Christianity because
the greater number of Christians seem to be persons
in humble walks of life, and are not always well
educated. They are humble Christians and they
hold humble positions as well. But those of lowly
station and humble circumstances are not to be
despised or looked down upon.

Paul wrote to the Christians in Corinth, "For
ye see your calling, brethren, how that *not many
wise men after the flesh, not many mighty, not
many noble, are called: but God hath chosen the
foolish things of the world to confound the wise;
and God hath chosen the weak things of the world
to confound the things which are mighty; and
base things of the world, and things which are
despised, hath God chosen, yea, and things which
are not, to bring to nought things that are: that
no flesh should glory in His presence.* But of Him
are ye in Christ Jesus, who of God is made unto
us wisdom, and righteousness, and sanctification,

and redemption: that, according as it is written, *He that glorieth, let him GLORY IN THE LORD"* (I Cor. 1:26-31).

Humility is one of the loveliest of all human dispositions, but humility is regarded by many proud, ungodly persons as nothing but commonness. The natural man cannot see that true humility comes from the Lord.

". . . in heaven their angels do always behold the face of my Father which is in heaven." However humble a believer may be in the world's estimation, that believer has angels attending him—angels sent from Almighty God. Hebrews 1:14 tells us that angels are "ministering spirits, sent forth to minister *for them who shall be heirs of salvation."* This applies to each and every true believer. Angels are never said to be "heirs of God," but *believers* are heirs of God and joint heirs with Christ (Rom. 8:17), and God sends forth His angels as ministering spirits for His saints, His born again ones. I personally believe that every born again believer has a guardian angel. Psalm 34:7 declares, *"The angel of the Lord encampeth round about them that fear Him, and delivereth them."*

In Acts chapter 12, King Herod had arrested Peter and put him in prison. While Peter, bound with two chains, slept between the two soldiers who were guarding him, the angel of the Lord came to him, released his chains, and led Peter out away from the sleeping guards and out of the prison. Peter was not fully aware of what was happening—he thought he was dreaming, or having a vision. When they were out on the street the angel departed and Peter then became fully conscious and realized that the angel of the Lord had delivered him out of the hand of Herod. He then went to the house of Mark where a prayer meeting was in session, and when the little maiden who answered his knock at the door told the saints within that Peter was at the door, they refused to believe her. They said, "It is his *angel.*" (Read the account in Acts 12:1-17.) Peter did not *see* the angel, but when he realized that he had been brought out from prison and was in the streets of the city, he immediately knew that an angel had delivered him.

We do not *see* angels today, but they are with us, ministering to "the heirs of salvation." In Psalm 91:11 we read, "(God) shall give His angels charge over thee, to keep thee in all thy ways." This was the Scripture Satan quoted to Jesus when he challenged the Lord to cast Himself down from the pinnacle of the temple (Matt. 4:6).

Angels are also present during our worship services. We learn this from Paul's inspired writing to the Corinthian church. He said, "For this cause ought the woman to have power on her head because of the angels"—that is, because of the *presence* of the angels (I Cor. 11:10).

In the great judgment the angels will be agents of God, separating the righteous from the wicked: "The Son of man shall send forth His angels, and they shall gather out of His Kingdom all things that offend, and them which do iniquity; and shall cast them into a furnace of fire. . . . And He shall send His angels with a great sound of a trumpet, and they shall gather together His elect from the four winds, from one end of heaven to the other" (Matt. 13:41, 42; 24:31).

In heaven, the angels of believers have a glorious position in the Father's house. They enjoy the highest dignity and consideration, and they continually behold the face of our heavenly Father. They are honored ministers of the courts of heaven.

However, in spite of the exalted position of angels, we must avoid all mere sentimental fantasies about them. We should feel deep gratitude for them, we may love them as God's ministering spirits and our exalted friends—but we must never *worship* angels (Col. 2:18; Rev. 22:8, 9). We are to worship *God*, and God alone.

While we are on the subject of angels, I would say this one more thing about those spiritual beings: There is a common idea or notion among many Christians that when a believer dies he (or she) becomes an angel. Many times when a baby dies it is said that the little one has "gone to be an angel." This is utterly unscriptural. There is not one word in the Bible to substantiate such belief. Believers do not become angels. In the life to come, believers will be like Jesus. This fact is made very, very plain in the Scriptures. I John 3:2 declares, "Beloved, *NOW are we the sons of God,* and it doth not yet appear what we shall be: *But WE KNOW that, when (Jesus) shall appear, we shall be LIKE HIM;* for we shall see Him as He is!" The redeemed in glory will *judge* angels (I Cor. 6:3). This denotes the superiority of the redeemed over angels. In this life, man is made "a little lower than the angels" (Heb. 2:7), but in the life to come, through our life in Christ, we will be superior to angels.

The Lost Sheep — the Seeking Lord

Verse 11: *"For the Son of man is come to save that which was lost."*

The meaning of this verse is unmistakeably clear—i. e., Jesus came into this world *to save the lost.* We find words similar to these in Luke 19:10, where Jesus told Zacchaeus, a publican, "The Son of man is come to seek and to save that which was lost." Of course it is entirely possible for a lost person to be attractive in personality, dress, personal habits, and even in his (or her) manner of life, because no one is saved by being attractive, intelligent, diligent, morally upright, or any other human trait. There is but one door to salvation and that Door is the Lord Jesus Christ. King and peasant alike must be saved through simple faith in Christ and His finished work. There is no other way. Therefore it is possible to say of a sinner that he, like the rich young ruler, lacks but one thing—God's gift of salvation.

On the other hand, a sinner can be—and often is—unattractive. I speak of those who are not only of lowly social position, but who have also gone so far in sin and degradation that they are indeed unlovely. But our present verse, the very words of the lovely Lamb of God, makes no distinction between the "lost." He does not put them in different classes. If they are lost, then they need salvation.

As we study the ministry of Jesus, we find time after time where He ministered to those who were lowly, helpless, degraded by both physical condition and by a life of sin. He healed a man who had been lying, unnoticed by mankind, for thirty-eight years by the pool of Bethesda—pitiful, needing mercy, but receiving none (John 5:1-15).

He touched and healed the lepers—outcasts, men feared and despised by their fellowmen, shut off from society and forced to live in ostracism. They came to Jesus and He cleansed them (Matt. 8:2,3; Luke 17:12-14).

At Jacob's well He opened the door of salvation to a woman whose life was so scarred by sin that she was shunned by the other women of her community. Jesus gave her living water, and because of her testimony a great revival broke out in Samaria (John 4:1-42).

He forgave the harlot, the woman taken in adultery, discomfited her accusers, and told her to go and sin no more (John 8:1-11).

To the lowly, the unlovely, the downtrodden and debased, Jesus afforded the same courtesy, the same loving kindness, as He showed to Nicodemus, a ruler of the Jews (John 3:1-16). He came to save the lost, and He loved them all, from the most elite to the lowliest sinner.

Jesus was speaking to His disciples—therefore He was also speaking to believers today. We are not to look down on or despise sinners. We may find their habits and way of life unattractive, but since believers are sinners saved by grace, we must be able to see that we, ourselves, were yet unlovely when Jesus loved us. Paul reminded the believers in the church at Ephesus that they, too, had at one time walked "according to the course of this world" until they were redeemed by the grace of God (Eph. 2:1-10).

Regardless of how lowly, poor and needy one may be, the soul of that person is very dear to God—"for the Lord seeth not as man seeth; for man looketh on the outward appearance, but *the Lord looketh on the heart*" (I Sam. 16:7). The heart may be sinful and the "outward appearance" unlovely, but in the eyes of God that *soul* is precious. The Lord Jesus cares for the most despised of men, as well as for the most honored and re-vered of men. If *He* loves them, are not *we, His followers,* to love them also? God forbid that we love only those who are wealthy, educated, at-tractive—and neglect to carry the Gospel to those who live in poverty and despair, sometimes even lacking the necessities of life. Jesus came to save sinners, and regardless of the position a sinner holds in this world, *he can become a child of God and a joint heir with the Lord Jesus Christ.* Christ died for the ungodly (Rom. 5:6). He came to save to the uttermost—yea, even to the most vile, miser-able, wretched person upon the face of this earth.

Verse 12: *"How think ye? if a man have an hundred sheep, and one of them be gone astray, doth he not leave the ninety and nine, and goeth into the mountains, and seeketh that which is gone astray?"*

Luke also records this parable of the lost sheep (representing a *lost* person—not a backslider), but in his account it is a threefold parable. I would like to give Luke's account here, so that you can read it in connection (and in comparison) with the words of Jesus as recorded here by Matthew. In the fifteenth chapter of Luke's Gospel, beginning at verse 3, we read:

"And He spake this parable unto them, saying: What man of you, having an hundred sheep, if he lose one of them, doth not leave the ninety and nine in the wilderness, and go after that which is lost, until he find it? And when he hath found it, he layeth it on his shoulders, rejoicing. And when he cometh home, he calleth together his friends and neighbours, saying unto them, Rejoice with me; for I have found my sheep which was lost. I say unto you, that likewise joy shall be in heaven over one sinner that repenteth, more than over ninety and nine just persons, which need no repentance.

"Either what woman having ten pieces of silver, if she lose one piece, doth not light a candle, and sweep the house, and seek diligently till she find it? And when she hath found it, she calleth her friends and her neighbours together, saying, Rejoice with me; for I have found the piece which I had lost. Likewise, I say unto you, there is joy in the presence of the angels of God over one sinner that repenteth.

"And He said, A certain man had two sons: And the younger of them said to his father, Father, give me the portion of goods that falleth to me. And he divided unto them his living. And not many days after the younger son gathered all together, and took his journey into a far country, and there wasted his substance with riotous living. And when he had spent all, there arose a mighty famine in that land; and he began to be in want. And he went and joined himself to a citizen of that country; and he sent him into his fields to feed swine. And he would fain have filled his belly with the husks that the swine did eat: and no man gave unto him. And when he came to himself, he said, How many hired servants of my father's have bread enough and to spare, and I perish with hunger! I will arise and go to my father, and will say unto him, Father, I have sinned against heaven, and before thee, and am no more worthy to be called thy son: make me as one of thy hired servants.

"And he arose, and came to his father. But when he was yet a great way off, his father saw him, and had compassion, and ran, and fell on his neck, and kissed him. And the son said unto him, Father, I have sinned against heaven, and in thy sight, and am no more worthy to be called thy son. But the father said to his servants, Bring forth the best robe, and put it on him; and put a ring on his hand, and shoes on his feet: and bring hither the fatted calf, and kill it; and let us eat, and be merry: for this my son was dead, and is alive again; he was lost, and is found. And they began to be merry.

"Now his elder son was in the field: and as he came and drew nigh to the house, he heard musick and dancing. And he called one of the servants, and asked what these things meant. And he said unto him, Thy brother is come; and thy father hath killed the fatted calf, because he hath received him safe and sound. And he was angry, and would not go in: therefore came his father out, and intreated him. And he answering said to his father, Lo, these many years do I serve thee, neither transgressed I at any time thy commandment: and yet thou never gavest me a kid, that I might make merry with my friends: But as soon as this thy son was come, which hath devoured thy living with harlots, thou hast killed for him the fatted calf.

"And he said unto him, Son, thou art ever with me, and all that I have is thine. It was meet that we should make merry, and be glad: for this thy brother was dead, and is alive again; and was lost, and is found" (Luke 15:3-32).

From the beginning of this eighteenth chapter of Matthew, Jesus has been teaching His disciples concerning the necessity for self-denial and humility in the Christian life. The Christian must put away pride and self-importance if he is to have the proper perspective in regard to other believers and the unsaved. He must learn proper evaluation of human worth as related to spiritual values. Having given an object lesson on the virtue of humility by using a little child as an illustration, Jesus now presents, in a parable, a lesson in the value of a soul.

"If a man have an hundred sheep, and one of them be gone astray . . . ." Certainly *one* sheep, by monetary value, would be of far less value than *ninety-nine* sheep. We might believe that a

183

shepherd would not place such value on the one that had strayed away. But the shepherd *leaves* the ninety-nine and sets out to find the one that was lost.

He *"goeth into the mountains"*—thus presenting a rugged, rough, dangerous journey in his search for the lost sheep. Certainly Jesus chose a rugged path when He left heaven's glories and came into this sin-cursed world to seek and to save the lost.

Verse 13: *"And if so be that he find it, verily I say unto you, he rejoiceth more of that sheep, than of the ninety and nine which went not astray."*

It would seem that the sensible thing to do would be for the shepherd to rejoice because he still had ninety-nine sheep left to him, thereby devaluating the one that was lost. But no—when he finds the sheep that went astray he rejoices more over finding *that one* than over all the ninety-nine that had not wandered away.

Verse 14: *"Even so it is not the will of your Father which is in heaven, that one of these little ones should perish."*

II Peter 3:9 tells us the Lord is "not willing that *any* should perish, but that *all* should come to repentance." The application here is very plain. Jesus was trying to get across to these disciples the value of one precious soul. Luke makes the comparison even stronger. He says "joy shall be in heaven *over ONE sinner that repenteth, more than over NINETY AND NINE just persons, which need no repentance.*"

When the lost *coin* was found, and the woman rejoiced, Luke recorded, "Likewise, I say unto you, *there is joy in the presence of the angels of God over ONE SINNER that repenteth.*"

In Luke's account of the *son* who went astray, we are told that when this son returned, and "was yet a great way off," the old father ran to meet him, and "fell on his neck and kissed him." The father had been looking, longing, waiting for that son's return, and when he finally returned there was great rejoicing—feasting and merry-making, thanksgiving because the son had returned. (The elder son, the older brother, played the part of a Pharisee by resenting the rejoicing over his lost brother's return.)

I would not be surprised if we have some "elder brothers" with us today. Sometimes Christians seem to become angry and skeptical when a sinner becomes a born again child of God, especially if that sinner is a "down-and-outer." Sometimes, instead of undergirding the newly saved one with prayer and guidance, some seem to wait and watch, until such time as that babe in Christ shall stumble and fall! That is the spirit of a Pharisee, not the spirit Christ wants His children to have. The way you and I, as Christians, feel toward fellow believers reveals to a great extent how spiritual we are and how much of the likeness of Christ we possess.

How We Should Deal With a Brother Who Has Wronged Us

Verse 15: *"Moreover if thy brother shall trespass against thee, go and tell him his fault between thee and him alone: if he shall hear thee, thou hast gained thy brother."*

When the disciples apparently had shown jealousy and selfish ambition, Jesus urged them to be humble and mutually kind toward each other and toward *all* believers. He pointed out the great wickedness of causing humble, lowly Christians to stumble, and He is here giving directions as to what course a believer should pursue toward a fellow believer who has sinned against him. In Matthew 5:23, 24 the admonition was to the *injurer*, the person who had wronged another. In this verse the instruction is to the *injured* one, the one who has been sinned against.

". . . if thy brother shall trespass against thee . . . ." The "brother" here is another believer—not a blood brother, but a brother in Christ.

". . . go and tell him his fault between thee and him alone . . . ." The case here is a personal offence, and notice that the offended is to seek the offender. We are not to wait for the one who offends us to come to us; we are to go and find

him. We are not to allow resentment of the offence to linger in our bosom by keeping silent, nor shall we announce the matter publicly. As a believer, we are to seek out the one who has offended us and tell him of the offence, even as though he were not aware of it—and indeed, in some instances he may not be.

"... *if he shall hear thee, thou hast gained thy brother."* If we approach our brother in the right Christian attitude, kindly and with a sincere desire to clear up the problem, he may at once rectify the offence. When that happens, we have definitely gained. We have not won an argument in our suit against a brother, but we have won something of far greater worth—we have won the brother, whereas we might have lost him had we kept silent and harbored the offence in our heart.

Verse 16: *"But if he will not hear thee, then take with thee one or two more, that in the mouth of two or three witnesses every word may be established."*

"If he will not hear thee...." Suppose the brother who has trespassed against us is hard and rebellious, rejecting even the kindest approach from the one against whom he has sinned. What then? If he displays hostility and refuses to be at peace, shall we give him up and turn from him? *Grace declares "No."* We must go the second mile and make another effort.

187

". . . take with thee one or two more, that in the mouth of two or three witnesses every word may be established." There is to be no false witnessing here. If the offending brother refuses to settle the affair between him and the offended one alone, then the offended brother shall go again to talk with him and he shall take one or two more believers with him; and in the presence of those witnesses the matter is to be taken up again. We see the practicality of this, and if we turn to Deuteronomy 19:15 we read: *"One witness shall not rise up against a man for any iniquity, or for any sin, in any sin that he sinneth: at the mouth of two witnesses, or at the mouth of three witnesses, shall the matter be established."*

Verse 17: *"And if he shall neglect to hear them, tell it unto the church: but if he neglect to hear the church, let him be unto thee as an heathen man and a publican."*

If in the presence of two or three witnesses the matter cannot be settled and the offending brother still refuses to make things right, we are instructed to make one more effort—a final effort—and *"tell it unto the church."* The entire assembly of faithful believers must hear the case, and they must plead with the one who has offended his brother. He is to have another opportunity by hearing the judgment and advice of the body of believers in his community. But

if that also fails? The answer is given to us:
". . . *if he neglect to hear the church, let him
be unto thee as an HEATHEN MAN and a PUB-
LICAN.*" In other words, *just leave him to himself.* There are no penalties prescribed here. The
offending brother is to be regarded as an un-
believer—"an heathen man and a publican." This
does not allow for personal revenge or the har-
boring of ill will toward him, and the entire matter
must be done without vindictiveness. We are not
to have fellowship or communion with the rebellious one, but neither are we to mistreat him.

In rebuking immorality in the Corinthian church,
the Apostle Paul wrote to that church: "I verily,
as absent in body, but present in spirit, have
judged already, as though I were present, concerning him that hath so done this deed, in the
name of our Lord Jesus Christ, when ye are gathered together, and my spirit, with the power of our
Lord Jesus Christ, *to deliver such an one unto
Satan for the destruction of the flesh, that the
spirit may be saved in the day of the Lord Jesus*"
(I Cor. 5:3-5).

To the Roman Christians Paul wrote: "Now
I beseech you, brethren, *mark them which cause
divisions and offences* contrary to the doctrine
which ye have learned; and *avoid them*" (Rom.
16:17).

To the church at Thessalonica, Paul wrote:
"But ye, brethren, be not weary in well doing.

189

And if any man obey not our word by this epistle, *note that man, and have no company with him, that he may be ashamed"* (II Thess. 3:13, 14).

Verse 18: *"Verily I say unto you, Whatsoever ye shall bind on earth shall be bound in heaven: and whatsoever ye shall loose on earth shall be loosed in heaven."*

In the first part of this chapter Jesus spoke to the disciples alone—to the twelve; but here the reference is to the entire church or body of believers. Whatever believers decide concerning a brother who has refused to make things right with another brother whom he has offended, the church decision is God's decision.

The true Church is led by the Holy Spirit. It is clearly declared that those who "bind" make up the whole of the assembly, assembled at that particular time in an attempt to make peace between two brethren. If this fails, then that same body of believers is to render a decision in the matter. Whatsoever they bind on earth shall be bound in heaven—that is, God honors whatsoever the Holy Spirit leads the assembly to do.

We must remember that this has nothing to do with forgiving sins. There is no man or group of men on earth, regardless of how spiritual they may be, who possess the power to forgive sins. Only God can do that. But God sanctions the deeds of the Church according to His holy Word.

This has to do with *the true Church,* a Church made up of born again believers who are led by the Holy Spirit of God, a Church that acts in the name of Jesus and rightly administers the rules and regulations for dealing with erring believers. The responsibility that thus rests upon an assembly of believers is very grave, and the assembly must be led by the Holy Spirit. When the Church acts under the absolute direction of the Spirit, God will sanction what the Church decides.

Some Bible scholars declare that this authority was given only to the apostles, but since God looks upon all believers in the same manner, then it seems reasonable that all believers in a local assembly would be included. There are no "uppers" and "lowers" in the true Church. The pastor is the undershepherd, it is true, and the deacons are elected to handle the business affairs of the Church; but when it comes to a case of discipline in the assembly, such as dealing with an erring believer, I believe that the entire body is included.

Verse 19: *"Again I say unto you, That if two of you shall agree on earth as touching any thing that they shall ask, it shall be done for them of my Father which is in heaven."*

This is very closely connected with the preceding verse, wherein divine approval is guaranteed to the Church when an opinion is rendered concerning a matter before the assembly. Jesus here adds even further assurance to God's approval of His Church:

"If two of you shall agree . . . ." The Greek word here used for "agree" has to do with sound, as the sound of musical instruments where the sounds agree and are in harmony even though they are not identical. This harmony is to be between two believers who agree *"as touching any thing that they shall ask . . . ."* Such harmony could only be as the Holy Spirit leads, and when such is the case, when two believers pray in perfect harmony of spirit, *"it shall be done for them"* by the heavenly Father. Thus Jesus sets His seal of approval upon assemblies, not only in acts of discipline concerning a wayward brother, but also in intercessory prayer where only two of God's children agree on the object of that prayer. In John 15:7 Jesus said, "If ye abide in me, and my words abide in you, ye shall ask what ye will, and it shall be done unto you."

The Simplest Form of the Local Church

Verse 20: *"For where two or three are gathered together in my name, there am I in the midst of them."*

The Church was promised in chapter 16, verse 18. At that time the Church was still future. But in this verse Jesus is speaking of the time when

He would be corporeally absent but spiritually present. He makes this clear in His farewell discourse in the Gospel of John. (Please study chapters 14 through 17 in John's Gospel.) He also makes it clear in His final words in Matthew, when He gave the great commission to His disciples:

"Go ye therefore, and teach all nations, baptizing them in the name of the Father, and of the Son, and of the Holy Ghost: teaching them to observe all things whatsoever I have commanded you: *and, lo, I am with you alway, even unto the end of the world.* Amen" (Matt. 28:19, 20).

"Where two or three are gathered together in MY NAME . . . ." Here Jesus speaks in general — not *"two,"* but *"two or THREE"* who gather *in HIS NAME.*

". . . there am I in the midst of them." Notice it does not say *"there I SHALL be,"* but *"there AM I,"* stating a fact. Jesus is the head of the Church and His presence is the center of the assembly. He is the reason for the Church to come together. If He were not present there would be no point in believers coming together.

Notice that the promise is not to a large assembly, but to the smallest gathering in His name. He is present where *thousands* of believers assemble in His name, but He is also present where only two or three individuals meet together to worship and honor Him. He does not *come* to be with them, He is *already* with them because He abides in the heart of every born again believer. That is what Jesus meant when He promised, "I will pray the Father, and He shall give you another Comforter, *that He may abide with you for ever;* even the Spirit of truth; whom the world cannot receive, because it seeth Him not, neither knoweth Him: but ye know Him; *for He dwelleth with you, AND SHALL BE IN YOU"* (John 14:16, 17).

Believers are to come together in one body, be of one mind, and in harmony of spirit. The gathering is to be in the name of Jesus, and the primary purpose of the assembly is to glorify His name, worship Him, listen to His Word, pray, and encourage one another.

In Hebrews 10:25 believers are admonished to forsake not *"the assembling of ourselves together,* as the manner of some is; but *exhorting one another:* and so much the more, as ye see the day approaching." Meeting together in oneness of spirit and oneness of purpose encourages Christians in their general Christian walk. Christian fellowship is one of God's greatest blessings to His people. We are to encourage each other, stir each other up to obey the will of God—and Jesus is there to help us in all that we do in His name and to His glory. If we as believers would be mindful of this Bible fact when we assemble in the house of God, I believe most assemblies would be quite different in attitude and actions. If we would be mindful of the fact that Jesus is in the midst of every assembly, we should dwell in peace and harmony and never allow frivolous things to cause strife among brethren. Surely if Jesus should weep today as He wept long ago over the city of Jerusalem, He would weep over His children because there is so little unity and harmony among us, and so much strife. The only reason for strife among brethren is lack of the spirit of Christ, and the presence of selfishness and self-seeking.

It should humble our hearts to know that God recognizes and respects such a small assembly. Many times we are prone to look down on a small church. Sometimes we say of a minister, "He is pastor of a little country church," or perhaps we say, "He is pastor of a little church out *in the sticks,*" thus belittling the work that minister is doing. God sees no "little" preachers or "little" churches. He sees the one true Church of which Jesus is the head, and all born again people are members of that one body, regardless of the size of the local assembly where they meet.

God's blessing on *"two or three"* who are gathered in the name of Jesus should also encourage our hearts in the interest of weekly prayer meetings. There is power in combined prayer, even if there are only two or three believers present. There is no excuse for Christians to become discouraged and dispense with prayer meeting. So often we say, "There are *so few* attending prayer meeting, it is hardly worthwhile to meet." God does not necessarily work with "crowds," and I sometimes wonder if the faithful few who show up for prayer meeting each week are not the actual powerhouse of the assembly! I am happy that God does not require numbers or "bigness" to bless His people.

The Christian Rule of Brother Forgiving Brother In This Dispensation of Grace

Verse 21: *"Then came Peter to Him, and said, Lord, how oft shall my brother sin against me, and I forgive him? till seven times?"*

Jesus had just been speaking of the proper Christian way for a believer to act when a brother sins against him, with special reference to *personal* offences. This suggested to Peter a practical question, and he approached Jesus to ask:

"How oft shall my brother sin against me, and I forgive him?" Suppose a brother commits the same wrong against us time after time. How many times should we forgive him? How long are we duty-bound to let this go on?

"Till seven times?" Bible history tells us that when a man sinned against another, the offended person would forgive the offender once, twice, three times—but *never* a *fourth* time. Peter probably knew this and thought *seven* a very liberal number of times to forgive someone who wronged him.

Verse 22: *"Jesus saith unto him, I say not unto*

thee, Until seven times: but, Until seventy times seven."

Jesus replied to Peter, "Seven times is not enough. Multiply that by seventy and make it *seventy TIMES seven*—four hundred and ninety times." This does not indicate that if a brother commit *more* than four hundred and ninety sins against us, we are not to forgive him the additional times. The number here suggests that there is *no limit* to forgiving one when he has wronged us and *sincerely repents* of the wrong. According to Luke 17:4, if the offender does not repent, we are under no obligation to him.

Verse 23: *"Therefore is the Kingdom of Heaven likened unto a certain king, which would take account of his servants."*

In all kingdoms there must be a king and a government—a tribunal. There must be judgment of those under the rule of the king. The personal servants of a king are expected to give special account as to how they have used the king's goods and his money. In this parable, the Greek word for *servants* means literally *slaves*. It has always been common in the east to call the subjects of the court *slaves of the king.* The king's slaves are dependent upon him as much as a true slave—that is, a slave in the true sense of the word—is dependent upon his master. They also served the king with even more diligence than a true slave

197

served the master who literally *owned* him. Since the servants in the parable were also officers of the king's government, they received the king's revenues and attended to the disbursement of those revenues. Thus it was quite possible for a servant to embezzle a great sum of money. The Lord Jesus purposely proposes a very strong case here, in order to more fully illustrate the vast difference between what God forgives *us* and what we are called upon to forgive our fellowman.

This *"certain king"* desired to *"take account of his servants."* This would be, I presume, much the same accounting as would be taken today when the paid auditors take account of the books and business records of a large corporation. If there has been any embezzling or false recording of accounts, it will be discovered in the process of auditing.

Verse 24: *"And when he had begun to reckon, one was brought unto him, which owed him ten thousand talents."*

Ten thousand talents was an immense amount of money for any person to owe, especially a servant. It has been estimated that this debt was equivalent to two million dollars of our money today. The important note here is that the debt could never be paid by a servant. It was overwhelming. And when it was discovered, that servant was brought before the king.

Can you imagine an ordinary servant standing before his king with a debt of two million dollars hanging over his head? But then, by comparison, can you imagine the debt Jesus paid for you and for me? Two million dollars is not a drop in an ocean when it is compared to the price of our sins which was paid on Calvary with the life blood of the Son of God!

Verse 25: *"But forasmuch as he had not to pay, his lord commanded him to be sold, and his wife, and children, and all that he had, and payment to be made."*

". . . he had not to pay . . . ." This servant had no money. In that day, when a man owed a debt he could not pay, his possessions were confiscated and sold, with the income thus received being applied on the amount of the debt. In this instance, the king ordered that the man, together with his family and his possessions, be sold—but even the amount obtained in such a sale would amount to very little compared with the huge debt that servant owed his king.

Verse 26: *"The servant therefore fell down and worshipped him, saying, Lord, have patience with me, and I will pay thee all."*

This servant was well aware that the act of his king was just. The king had a perfect right, legally, to sell him, and his family, and all that he owned. The Lord Jesus does not justify the act of the king in the parable. He simply uses the custom as part of the illustration to drive home the lesson of forgiveness on the part of His disciples— and of course, all believers. The servant was pitiful beyond description. He was in a sad plight indeed. He could not pay, nothing remained his own—not even his own personality. He was to be sold and all that he had would be taken away. Yet, by royal order, *payment must be made.*

"The servant therefore fell down and worshipped him . . . ." The poor man could not pay, but he could humble himself befo 'e his lord and beg for mercy. He did not deny owing the debt, but he pleaded, *"Lord, have patience with me, and I will pay thee all."*

Anyone knows that the promise this man made to his lord was not worth the breath and energy required to speak the words! What man who had not one penny could earn two million dollars to pay a debt, even in the length of a lifetime? Men who make large debts also make large promises—but as a rule they also have large incomes from which to meet their obligations. Therefore they can assure their creditors that they will pay the debt in full if given time. The only possible chance for this king's servant to survive and keep the liberty of himself and his family was to beg—not for time, not for patience, but for *forgiveness.*

Verse 27: *"Then the lord of that servant was moved with compassion, and loosed him, and forgave him the debt."*

The servant received far more than he had asked for. He had not asked that the debt be wiped out. He had asked only for time and patience. But his prayer for mercy and his outward signs of humility moved the heart of the king, and he commanded that the servant should be released, and *"forgave him the debt."* I doubt that such a liberal, compassionate monarch could be found on earth today!

Under the Law of Moses a man could be sold for a theft or a debt (Ex. 22:3; Lev. 25:39; II Kings 4:1). If this forgiven servant had been a man indeed, if he had had any feeling at all toward his fellowman, he would have realized that his lord had exercised grace and kindness that could neither be earned nor bought. No greater act of kindness could have been done for him. Such treatment from his compassionate king should have caused the servant to resolve in his heart that he would hereafter *imitate,* in his own life, the example the king had set before him. He would be humble, he would forgive, he would be kind, gracious, and compassionate to others. But it is evident that his heart was not moved in that direction.

Verse 28: *"But the same servant went out, and*

found one of his fellowservants, which owed him an hundred pence: and he laid hands on him, and took him by the throat, saying, Pay me that thou owest."

"The same servant . . . ." Yes, the same man who a short while ago was prostrate on his knees before his king, begging for mercy, is now a brutal tyrant. He went from the presence of his compassionate king and *"found one of his fellowservants,"* not *his* servant, mind you, not a man who was inferior in position, but one who was in the same category with him—his equal, his companion in service in the king's court.

". . . which owed him an hundred pence . . . ." The fellowservant's debt was but pennies in comparison with the debt the king had forgiven. One would expect that the ungrateful servant would at once mark this small debt paid. But no—*"he laid hands on him, and took him by the throat."* He used violence against his fellowservant, and began to make demands that the debt be paid.

Verse 29: *"And his fellowservant fell down at his feet, and besought him, saying, Have patience with me, and I will pay thee all."*

"His fellowservant fell down at his feet, and besought him . . . ." How hard the servant's heart must have been! Only a short time before, he himself had been on his knees before the king, pleading for mercy—and the king had forgiven him

a debt so great it would have been impossible for him to pay it even if he had labored a lifetime to do so. This fellowservant owed only a small debt and could have paid it in full if he had been granted time to do so. Even if the servant to whom the debt was owed had not forgiven the entire debt, he could at least have granted the time and patience asked for. But not so!

Verse 30: *"And he would not: but went and cast him into prison, till he should pay the debt."*

"He would not . . . ." Notice the interesting fact that the words of the parable do not say *"he COULD not,"* but *"he WOULD not."* He would not have patience with his fellowservant, he would not have mercy on him and give him time to pay the debt. He demanded immediate payment.

". . . but went and cast him into prison, till he should pay the debt." Notice the man did not call one of the king's officers to arrest his fellowservant. From the wording here we are to conclude that he personally took it upon himself to arrest and imprison the debtor. Not only was the action unjust, in the light of the recent forgiveness of so great a debt to this servant, it was also foolish. How could the fellowservant pay a debt when he was confined in a debtor's dungeon?

Verse 31: *"So when his fellowservants saw*

what was done, they were very sorry, and came and told unto their lord all that was done.''

No doubt the incident of the king's forgiveness of the great debt of his servant was known throughout the king's court. Therefore when the other servants saw the evil of that wicked servant toward the man who owed him but a small debt, *"they were very sorry, and came and told unto their lord all that was done."* They recognized the wrongdoing of the servant who had been forgiven so much, and they felt that the king should know about it. The one servant had been forgiven a debt of two million dollars, but had refused to allow his fellowservant time to repay a debt which would have amounted to about seventeen dollars. Since he had been forgiven so much and yet had refused to forgive so little, his fellowservants went to the king and reported what had happened.

Verses 32 and 33: *"Then his lord, after that he had called him, said unto him, O thou wicked servant, I forgave thee all that debt, because thou desiredst me: shouldest not thou also have had compassion on thy fellowservant, even as I had pity on thee?"*

"Then his lord, after that he had called him . . . ." Notice that this wretched creature was not condemned until the king had first heard him. The king sent for him, made the matter known, and then reminded him of what he had done for him.

"O thou wicked servant!" Words of indignation these. The servant had committed wickedness as must have proceeded from a wicked heart. It was not an action of impulse, but of design and determination. He could have given his debtor time to pay, but he would not.

"I forgave thee ALL that debt . . . ." Not *almost* all, but *ALL* of the extremely large debt, and not because the servant *deserved* forgiveness, but out of the goodness of the king's own heart, moved with compassion, he forgave the debt.

"Shouldest not THOU ALSO have had compassion . . . ?" The king had set the example. He had forgiven so much, so freely, should not this servant have forgiven his fellowservant who owed so little in comparison?

What could the wicked servant say? He could offer no defense or excuse. He could offer no argument in favor of his actions. He could not even ask for mercy a second time. Mercy had been extended to him but he had not appropriated it, because he had no mercy on one who owed him a much smaller debt than he himself had been forgiven.

Verse 34: *"And his lord was wroth, and delivered him to the tormentors, till he should pay all that was due unto him."*

"His lord was wroth." The king's compassion turned toward the poor debtor who had been

imprisoned by the servant who had been forgiven an enormous debt. It was righteous wrath which caused the king to deliver the wicked servant *"to the tormentors"* (or the proper officers of justice).

If we look deeply enough into this sentence passed upon the ungrateful servant, we understand that his punishment was never to end. It was eternal. Why? Because he was turned over to the tormentors *"till he should pay all that was due."* He could never pay a debt of such magnitude, even if he had been left free to do his best to pay it. And since he was to remain in prison until that debt was paid, it would be impossible for him to pay one penny of what he owed. Therefore his torment would be unending.

Verse 35: *"So likewise shall my heavenly Father do also unto you, if ye from your hearts forgive not every one his brother their trespasses."*

In this verse Jesus drives home the lesson of forgiveness. He Himself is that "certain King, which would take account of His servants." The Lord Jesus, King of kings and Lord of lords, will surely call His own servants to a just and righteous settlement. He has forgiven our sins, our grievous transgressions against Him—a debt so great there was no way by which we could pay it. No offence that anyone could commit against us can be compared with the sin-debt which our Lord paid in full. Since He paid it all and forgave us, should we not follow His steps and forgive offences of our fellow believers against us?

Jesus has set before us a model of compassion and forgiveness which we cannot overlook or ignore. We have no right to hold a grudge or grievance against a Christian brother when we claim the name of Jesus and He has forgiven us our trespasses. We all belong to the same Lord. Since we are His because He gave so much, we should— *and we MUST*—forgive one another.

When we willingly and freely forgive one who has wronged us, we express our thanksgiving to God, our gratitude for His forgiveness toward us. How much shall we forgive? *We are to forgive ALL;* and notice, our forgiveness must be *from the heart.* We must forgive as God for Christ's sake has forgiven us.

The sovereignty of God is never unjust. The righteous God will judge right and righteously. He cannot judge wrongly. God delivers to the tormentors only those who rightly belong there because of their rejection of God's love, mercy, and salvation. It is the good pleasure of God to forgive all who will come in the name of Jesus, but all who refuse to come must suffer eternally in the lake of fire. To ignore the love of God is sin enough to bring condemnation to the lowest hell. Our Lord Jesus is compassionate, tender, kind, and longsuffering. He forgives when we *seek* forgiveness—but the same God who is love is also a consuming fire (Heb. 12:29).

In Ephesians 4:30-32 we are admonished: "Grieve not the Holy Spirit of God, whereby ye are sealed unto the day of redemption. Let all bitterness, and wrath, and anger, and clamour, and evil speaking, be put away from you, with all malice: *and be ye kind one to another, tenderhearted, forgiving one another, even as God FOR CHRIST'S SAKE hath forgiven you!*"

Paul instructed the Christians in Rome that they be *"kindly affectioned one to another with brotherly love; in honour preferring one another"* (Rom. 12:10).

Each of us who name the name of Jesus and who are truly born again should pray daily, "Lord, make me meek and lowly in heart *and give me a forgiving spirit."*

Chapter XIX

1. And it came to pass, that when Jesus had finished these sayings, he departed from Galilee, and came into the coasts of Judaea beyond Jordan;

2. And great multitudes followed him; and he healed them there.

3. The Pharisees also came unto him, tempting him, and saying unto him, Is it lawful for a man to put away his wife for every cause?

4. And he answered and said unto them, Have ye not read, that he which made them at the beginning made them male and female,

5. And said, For this cause shall a man leave father and mother, and shall cleave to his wife: and they twain shall be one flesh?

6. Wherefore they are no more twain, but one flesh. What therefore God hath joined together, let not man put asunder.

7. They say unto him, Why did Moses then command to give a writing of divorcement, and to put her away?

8. He saith unto them, Moses because of the hardness of your hearts suffered you to put away your wives: but from the beginning it was not so.

9. And I say unto you, Whosoever shall put away his wife, except it be for fornication, and shall marry another, committeth adultery: and whoso marrieth her

which is put away doth commit adultery.

10. His disciples say unto him, If the case of the man be so with his wife, it is not good to marry.

11. But he said unto them, All men cannot receive this saying, save they to whom it is given.

12. For there are some eunuchs, which were so born from their mother's womb: and there are some eunuchs, which were made eunuchs of men: and there be eunuchs, which have made themselves eunuchs for the kingdom of heaven's sake. He that is able to receive it, let him receive it.

13. Then were there brought unto him little children, that he should put his hands on them, and pray: and the disciples rebuked them.

14. But Jesus said, Suffer little children, and forbid them not, to come unto me: for of such is the kingdom of heaven.

15. And he laid his hands on them, and departed thence.

16. And, behold, one came and said unto him, Good Master, what good thing shall I do, that I may have eternal life?

17. And he said unto him, Why callest thou me good? there is none good but one, that is, God: but if thou wilt enter into life, keep the commandments.

18. He saith unto him, Which? Jesus said, Thou shalt do no murder, Thou shalt not commit adultery, Thou shalt not steal, Thou shalt not bear false witness,

19. Honour thy father and thy mother: and, Thou shalt love thy neighbour as thyself.

20. The young man saith unto him, All these things have I kept from my youth up: what lack I yet?

21. Jesus said unto him, If thou wilt be perfect, go and sell that thou hast, and give to the poor, and thou shalt have treasure in heaven: and come and follow me.

22. But when the young man heard that saying, he went away sorrowful: for he had great possessions.

23. Then said Jesus unto his disciples, Verily I say unto you, That a rich man shall hardly enter into the kingdom of heaven.

24. And again I say unto you, It is easier for a camel to go through the eye of a needle, than for a rich man to enter into the kingdom of God.

25. When his disciples heard it, they were exceedingly amazed, saying, Who then can be saved?

26. But Jesus beheld them, and said unto them, With men this is impossible; but with God all things are possible.

27. Then answered Peter and said unto him, Behold, we have forsaken all, and followed thee; what shall we have therefore?

28. And Jesus said unto them, Verily I say unto you, That ye which have followed me, in the regeneration when the Son of man shall sit in the throne of his glory, ye also shall sit upon twelve thrones, judging the twelve tribes of Israel.

29. And every one that hath forsaken houses, or brethren, or sisters, or father, or mother, or wife, or children, or lands, for my name's sake, shall receive an hundredfold, and shall inherit everlasting life.

30. But many that are first shall be last; and the last shall be first.

Jesus Departs From Galilee

Verse 1: *"And it came to pass, that when Jesus had finished these sayings, He departed from Galilee, and came into the coasts of Judaea beyond Jordan."*

"When Jesus had finished these sayings"—that is, when He had finished His teaching on forgive-

ness, He hastened on to other work yet to be finished.

"... *He departed from Galilee, and came into the coasts of Judaea beyond Jordan.*" Jesus left Galilee and turned toward the south, to come into the coasts of Judaea. Matthew and Mark do not mention anything intervening, but we know from Luke's Gospel that some time elapsed between the departure from Galilee and the arrival in Jerusalem. Luke, after completing his account parallel to Matthew and Mark on Christ's ministry in Galilee, describes Jesus as going from Galilee into Judaea through Samaria on the way to Jerusalem (Luke 9:51-56).

John's Gospel agrees with Luke (John 7:2-10)— that is, Jesus' going in secret from Galilee to Jerusalem to attend the feast of tabernacles six months before the final Passover and His crucifixion.

Luke then records a list of the Saviour's sayings, miracles, and ministries (Luke 10:1—18:14), after which He again parallels Matthew and Mark. (Notice Luke 18:15, Matthew 19:13, and Mark 10:13.)

The Gospels of Matthew and Mark deal with the ministry of Jesus in Galilee and vicinity, except for the final Passover and a few incidents on the journey thereto, whereas Luke and John record many incidents that we do not find in Matthew and Mark. That is why we have four Gospels.

They harmonize, yet each one has a message that is very important, and many times *one Gospel* makes known to us what another does not.

Verse 2: *"And great multitudes followed Him; and He healed them there."*

Jesus never lacked for crowds. It is true that on some occasions He preached to only one person, and on other occasions He spoke to a very small group. But there was almost always the press of crowds around Him, and from the Scriptures we learn that while the religious leaders opposed Him vigorously, "the common people heard Him gladly" (Mark 12:37), and *"great multitudes followed Him."* Even His enemies declared, "Never man spake like this Man" (John 7:46).

". . . and He healed them there." Jesus was now coming near to Jerusalem and His enemies were constantly observing Him. But He did not restrain His miracles of mercy because of the jealousy and hatred of those who opposed Him and sought reason (or excuse) to put an end to His ministry. Wherever He found a need He met that need, going on toward Calvary but at the same time performing the work God had sent Him to do.

Jesus Gives Instruction Concerning Divorce

Since divorce is such an important subject, especially in our day, I feel that it would be wise and profitable for us to give here other Scriptures pertaining to divorce and remarriage. Then we will discuss all of these Scriptures together as we go through our present chapter, verse by verse:

Mark 10:1-12: "And He arose from thence, and cometh into the coasts of Judaea by the farther side of Jordan: and the people resort unto Him again; and, as He was wont, He taught them again. And the Pharisees came to Him, and asked Him, Is it lawful for a man to put away his wife? tempting Him.

"And He answered and said unto them, What did Moses command you? And they said, Moses suffered to write a bill of divorcement, and to put her away. And Jesus answered and said unto them, For the hardness of your heart he wrote you this precept. But from the beginning of the creation God made them male and female. For this cause shall a man leave his father and mother, and cleave to his wife; and they twain shall be one flesh: so then they are no more twain, but one flesh. What therefore God hath joined together, let not man put asunder.

"And in the house His disciples asked Him again of the same matter. And He saith unto them, Whosoever shall put away his wife, and marry another, committeth adultery against her. And if a woman shall put away her husband, and be married to another, she committeth adultery."

Please notice also *Luke 16:18:* "Whosoever putteth away his wife, and marrieth another, com-

214

mitteth adultery: and whosoever marrieth her
that is put away from her husband committeth
adultery."

To the believers at Corinth, Paul gave the
following instruction: "Unto the married I command, yet not I, but the Lord, Let not the wife
depart from her husband: but and if she depart,
let her remain unmarried, or be reconciled to her
husband: and let not the husband put away his
wife. But to the rest speak I, not the Lord: If
any brother hath a wife that believeth not, and
she be pleased to dwell with him, let him not
put her away. And the woman which hath an
husband that believeth not, and if he be pleased
to dwell with her, let her not leave him. For
the unbelieving husband is sanctified by the wife,
and the unbelieving wife is sanctified by the husband: else were your children unclean; but now
are they holy. But if the unbelieving depart, let
him depart. A brother or a sister is not under
bondage in such cases: but God hath called us
to peace" (I Cor. 7:10-15).

We have already studied the words of Jesus in
the Sermon on the Mount, but here they are again.
Read them carefully:

"It hath been said, Whosoever shall put away
his wife, let him give her a writing of divorcement:
but I say unto you, That whosoever shall put away
his wife, saving for the cause of fornication, causeth
her to commit adultery: and whosoever shall

marry her that is divorced committeth adultery"
(Matt. 5:31, 32).

Verse 3: *"The Pharisees also came unto Him,
tempting Him, and saying unto Him, Is it lawful
for a man to put away his wife for every cause?"*

This is what we might call a "loaded" question.
Whenever the Pharisees questioned Jesus their questions were designed to entrap Him, to get Him to
say something they could use against Him to
discredit Him and cause public opinion to become
prejudiced against Him. In the question they
asked Him in this verse, they fully expected Him
to become entangled in a discussion about the
law.

*"Is it lawful for a man to put away his wife
for every cause?"* It was the intention of the
Pharisees to lead Jesus in one of two directions
here. Either He would reply to their question in
a manner too severe, or He would say something
that could be interpreted as a contradiction to
the Law of Moses. John the Baptist, who had
also troubled them, had criticized King Herod
for having married his brother's wife, and that
criticism had brought the wrath of Herod down
upon John and had cost him his head. Would this
Nazarene also say something that could be con-
strued as criticism of Herod, thus turning Herod's
anger upon Himself? Or would He be bold enough
to contradict the Law of Moses?

We saw this opposition at work in Matthew 12:2-42 as they tried time after time to establish damaging evidence against Jesus. They tried again in Matthew 15:1-9 and again in chapter 16:1-4. Now they renew their attack on Him.

Jesus had clearly stated His position on the question of divorce when He preached the Sermon on the Mount. (See Matthew 5:31, 32.) These religious "vipers" were not seeking spiritual instruction. In fact, they were ready to argue with Jesus no matter what He said. They were seeking but one thing—something, *anything*, that could be used against Him.

Not only did the Pharisees know what Jesus had to say about divorce, they also knew what the Law of Moses said about it—or at least they *should* have known, for they boasted of their knowledge of the law in general, and the law concerning divorce was very clearly stated in Deuteronomy 24:1-4:

"When a man hath taken a wife, and married her, and it come to pass that she find no favour in his eyes, because he hath found some uncleanness in her: then let him write her a bill of divorcement, and give it in her hand, and send her out of his house. And when she is departed out of his house, she may go and be another man's wife. And if the latter husband hate her, and write her a bill of divorcement, and giveth it in her hand, and sendeth her out of his house; or if the latter husband die, which took her to be his wife; her former husband, which sent her away, may not take her again to be his wife, after that she is defiled; for that is abomination before the Lord: and thou shalt not cause the land to sin, which the Lord thy God giveth thee for an inheritance."

When Christ ministered on earth, there had sprung up two schools of thought on the subject of divorce.   One group taught that a man might divorce his wife for any offence whatsoever or for any dislike he might have toward her. Even if he tired of her, or saw someone else he thought more beautiful and desirable, he could divorce his wife in favor of the other woman. The second group declared that divorce was definitely unlawful except for the cause of adultery. So regardless of what Jesus might have said, His enemies would have differed with Him. They did not ask Him for what cause a man might put away his wife, but if he might put her away *"for EVERY cause."* The question was loosely formed, and of course the looser the terms of any question, the more likely is that question to entangle the person questioned.

Verse 4:   *"And He answered and said unto them, Have ye not read, that He which made them at the beginning made them male and female?"*

"Have ye not read . . . ?" Jesus in answering

218

did not refer to either of the two schools of thought which were prevalent at that time. He simply called their attention to the authority of the writings of Moses.

"He which made them at the beginning . . . ." — here going back to God's original plan of marriage, when He created Adam and then removed a rib from Adam's side and created Eve (Gen. 1:27; 2:21-24).

". . . made them male and female." In the beginning God created one man, and then for that one man He created *one woman.* He could have created any number of women and let Adam choose one or more of those women for his wife—but He did not. He created one of each—one man, one woman, definitely setting the pattern for all men because Adam and Eve are the parents of all living. They are the parents of the human race.

Verse 5: *"And said, For this cause shall a man leave father and mother, and shall cleave to his wife: and they twain shall be one flesh."*

The meaning here is that the man shall bind himself more strongly to his wife than to his own father and mother. There is a tendency on the part of mankind to put emphasis on the close bond between child and parent, and between parent and child. It is true that *there IS a bond* between child and parent as we will see a bit later, but Jesus declares that the marriage connection between man and wife is more endearing and binding than any other human relationship.

According to the words of Jesus, when a man takes a wife he is to love her more than anyone else on earth. He is to *"CLEAVE to his wife"*— and the word *cleave* as used here denotes union of the strongest and most binding kind, *a union that cannot be broken.* The Greek word comes from the word meaning "to glue," indicating that when a man and woman are married they are *glued together* and can never be separated.

". . . they twain shall be one flesh." They who were formerly *two* shall be *one*—one in love, one in desire, one in interest, one in life. They shall no longer go their individual ways or have separate interests. In all things they are to act in accord with each other, as if they were one.

Verse 6: *"Wherefore they are no more twain, but one flesh. What therefore God hath joined together, let not man put asunder."*

The teaching of Jesus is clear—that is, God *created* one man and one woman and declared that they should be so intimately united as to be one flesh, joined by the authority of Almighty God. Therefore it must follow that they cannot be *separated* but by the authority of Almighty God. *"What therefore GOD hath joined together let not MAN put asunder."*

Verse 7: *"They say unto Him, Why did Moses*

then command to give a writing of divorcement, and to put her away?"

The Pharisees of course immediately found fault with what Jesus said concerning divorce. Since Moses had allowed it, how could *He,* merely a teacher from Nazareth, declare divorce to be unlawful?

"Why did Moses then COMMAND . . ?"—but if we look at what the *Pharisees* said in the light of what Moses *actually said,* we see an unfair rendering of the words of Moses. We find these words in Deuteronomy 24:1-4 and that passage has already been quoted; but let us paraphrase it here:

Moses said that when a man married, and after the marriage he found some uncleanness in his wife (meaning that she was not a virgin), then that man could write a bill of divorcement and give it to her and send her out of his house. She could then go and marry another man—that is, if she could find another who would marry her.

Please notice that Moses *did not COMMAND* this. He merely *tolerated* a custom which was then in vogue, and he greatly *limited* that custom. He did not allow such a practice because it was right or because it was according to God's plan, but because of the hardness of the hearts of men. We see this further explained in the next verse.

Verse 8: *"He saith unto them, Moses because of*

the hardness of your hearts suffered you to put away your wives: but from the beginning it was not so."

When Moses led Israel out of Egyptian bondage, he was, in the fullest sense, leading a nation of emancipated slaves who had fallen into great laxity concerning many moral standards, including the marriage vows. Moses was wise enough to know that it would be difficult, if not impossible, to abruptly change their beliefs and practices concerning these things. Therefore, because of the hardness of their hearts, he "suffered" *(permitted)* them to put away their wives. The law did not *command* a husband to divorce his unfaithful wife. It might be that she would repent, the husband would accept her repentance and continue to live with her. In the prophets, Israel is spoken of as Jehovah's adulterous wife, but it is clearly declared that God would forgive His spouse if that nation would repent. (Read Hosea chapter 2.) The law did not *command* a man to put away an unfaithful wife, but it did command that he give her a "writing of divorcement" if he did put her away.

Moses had found divorce in existence to an almost unlimited extent and he knew that this was not according to God's plan in the beginning. Therefore he began to overthrow this loose law concerning divorce by *limiting* the custom, rather than absolutely forbidding it *suddenly*. Men were not allowed to simply send their wives away—

that is, they could not simply tell her to get out of the house. Moses demanded a solemn cere-monial separation. A writing of divorcement must be prepared and placed in the hand of the wife who was being sent away—and even this was to be done only if he had found some uncleanness in her.

It was no new device for the Pharisees to set Moses against *Jesus.* They had done it before. But wicked as they were, they would hardly dare set Moses against *Jehovah God* and thus force an alteration to the divine law ordained of God from the beginning. Jesus made these teachers of the law see that they would be forced to do exactly that to maintain their theory of quick and easy divorce for *every* reason or cause.

Verse 9: *"And I say unto you, Whosoever shall put away his wife, except it be for fornication, and shall marry another, committeth adultery: and whoso marrieth her which is put away doth commit adultery."*

"I say unto you . . . ." In other words, Jesus said, "Regardless of what the law may have said, and regardless of what Moses may have taught, *I want you to listen to ME."* Jesus taught "as one having authority, and not as the scribes" (Matt. 7:29; Mark 1:22). He certainly spoke with authority here on the subject of divorce. He made it crystal clear that divorce is not allowable "for

every cause," and furthermore, divorce is not allowable *at all* "except it be for *fornication."*

It has been said that it seems strange that the only ground for divorce is mentioned here, briefly, and in Matthew 5:31, 32, whereas Mark and Luke do not mention it at all. Remember, when Jesus made the statement to the Pharisees there was in reality no question concerning divorce, because the strictest school of the rabbis, the school of Shammai, *permitted* divorces for fornication and other disgraceful acts. It was clear that one could divorce his wife if she were a fornicator. Therefore the matter did not need to be enlarged upon. It was taken for granted. So although the one scriptural ground for divorce is mentioned by Jesus only twice, both times in the Gospel of Matthew, I would remind you that Jesus does not need to say anything but *once* to make it true!

"Whosoever shall put away his wife, except it be for fornication, and shall marry another, committeth adultery." The question arises, How could there be a *divorce* granted on the ground of fornication, when the *law* commanded that the one *guilty* of fornication be brought forth and put to death? If a man and a woman were taken in *adultery, both were put to death:* "The man that committeth adultery with another man's wife, even he that committeth adultery with his neighbour's wife, *the adulterer and the adulteress* shall surely be put to death" (Lev. 20:10). Why was not

224

this decree carried out in the case of a man who found his wife not to be a virgin?

Note that the law regarding this did not compel the *husband* to bring forth his adulterous wife. If a man married and then found his wife not to be a virgin, he was not commanded to bring her forth to be put to death. Remember Joseph, when he discovered that his bride-to-be (Mary) was with child, was minded to put her away privily, thus taking her out of the public eye. But the angel of the Lord came to Joseph and assured him that Mary's condition involved no guilt whatsoever, and that the Child she would bring forth was the Son of God. (Study Matthew 1:18-25.)

According to the words of Jesus—and His Word is final—fornication is the one and only scriptural ground for divorce. When a man can prove that his wife has committed fornication he is under no obligation to keep her, and he may divorce her. Any other basis for divorce is, by the law of God, null and void.

". . . and whoso marrieth her which is put away doth commit adultery." One who marries a divorced person, even though that individual may not have been married before, commits adultery. Man cannot alter the law of God. The King of kings does not tolerate what men tolerate. A man and woman, united in matrimony, are married for life. The only exception is fornication, and even that must occur the first day, or perhaps even the

first hours, of the marriage, the moment the man discovers that he has not married a virgin. In that case, that woman can marry again, and so can the man; but how many cases do you know like that in our day? *

Verse 10: *"His disciples say unto Him, If the case of the man be so with his wife, it is not good to marry."*

It is interesting that these disciples apparently went along with the Jewish belief concerning marriage—that is, they had come to look upon the ease of getting rid of a wife as a sort of relief from marriage, and if that privilege were taken away, then they considered that it would be better for a man not to marry at all if he had to tie himself down to one woman for life. Thus weighing the risk of an unhappy married life without possibility of change, they concluded, *"If this be so . . . it is not good to marry."*

Verse 11: *"But He said unto them, All men cannot receive this saying, save they to whom it is given."*

"All men cannot receive this saying . . . ." Granting that there are some, though certainly not many, who could find it expedient *not* to marry, that

* Write for our 72-page booklet on *Marriage, Divorce, and Remarriage.*

would be the exception, not the rule. Jesus had spoken on the subject of divorce as viewed from the divine purpose in the creation of man—i. e., *in the beginning* God created them male and female, and when God joined them in marriage *they were ONE.* However, not all men could "receive" what Jesus said.

The word "receive" here does not mean to accept this teaching as truth. Rather, the Greek word here used signifies *space in one's nature* for something. For example, a vessel will hold only so much. When it is filled to capacity it will hold no more. Just so, "receive" here is used in the sense of a person having the *capacity* to *act* according to the saying of Jesus. "Capacity" thus used depends upon many things. Not all have the capacity for marriage.

"*. . . save they to whom it is given.*" I believe there are some people whom God *calls* to remain single for a specific ministry. There are some very peculiar ministries which, though very honorable, can be carried out much more effectively without a mate. By like token, there are other ministries which can be carried out much more effectively if a person is married. God made woman for man and man for woman; and except in rare cases, one life is not complete without the other. A true marriage is ordained of God and brings joy, peace, happiness, and fulfillment that only heaven can afford. The Jews regarded marriage as universally desirable, but Jesus told them that for some persons it was expedient that they refrain from marriage.

There are some Bible scholars and teachers who maintain that the Apostle Paul was never married. They base this interpretation on Paul's declaration in I Corinthians 7:6, 7 where he said: "I speak this *by permission,* and not of *commandment. . . . I would that ALL men were even AS I MYSELF.* But every man hath his proper gift of God, one after this manner, and another after that." We know from this testimony that Paul was not married at that time, but I personally believe that he was married at some time previously, because it appears that when he was Saul of Tarsus he was a member of the Sanhedrin in good standing, and only married men could be members of that body. It is impossible to prove whether he was ever married or not, but it seems reasonable to me that he was. Perhaps his wife had died. At any rate, he found it profitable to serve the Lord unhampered by wife and family.

On the other hand, we know that *Peter* was *married.* In Matthew 8:14, 15, Jesus came into Peter's home and healed *Peter's wife's mother* who was "sick of a fever." Also, in I Corinthians 9:5 Paul speaks of Peter (Cephas) and others of the apostles taking a sister or a wife with them on their missionary journeys.

The capacity for marriage depends upon psychological constitution and general temperament, and there are some people who can be happy and useful *without* marriage. For instance, suppose God calls a young man to service on savage fields—in jungles, in areas where life is hazardous and disease is rampant. Living conditions may be very primitive and the bare necessities of life hard to come by. It seems to me that under such conditions the missionary could carry out his work much more effectively unmarried than it could be done if he had a wife—and perhaps little children to consider.

I know there are churches which could support one missionary on the field whereas those churches cannot send a man, his wife, and two or three children to the field and support them. I am also convinced, from personal knowledge, that the children of missionaries in some very primitive areas must be sent back to the states for educational purposes, sometimes after they have reached high school or college age, and in such instances these young people are thrown into a society that has no mercy on them nor understanding of them. At best, it is a traumatic experience for them, and at the worst it has resulted in boys and girls falling into sin. God forbid that I should judge—and I do not mean to judge. But I do know that God has a perfect, *directive* will for every one of His children, and He also has a *permissive* will under which He *permits* us to do things that do not come under His directive will.

I believe this to be the case with many ministerial students and missionary candidates who cut short their education and time of preparation for service because they have found the girl they want to marry and they are not willing to postpone the marriage for awhile until their preparation for God's service is complete. It is a wonderful thing for young people to fall in love and marry to the glory of God; but the person whom God has called to service in a special way must put God first if he (or she) expects to have God's best. I have known young ministers who have chosen God's permissive will instead of following His directive will and then, as time passed and children came into the home, the burden of the little family discouraged that young preacher and hindered his ministry.

I repeat—I am not judging; but the servant of God must be positive in his heart that God is leading in whatever course he chooses to follow.

From the standpoint of service, I believe that a *pastor* can serve in a greater, much more effective way if he is married. There are so many, many ways and so many places in which a wife could enrich that pastor's ministry. I offer this comment because of the experience through my many years in the ministry. I have seen places where only a single person could effectively serve God, and

I have known other instances where a man's service to God has been rendered more effective and given a much broader scope because of that man's wife and the contribution she makes to his ministry.

However, I declare upon the authority of God's Word that this is a decision which must be made by the individual under God's direction through the ministry of the Holy Spirit. Paul warns us that there will come a false teaching of the worst kind, when men will take it upon themselves to forbid other men to marry. In Paul's first letter to young Timothy, chapter 4, verses 1-5, we read:

"Now the Spirit speaketh expressly, that in the latter times some shall depart from the faith, giving heed to seducing spirits, and doctrines of devils; speaking lies in hypocrisy; having their conscience seared with a hot iron; *forbidding to marry,* and commanding to abstain from meats, which God hath created to be received with thanksgiving of them which believe and know the truth. For every creature of God is good, and nothing to be refused, *if it be received WITH THANKSGIV-ING: for it is sanctified by the Word of God and prayer.*"

The institution of marriage is holy, and no group of religious leaders, no religious governing body, has any right to forbid it. There are such men with us today, just as Paul said there would be. Celibacy for its own sake is not taught any-where in the Holy Scriptures.

Verse 12: *"For there are some eunuchs, which were so born from their mother's womb: and there are some eunuchs, which were made eunuchs of men: and there be eunuchs, which have made themselves eunuchs for the Kingdom of Heaven's sake. He that is able to receive it, let him receive it."*

A *eunuch,* by general definition, is a man who, by emasculation, has been rendered sexually impotent. However, in this verse Jesus applies the term in a broader sense as He speaks of *three classes* of eunuchs:

"There are some eunuchs, which were so born from their mother's womb . . . ." Used here, "eunuch" is a comparative term—that is, there are some men who, because of their lack of interest in marriage, might well *be* eunuchs. Admittedly they are in the extreme minority, but some men have no desire whatsoever to marry. They may be constitutionally unsuited for marriage, or they may be indisposed toward that institution. Some men do not care to undertake the *responsibility* of marriage. Others remain single because of devotion to their chosen vocation, feeling that they follow their occupation so closely that they have no time for wife or family. I do not doubt that some men remain single because of heritage or some experience in early life. For one reason or another they *choose* to remain single.

". . . there are some eunuchs, which were made

eunuchs of men.'' Here Jesus speaks of true
eunuchs—those who have, either by self-mutilation
or by force of other men, been rendered impotent.
We find this in both sacred and secular history.
Josephus tells us that eunuchs of this type were
a very common feature of the courts of the Herods.
Secular history tells us that throughout the Orient
the warlords and potentates selected good physical
specimens from among their servants, men who
were considered handsome and physically attractive,
and subjected them to emasculation. Thus rendered impotent from the standpoint of masculinity,
they were then placed in charge of the warlord's
harem. Sometimes a eunuch was the victim of
self-mutilation committed in idol worship. Christ's
reference here indicates that the existence and
purpose of eunuchs as a class were known to the
Jews in that day, although they themselves ab-
horred the practice of such mutilation. There was
a reason for this:

Under the law, God demanded *perfection.* Every
sacrifice or offering made to God must be done
with animals which were perfect and "without
blemish." We find this throughout the books of
the law and the prophets. Because of this law of
perfection, a eunuch could not serve in the congregation, nor could he even *enter* the congregation
(Deut. 23:1). The fact that any maimed creature,
whether man or beast, was not acceptable for
service to Jehovah, caused the Jews *as a people*

to refrain from the practice of such mutilation as prevailed among the eunuchs. However, the kings of Israel and Judah did use eunuchs as guardians (chamberlains) of the harem.

For example, eunuchs were used in service to Jezebel in Ahab's kingdom, and it was eunuchs who cast her down to her death: "When Jehu was come to Jezreel, Jezebel heard of it; and she painted her face, and tired her head, and looked out at a window. And as Jehu entered in at the gate, she said, Had Zimri peace, who slew his master? And he lifted up his face to the window, and said, Who is on my side? who? And there looked out to him *two or three eunuchs*. And he said, Throw her down. *So they threw her down:* and some of her blood was sprinkled on the wall, and on the horses: and he trode her under foot" (II Kings 9:30-33).

Eunuchs were used in the court of Babylon, as revealed in Daniel 1:3.

In Esther 1:10, 2:21, and 4:5 the eunuchs who served were referred to as "chamberlains."

It was a eunuch who was responsible for Jeremiah's deliverance from the dungeon where he had been imprisoned: "When Ebed-melech the Ethiopian, *one of the eunuchs which was in the king's house,* heard that they had put Jeremiah in the dungeon . . . Ebed-melech went forth out of the king's house, and spake to the king, saying, My lord the king, these men have done evil in all that they have done to Jeremiah the prophet, whom they have cast into the dungeon; and he is like to die for hunger in the place where he is: for there is no more bread in the city. Then the king commanded Ebed-melech the Ethiopian, saying, Take from hence thirty men with thee, and take up Jeremiah the prophet out of the dungeon, before he die. So Ebed-melech took the men with him, and went into the house of the king under the treasury, and took thence old cast clouts and old rotten rags, and let them down by cords into the dungeon to Jeremiah. And Ebed-melech the Ethiopian said unto Jeremiah, Put now these old cast clouts and rotten rags under thine armholes under the cords. And Jeremiah did so. So they drew up Jeremiah with cords, and took him up out of the dungeon . . ." (Jer. 38:7-13).

We notice eunuchs are mentioned in Jeremiah 29:2, 34:19, and 41:16. Many times these men rose to places of prominence. The eunuch to whom Philip preached in Acts 8:26-39 was a man "of great authority under Candace queen of the Ethiopians." He had charge of all the queen's treasure.

"... and there be eunuchs which have MADE THEMSELVES eunuchs for the Kingdom of Heaven's sake." Here Jesus speaks of those men who have accomplished victory and self-control over sexual passion, thus achieving a much greater victory than those who resorted to self-mutilation. Here our Lord presents the fact that it is entirely possible for one to become so completely absorbed in God's work as to have neither time, opportunity, nor desire for fleshly lusts. Such men are possessed of a high and holy purpose. In I Corinthians 7:29-31 the Apostle Paul admonishes:

"This I say, brethren, the time is short: it remaineth, that both they that have wives be as though they had none; and they that weep as though they wept not; and they that rejoice, as though they rejoiced not; and they that buy, as though they possessed not; and they that use this world, as not abusing it: for the fashion of this world passeth away."

For Paul, this was possible. He was so possessed by the fervor of his service to God that he was not closely allied with things of this life. To the Thessalonians Paul stressed the fact that every one "should know how to possess his vessel in sanctification and honour" (I Thess. 4:4), and to the Corinthians he wrote: "I say therefore to the unmarried and widows, It is good for them if they abide even as I. But if they cannot contain, let them marry: for it is better to marry than to burn" (I Cor. 7:8, 9).

"Marriage is honourable in all, and the bed undefiled . . ." (Heb. 13:4). Next to redemption or damnation, marriage is either the *greatest blessing* that can come into the life of a human being, or else it becomes the greatest *curse* that can come to a life. As God said in the beginning, "It is not

236

good that the man should be alone . . ." (Gen.
2:18). That still stands. But it is better not to
marry at all than to marry out of the will of God.
Those who marry need the grace of God and the
leadership of the Holy Spirit to guide them in the
way they should walk as a married couple. Those
who elect to remain *unmarried* need an *extra
portion* of grace and the guidance of the Holy
Spirit lest they fall into sin. *"He that is able
to receive it, let him receive it!"*

Jesus Receives and Blesses Little Children

Verse 13: *"Then were there brought unto Him
little children, that He should put His hands on
them, and pray: and the disciples rebuked them."*

"Then"—when Jesus had finished His disserta-
tion concerning marriage and divorce—*"were there
brought unto Him little children."* We have no
taken-from-life photographs of the Lord Jesus Christ.
We have only the portraits brought to life on
canvas, by which artists down through the ages
have attempted to portray their conception of the
face and figure of the Christ. I would in no way
belittle the efforts of those men who have pre-
sented, to the best of their great ability, their
conception of the love, tenderness, compassion,
or suffering as it might have been mirrored in the
face of Jesus. But I do not believe that any
mortal, no matter how great his God-given talent,

could ever begin to put on canvas the actual expression of holy love and yearning for mankind that would of necessity have been an integral part of the personality of our Lord.

It has been said that the *eyes* are "the windows of the soul." If this be true, considering the great heart of Jesus, very God in flesh, what must have been the impression the parents of these children received when they looked into His eyes! No wonder they brought their children to Him to be blessed.

"*. . . that He should put His hands on them, and pray . . . .*" To me, this is one of the most blessed scenes in our Lord's ministry. How gentle was His touch, how all-encompassing His prayer. We cannot bring our children to Him today to be touched in a physical way, as He touched those children; but we can certainly bring them to Him in prayer—and who can deny that He touches lives today just as surely as He touched the little children brought to Him when He walked this earth? It is perfectly in order for parents today to dedicate their babies to God. When a baby is born into this world, the parents should surrender that baby to Jesus, whether it be done publicly, or in private between the parents and God alone. It is perfectly in order to bring a little one to the church and have the pastor pray *with the parents* at the altar in the church.

You will notice Jesus did not baptize the children, and I find no place in the Bible where infant baptism is taught. It is my opinion that one should know the meaning of baptism before that rite is administered. To baptize an infant neither helps nor hurts it, but a Christian service of dedication is profitable to the child and to the parents.

"*. . . and the disciples rebuked them.*" It is strange that the disciples would rebuke the parents for bringing their little children to Jesus, especially after the lesson He had taught them concerning the childlike faith necessary for entrance into the Kingdom of Heaven. How far they yet were from understanding the nature of His Kingdom! Perhaps they were jealous of the time taken up by the children and their parents. Or perhaps they thought Jesus was too busy and had other things more important to do. Whatever their reasoning, even if it were merely a matter of protecting Him from the pressure of the crowd, "*when Jesus saw it, He was much displeased*" (Mark 10:14).

Verse 14: "*But Jesus said, Suffer little children, and forbid them not, to come unto me: for of such is the Kingdom of Heaven.*"

"*Suffer* (allow) *little children, and forbid them not, to come unto me.*" Jesus had already explained to the disciples that unless they came to Him with the faith of a little child, they could not enter the Kingdom of Heaven. In Luke 18:17 He said, "Verily I say unto you, Whosoever shall not

239

receive the Kingdom of God as a little child shall in no wise enter therein." ". . . *for of such is the Kingdom of Heaven."*

Verse 15: *"And He laid His hands on them, and departed thence."*

Thank God for little children and for parents who surrender their children to the Lord when the little ones come into this world. Jesus laid His hands on these children, and then *"departed thence"* to other ministries that still awaited Him.

The Rich Young Ruler

Verse 16: *"And, behold, one came and said unto Him, Good Master, what good thing shall I do, that I may have eternal life?"*

Mark tells us that this young man came *running* and *kneeled* to Jesus (Mark 10:17), and Luke tells us that this was "a certain *ruler"* (Luke 18:18). He might have been a ruler in one of the synagogues, or perhaps a ruler in the council of the nation, a place to which he had been chosen because of his unquestionable character. He must have been a man of outstanding talents, also, or he would not have acquired his wealth and position in so few years.

This young man came *running* to Jesus, indicating his eagerness to talk with Him. He immediately *knelt* before Jesus, indicating—not an attitude of worship, because he did not realize that he was in the presence of Deity, but an attitude of humility and willingness to be *taught* of Jesus.

"Good Master...." The Greek word used here for "good" means *excellent*—referring not to the moral character of Jesus but to His outstanding position as a teacher of religion who had come to the nation Israel. The term was commonly used in referring to the rabbis and teachers.

"What good thing shall I do, that I may have eternal life?" This young man had been well taught, but the Jewish teachers had led him to believe that the only way he could reach heaven was by *"doing good"*—by performing works of righteousness. He had done all that he *knew* to do, but his present action showed that his heart hungered for something more. He had no peace in his heart.

Nothing in this world can truly satisfy the heart of man. Nothing save the right relationship with God can bring peace and satisfaction. Until one comes into fellowship with his Maker, he will never know true joy and contentment. This young man wanted to know of Jesus if there was anything else he could do to complete his work of righteousness and have assurance of eternal life.

Verse 17: *"And He said unto him, Why callest thou me good? There is none good but one, that is, God: but if thou wilt enter into life, keep the commandments.''*

"Why callest thou me GOOD?'' In His omniscience, Jesus knew that this young man did not believe that He was God in flesh, the true Messiah. He believed that Jesus was a great Teacher who could instruct him in spiritual matters in a greater way than the teachers he had previously known, but he did not believe that Jesus was very God in flesh.

"There is none good but one, that is, God...." What Jesus actually said to the young man was: "If I am *good,* I am *God,* and if I am not *GOD,* then I am not *GOOD.* If I am not God, I am the world's vilest impostor and liar. I have repeatedly announced that I am the Son of God, equal with God. *I and my Father are one''* (John 10:30).

"... but if thou wilt enter into life, keep the commandments.'' Can one be saved by keeping the commandments? Did Jesus mean to tell this young man that if he kept the commandments he would enter heaven and have eternal life? No, He did not mean to say that man can be saved by the works of the law. God's Word teaches clearly that man cannot be saved by keeping the law. The following Scriptures prove this:

Romans 3:20-28: *"Therefore by the deeds of the law there shall no flesh be justified in His sight:* for by the law is the knowledge of sin.

But now the righteousness of God *without* the law is manifested, being witnessed by the law and the prophets; even the righteousness of God which is by faith of Jesus Christ unto all and upon all them that believe: for there is no difference: *for ALL have sinned, and come short of the glory of God;* being justified freely by His grace through the redemption that is in Christ Jesus: whom God hath set forth to be a propitiation through faith in His blood, to declare His righteousness for the remission of sins that are past, through the forbearance of God; to declare, I say, at this time His righteousness; that He might be just, and the justifier of him which believeth in Jesus. Where is boasting then? It is excluded. By what law? of works? Nay: but by the law of faith. *Therefore we conclude that a man is JUSTIFIED BY FAITH WITHOUT THE DEEDS OF THE LAW."*

Galatians 2:16: "Knowing that a man is not justified by the works of the law, but by the faith of Jesus Christ, even we have believed in Jesus Christ, that we might be justified *by the faith of Christ, and NOT by the works of the law: for BY THE WORKS OF THE LAW shall NO flesh be justified."*

Ephesians 2:8, 9: "For *by GRACE are ye saved through FAITH; and that not of yourselves: it is the gift of God: NOT OF WORKS, lest any man should boast."*

243

II Timothy 1:8, 9: "Be not thou . . . ashamed of the testimony of our Lord . . . but be thou partaker of the afflictions of the Gospel according to the power of God; who hath saved us, and called us with an holy calling, *not according to our WORKS, but according to His own PURPOSE AND GRACE,* which was given us in Christ Jesus before the world began."

These Scriptures assure us that one certainly cannot reach heaven by keeping the commandments and observing the law. *Salvation is by GRACE through FAITH.* It is not by works of the law. Jesus told the rich young ruler to keep the commandments in order to wake him up to the fact that he was a sinner and that the only way he could *"do"* his way to heaven was by keeping the commandments—and of course he would have to keep them *perfectly,* which none save Jesus could ever do.

Jesus was God in flesh. Only God could satisfy the law, and what God *demanded* to satisfy His righteousness, He *provided* in His only begotten Son, the Lord Jesus Christ, who came not to destroy the law but that the law through Him might be fulfilled (Matt. 5:17). If it were *possible* for any man to keep the law perfectly, the man who could do that would be saved; but no mortal man ever *has kept,* nor ever *will* keep, the law perfectly. Only Jesus, God in flesh, could—and did—do that.

Verses 18 and 19: *"He saith unto Him, Which? Jesus said, Thou shalt do no murder, Thou shalt not commit adultery, Thou shalt not steal, Thou shalt not bear false witness, Honour thy father and thy mother: and, Thou shalt love thy neighbour as thyself."*

Jesus gave the rich young ruler six commandments:

1. "Thou shalt do no murder."
2. "Thou shalt not commit adultery."
3. "Thou shalt not steal."
4. "Thou shalt not bear false witness."
5. "Honour thy father and thy mother."
6. "Thou shalt love thy neighbour as thyself."

If you will read these commandments carefully you will see that they pertain to one's fellowman, not to Almighty God. Jesus did not give the young man the *first* commandment—"Thou shalt have no other gods before me" (Ex. 20:3). He knew the young man had another god—his wealth. He loved his riches more than he loved God, therefore Jesus did not give him any of the commandments pertaining to man's relationship to Deity. Now let us look at these commandments individually:

"Thou shalt do no murder." I believe Jesus was referring here to what we would call murder— premeditated killing. It is possible to kill accidentally or in self-defense and not be a murderer. According to the words of Jesus in Mark 7:21-23, *murder* (along with numerous other sins) comes

from the heart. So it is entirely possible that the rich young ruler had kept this commandment. He had murdered no one, he was free from the guilt of the blood of his fellowman.

"Thou shalt not commit adultery." In Matthew 5:27,28 Jesus declared: "Ye have heard that it was said by them of old time, Thou shalt not commit adultery: *but I SAY UNTO YOU, That whosoever looketh on a woman to lust after her hath committed adultery with her already in his heart."* God looks upon the heart, and it is possible for a man to live out a lifetime here on earth and not commit adultery, even in his heart. It is possible that this young man had never committed physical adultery nor even lusted with his eyes or heart after a woman. It seems evident from his own testimony that he had never broken up a home or taken another man's wife.

"Thou shalt not steal." To steal is to take property from one's fellowman without his knowledge or consent. To steal is to take from another what does not belong to us. The item stolen may be worth a few cents or it may be worth a million dollars. God does not measure stealing by the value of the article stolen. All thieving comes from the heart. Certainly it is possible for a person to live for a full threescore and ten years and never take one single item unjustly. This young ruler had great wealth, but it is possible that he earned it honestly without one incident of stealing.

"Thou shalt not bear false witness." To bear false witness is to give testimony that is not true. One may bear false witness in the civil courts. Such testimony is called perjury and it carries a heavy legal penalty. One may also bear false witness against a fellowman by telling things which are not true and thus damaging or slandering the character of a person. But it would be possible to refrain from such testimony, and it is possible that this young man had not been guilty of bearing false witness against anyone.

"Honour thy father and thy mother." How does one honor his father and mother? By obedience, by keeping or obeying the commands of father and mother. I am not saying that the commands of parents are inspired, certainly not; and the commands of unregenerated fathers and mothers may not be according to *God's* commandments. But the instructions of parents, when not directly against God's commands, are to be obeyed by their children. Colossians 3:20 commands, "Children, *obey your parents in all things:* for this is well pleasing unto the Lord." In Ephesians 6:1-3 Paul instructs, "Children, *obey your parents in the Lord:* for this is right. Honour thy father and mother, which is the first commandment with promise; that it may be well with thee, and thou mayest live long on the earth."

To honor father and mother also means to show respect for them and give them due reverence—

not as we reverence God, but with reverence due father and mother because they brought us into this world and cared for us while we could not care for ourselves. Godly parents constitute a gift that cannot be valued by earthly standards. Our parents may not dress or act exactly as we think they should, they may be what we choose to call "a little bit old-fashioned." But they are our parents and we are duty-bound to honor and respect them. Do not speak disrespectfully of them, do not ridicule or rebuke them, for they have the wisdom that only age can bring.

We should also honor father and mother when they are old and cannot always care for themselves as they need to be cared for. We should stand by and take care of them when they need us most. They cared for us when we were small and helpless, and when they are old and need us we need to bear with them and be patient with them. There are many, many ways by which we may honor father and mother.

"Thou shalt love thy neighbour as thyself." First of all, *who is* our neighbor? Our neighbor is, of course, the person who lives next door to us; but in the true sense of the word and according to the teachings of Jesus, our neighbor is the person with whom we come in contact in business, social, or Christian life.

In Luke 10:29-37, Jesus teaches us who our neighbor is. A certain lawyer asked, *"Who IS my neighbour?"* By way of reply, Jesus gave the parable of the good Samaritan. He said:

"A certain man went down from Jerusalem to Jericho, and fell among thieves, which stripped him of his raiment, and wounded him, and departed, leaving him half dead. And by chance there came down a certain priest that way: and when he saw him, he passed by on the other side.

"And likewise a Levite, when he was at the place, came and looked on him, and passed by on the other side.

"But a certain Samaritan, as he journeyed, came where he was: and when he saw him, he had compassion on him, and went to him, and bound up his wounds, pouring in oil and wine, and set him on his own beast, and brought him to an inn, and took care of him. And on the morrow when he departed, he took out two pence, and gave them to the host, and said unto him, Take care of him; and whatsoever thou spendest more, when I come again, I will repay thee."

Then Jesus asked the lawyer, "Which now of these three, thinkest thou, was neighbour unto him that fell among the thieves?"

The lawyer replied, "He that shewed mercy on him." Then Jesus said to him, *"Go, and do thou likewise."*

To love one's neighbor is to be sure not to injure him, his person, his character, or his property.

To love one's neighbor is to help him when he has need, when adversity befalls. To love one's neighbor as oneself is to treat the neighbor's character, his name, his property and all that he has as we would treat ourselves and our very own according to what is right.

This does not mean that we are to neglect our own needs and the needs of our own family. It does not mean that we should neglect our business or bankrupt ourselves while we take care of our neighbor. It simply means that we are to love, respect, and help our neighbor in times of need. It is our duty to provide for our own family first. We are not to allow our own family to suffer in order to provide for our neighbor. The Scripture plainly declares, "If any provide not for his own, and specially for those of his own house, he hath denied the faith, and is worse than an infidel" (I Tim. 5:8). But in the majority of homes, even though those homes be poor, there are things that can be shared with others and consideration that can be shown to others.

It is possible to keep this commandment of our Lord and love one's neighbor as oneself, and it is possible that this rich young ruler had done all that he could for his neighbors.

Notice I have said it is *possible* for a person to keep these six commandments. I will also say that while it is possible, it is indeed not *probable*. In addition to the six commandments Jesus gave this young man, it would also be possible—though not probable—to keep the commandment which forbids covetousness: *"Thou shalt not covet* thy neighbour's house, thou shalt not covet thy neighbour's wife, nor his manservant, nor his maidservant, nor his ox, nor his ass, nor any thing that is thy neighbour's"* (Ex. 20:17). But when we look at the other commandments we realize that mortal man would fail the test:

"Thou shalt have no other gods before me. Thou shalt not make unto thee any graven image . . . . Thou shalt not bow down thyself to them, nor serve them: for I the Lord thy God am a jealous God . . . . *Thou shalt not take the name of the Lord thy God in vain;* for the Lord will not hold him guiltless that taketh His name in vain. *Remember the sabbath day, to keep it holy"* (Ex. 20:1-8 in part).

There are thousands upon untold thousands of idol-worshipers in America, and other thousands around the world. Anything that stands between man and God, keeping man from surrendering soul, spirit, and body to God, is an idol. It may be money, a home, business, wife, or children. It could be a race horse or a speedboat. It could be a set of golf clubs. In other words, *anything* that occupies so much of one's time that that one does not have time to serve God becomes an idol. Jesus did not mention any of the commandments pertaining to Deity when He instructed the rich young ruler. The six commandments He quoted to him had to do only with the attitude toward and treatment of his fellowman.

Verse 20:   *"The young man saith unto Him, All these things have I kept from my youth up: what lack I yet?"*

It was *possible*, though not *probable*, that this young man *had* kept all of those commandments. I would not accuse him of being a hypocrite. It appears that he came to Jesus in all sincerity. He fell at the feet of Jesus in humility, and he honestly and earnestly asked what he must do to inherit eternal life.   When he said he had kept all of the commandments Jesus quoted to him, he was evidently testifying to what he sincerely thought to be true.

There are many people today who believe in their own heart that they keep the ten commandments and live by them.   Some religions *major* on commandment keeping.   Fundamental ministers of the Gospel of the grace of God are accused of *doing away with* or *destroying* the law.   Such is not the case.   Fundamental preachers do not teach that God has destroyed His law.   The law of God "is holy, and the commandment holy, and just, and good" (Rom. 7:12).   The law of God is perfect and powerful, but the law was not given to save souls.   ". . . the law was our schoolmaster to bring us unto Christ, *that we might be justified by faith"*

(Gal. 3:24). Paul said, ". . . I had not known *sin*, but by the law" (Rom. 7:7 in part). The law brings the knowledge of sin—but by the deeds of the law there shall no flesh be justified. I am not attempting to destroy or minimize the law and its importance. I am simply teaching what *Jesus* taught—that is, that He fulfilled every jot and tittle of the law (Matt. 5:17). *WE are lawkeepers IN CHRIST, and only in Christ.*

Paul, longing to see his people saved, declared: "Brethren, my heart's desire and prayer to God for Israel is, that they might be saved. For I bear them record that they have a zeal of God, but not according to knowledge. *For they being ignorant of God's righteousness, and going about to establish their own righteousness, have not submitted themselves unto the righteousness of God. For CHRIST is the END of the law for righteousness to every one that believeth*" (Rom. 10:1-4).

We are not saved by commandment keeping. We are saved by God's grace, through faith.

"What lack I yet?" This young man had been taught according to the Jewish religion, and he had been taught well. To the best of his ability he had lived by what he had been taught. But perhaps this great Teacher could tell him something else to do, in addition to what he had already done, that would assure him of a place in the Kingdom of Heaven.

Verse 21: *"Jesus said unto him, If thou wilt be*

perfect, go and sell that thou hast, and give to the poor, and thou shalt have treasure in heaven: and come and follow me."

"*If thou wilt be perfect . . . .*" The Greek word translated "perfect" means "complete in all its parts, finished, having no part lacking." Suppose we illustrate thus: A very expensive watch or clock—or even an automobile—is not completed or finished until every little screw, spring, and wheel is properly installed by a master mechanic. What God Almighty demands, only God Almighty could provide. Therefore one is not complete *IN the law, THROUGH the law,* nor *by WORKS.* We are complete *in CHRIST:* "For in Him dwelleth all the fulness of the Godhead bodily. And ye are complete in Him, which is the head of all principality and power" (Col. 2:9, 10).

That is why the Word of God declares, ". . . whosoever shall keep *the whole law,* and yet offend *in ONE POINT, he is guilty of ALL"* (James 2:10). If you remove the least screw from a watch, the watch is no longer complete and will not run. This young ruler had lived a life as nearly perfect as it is possible to live. In Mark 10:21 we read, "Then Jesus beholding him loved him, and said unto him: *ONE THING thou lackest:* go thy way, sell whatsoever thou hast, and give to the poor, and thou shalt have treasure in heaven: and come, take up the cross, and follow me."

Any young man as exemplary in his manner of

life as this young ruler was, would surely be considered a righteous man by his friends and family. But Jesus, looking on his heart, knew that this *one thing* the young man lacked was separating him from God. To be complete and perfect in the sight of God, he must separate himself from that which meant more to him than his soul's salvation, that which kept him from loving God supremely.

We are so prone to judge from outward appearance! Saul of Tarsus, the mighty Jew who became the Apostle Paul, declared that before his conversion he had lived "in all good conscience" through his religious endeavors (Acts 23:1). Writing to the Philippians he said, "Concerning zeal, persecuting the Church; *touching the righteousness which is in the law, BLAMELESS*" (Phil. 3:6).

The Scripture tells us that *Job* was a perfect man—"*perfect and upright,* and one that feared God and eschewed evil" (Job 1:1). Yet we know that Job was not *sinless,* because God reproved him. (Read Job chapters 38, 39, and 40.) Job was pious—he was a pious father, a pious lawman (magistrate), a pious citizen, and a pious neighbor. His religion was not confined to one thing, but was well-rounded.

"Perfect" sometimes means "carrying out or filling up," an expression of a principle of action. We see an example of this in I John 2:5: "Whoso keepeth His Word, in him verily is the love of God *perfected . . . .*" Jesus left the Father's bosom,

the streets of gold, the singing of the angels, and all the glory of God's house, and came into this world to die for the ungodly. Thus God declared His love—not only in words, but in action as well. Jesus on Calvary, suffering, bleeding, dying for sinners, was God's love on display.

Jesus knew the heart of this young ruler. He knew the young man would reject Him. But in spite of that, *He loved him*—with love such as only Jesus could know. He dealt with this one graciously, calmly, affectionately. The young man asked, "What lack I yet?" and Jesus told him what he lacked:

"Go and SELL that thou hast, and give to the poor, and thou shalt have treasure IN HEAVEN: and come and follow me."

Notice please, the "one thing" this young man lacked, the one thing that would have made him complete, consisted of six steps:

1. Going back to his property.
2. Selling that property—real estate and other possessions.
3. Giving the proceeds of the sale (money) to the poor.
4. Returning to Jesus.
5. Taking up the cross which Jesus would give him.
6. Following Jesus—presumably as He traveled from place to place, as the other disciples did.

In return, Jesus promised the young man that

he would have "treasure in heaven," treasure such as no mortal man could ever attain on this earth.

Verse 22: *"But when the young man heard that saying, he went away sorrowful: for he had great possessions."*

What this young man really lacked was *faith.* Jesus did not call upon him to sell his possessions, give the proceeds to the poor—*and receive NOTHING in return.* Jesus promised him a treasure in *heaven.* He had asked Jesus to instruct him as to how he might obtain eternal life, but he did not believe what Jesus told him. He evidently did not believe there would *be* a treasure. He did not believe that selling his property and distributing the money to the poor would be for his good, as well as blessing hundreds of poor people. *God is not cheap.* He has never called upon anyone to do anything for Him without repaying as only God can repay! One who gives even a cup of cold water in the name of Jesus will not lose his reward (Mark 9:41).

This young man had been blessed abundantly. Even the ability to accumulate the riches he possessed was God's gift to him. *"Every good gift and every perfect gift is from above, and cometh down from the Father of lights,* with whom is no variableness, neither shadow of turning" (James 1:17). But when Jesus told him to sell all that he had, give the money to the poor, and take up his cross and follow Jesus, *"he went away sorrowful: for he had great possessions."*

Matthew tells us that this young man "had great possessions." *Mark* tells us that "he had great possessions" (Mark 10:22). *Luke* tells us that "he was *very rich*" (Luke 18:23). Certainly this was a very wealthy young man! He was very rich—and his riches had become his idol, his god. He loved what he had more than he loved Almighty God, and he would not turn his back on what he had in order to know God in forgiveness of sin—no, not even to possess eternal life, which he had come to Jesus in search of.

Thus he proved his unbelief. Faith comes by hearing, and hearing by the Word of God (Rom. 10:17). This young man heard the Word—Jesus promised him a treasure if he would dispose of his earthly possessions and follow HIM. But he rejected that treasure because of unbelief. Every soul that screams in hell today is there because of unbelief, and every soul that drops into hell from this day until the last moment of time will do so because of unbelief. Unbelief is the sin that damns the soul of man: "He that believeth on (Jesus) is not condemned: but *he that believeth not is condemned already, because he hath not believed in the name of the only begotten Son of God"* (John 3:18).

A few moments ago this young man had come

running to Jesus, so eager was he to know the way of eternal life. Now he slowly rises from his knees. His face is no longer filled with bright anticipation, his heart no longer pounding with excitement. His countenance is sad and his heart is grieved. He was married to his riches and he loved his great possessions more than he loved God, more than he loved his own soul. What a sad, sad picture! And yet it is repeated over and over again every day of this world. There are many people today who love worldly possessions and temporal things more than they love God. They are more interested in acquiring more temporal possessions than they are in the heavenly treasure of *spiritual* wealth for all eternity.

Verse 23: *"Then said Jesus unto His disciples, Verily I say unto you, That a rich man shall hardly enter into the Kingdom of Heaven."*

Jesus said, *"VERILY, I say unto you . . . ,"* again stressing the urgency and importance of what was to follow, *"a rich man shall hardly enter into the Kingdom of Heaven."* Thank God Jesus did not say that a rich man *cannot* enter heaven. He said a rich man shall "hardly enter" into the Kingdom, meaning that it is difficult for the rich to break away from their treasures to serve God by faith. The natural man craves the things money can buy, and many times money buys things which bring such pleasure to a man and his family that even on the Lord's day, when he should be praying, reading his Bible, and worshiping God, he is out away from the house of God *enjoying* the things his money has bought.

Lest I be misunderstood, I hasten to declare that it is not wealth or money, as such, that is "the root of all evil." It is *the LOVE of money* that is the root of all evil (I Tim. 6:10). There are some people who love money who have very little of it. There are others who have money but do not love it.

It is certainly not a sin to own a home, an automobile, a boat, an airplane, saddle horses—and many other things that come under the heading of comfort, convenience, or even pleasure. But when an automobile takes one away from the house of God when he should be there to worship, and instead, transports him to places of worldly pleasure and sin, then that automobile becomes that person's idol or false god.

There are business men who never attend church, and they excuse themselves by declaring that they have business obligations which demand their time even on Sunday. Beloved, if you are so big in business that you have no time to serve God, then that business has become your idol! There are many wealthy men who love God supremely and support the work of the Lord with their money; but there are many others—by far in the majority— who have no time for God, no time for the church, no time for anything save making money. They devote all their time to making more millions and satisfying the lusts of the flesh.

Shall we allow the Word of God to instruct us concerning this matter? In I Timothy 6:6-12 we read:

"Godliness with contentment is great gain. For we brought nothing into this world, and it is certain we can carry nothing out. And having food and raiment let us be therewith content. But they that will be rich fall into temptation and a snare, and into many foolish and hurtful lusts, which drown men in destruction and perdition. *For THE LOVE OF MONEY is the root of all evil:* which while some coveted after, they have erred from the faith, and pierced themselves through with many sorrows. But thou, O man of God, flee these things; and follow after righteousness, godliness, faith, love, patience, meekness. Fight the good fight of faith, lay hold on eternal life, whereunto thou art also called, and hast professed a good profession before many witnesses."

Verse 24: *"And again I say unto you, It is easier for a camel to go through the eye of a needle, than for a rich man to enter into the Kingdom of God."*

The statement here concerning a camel and the eye of a needle was a proverb greatly used among the Jews in the time when Jesus walked among men, and it is still used by the Arabs with reference to something impossible. The statement means that it is as impossible for a person to be saved while he is enslaved by his wealth and material treasures as it is for a camel to go through the eye of a needle.

It has been suggested that this proverb refers to a little gate and a *rope* which was called a camel, but I cannot accept that suggestion. I personally believe Jesus meant exactly what He said. A camel is a large, ungainly animal, and it also has humps on its back. For such a creature to pass through the eye of a needle would be so impossible as to defy imagination! When a person has his eyes on riches and treasures of this earth, when his consuming ambition is directed toward this world and what this world affords, it is as impossible for that person to be saved as it is for a camel to go through the eye of a needle. He must turn his eyes upon Jesus and see (with the inner eye) the treasures heaven holds.

According to Jesus, the wealth of this world is a much greater hindrance than it is a help to those who would enter into the Kingdom of God. The *rich* man is shielded from a sense of need. He has all that money can buy, and it takes a miracle wrought through God's saving grace to make him stop and consider where he will spend eternity. On the other hand, a *poor* man who meets with many heartaches, disappointments, and deprivations will compare the heavenly treasure to his earthly poverty and reach out for God.

Verse 25: *"When His disciples heard it, they were exceedingly amazed, saying, Who then can be saved?"*

I like the way Mark records this. Notice what he has to say:

"And Jesus looked round about, and saith unto His disciples, How hardly shall they that have riches enter into the Kingdom of God! And the disciples were astonished at His words. But Jesus answereth again, and saith unto them, Children, how hard is it for them that trust in riches to enter into the Kingdom of God! It is easier for a camel to go through the eye of a needle, than for a rich man to enter into the Kingdom of God. And they were astonished out of measure, saying among themselves, Who then can be saved? And Jesus looking upon them saith, With men it is impossible, but not with God: for with God all things are possible" (Mark 10:23-27).

These disciples, like most men, thought that wealth was an asset and a great advantage. They had just heard Jesus declare that money is more likely to be a curse than a blessing, and they did not understand His words. They reasoned that if *rich* men could be saved only through great difficulty, then *poor* men such as *they* were, men devoid of this world's goods, had no chance at all!

Hence the question, *"Who then CAN be saved?"*

Verse 26: *"But Jesus beheld them, and said unto them, With men this is impossible; but with God all things are possible."*

"With men this is impossible . . . ." Certainly the comparison Jesus had just given them was impossible. There was no way open to the imagination whereby a camel might pass through the eye of a needle. And it is just as impossible for man to be saved apart from the grace of God. For the rich man, it would be equally impossible for him to be saved without the work of the Holy Spirit in his heart, but so many times riches blind one's eyes to the need of the soul. Like the Laodiceans, a wealthy person is prone to say, "I am rich, and increased with goods, and have need of nothing," not realizing that he is "wretched, and miserable, and poor, and blind, and naked" (Rev. 3:17). As long as *physical* needs are supplied, the natural man is not likely to be aware of the need of the soul. The spiritual need is not much in the mind of a person whose every physical need and desire are at his fingertips.

". . . but with God ALL THINGS are possible." It is not a divine necessity that men spend eternity in the lake of fire because of their wealth. God does not condemn a man because that man has riches. Many men have become wealthy by honest measures, and without making money their god.

But it is *difficult* to acquire riches and at the same time withstand the temptation of avarice, covetousness, fraud, and oppression of one's fellowman. As Paul explained in I Timothy 6:8-10, "Having food and raiment let us be therewith content. But *they that will be rich fall into temptation and a snare, and into many foolish and hurtful lusts,* which drown men in destruction and perdition. *For the LOVE of money is the root of all evil:* which while some coveted after, they have erred from the faith, and pierced themselves through with many sorrows."

Then in verse 17 of that same chapter, Paul admonishes Timothy, "Charge them that are rich in this world, that they be not highminded, nor trust in uncertain riches, but in the living God, who giveth us richly all things to enjoy."

James issues a stern rebuke to those who have acquired riches by unethical practices. In James 5:1-6 we read:

"Go to now, ye rich men, weep and howl for your miseries that shall come upon you. Your riches are corrupted, and your garments are motheaten. Your gold and silver is cankered; and the rust of them shall be a witness against you, and shall eat your flesh as it were fire. Ye have heaped treasure together for the last days. Behold, the hire of the labourers who have reaped down your fields, which is of you kept back by fraud, crieth: and the cries of them which have reaped are entered into the ears of the Lord of sabaoth. Ye have lived in pleasure on the earth, and been wanton; ye have nourished your hearts, as in a day of slaughter. Ye have condemned and killed the just; and he doth not resist you."

God can give grace if the rich will realize their need of a Saviour, a need *beyond anything money can provide.* All things are possible with God. It is just as easy for God to save a rich man as it is for Him to save a pauper. His grace is sufficient for all. Rich or poor, bond or free, wise or unwise, we are saved *by GRACE through FAITH.* Then we *overcome the world* by faith, we *live* by faith, and *"whatsoever is NOT of faith is sin"* (Rom. 14:23).

Rewards Promised to Those Who Leave All for Jesus' Sake

Verse 27: *"Then answered Peter and said unto Him, Behold, we have forsaken all, and followed thee; what shall we have therefore?"*

Mark records this conversation as follows: "Then Peter began to say unto Him, Lo, we have left all, and have followed thee. And Jesus answered and said, Verily I say unto you, There is no man that hath left house, or brethren, or sisters, or father, or mother, or wife, or children, or lands, for my sake, and the Gospel's, but he shall receive an hundredfold now in this time, houses, and brethren, and sisters, and mothers, and children, and lands, with persecutions; and in the world to come eternal life. But many that are first shall be last; and the last first" (Mark 10:28-31).

Luke puts it in these words: "Then Peter said, Lo, we have left all, and followed thee. And He said unto them, Verily I say unto you, There is no man that hath left house, or parents, or brethren, or wife, or children, for the Kingdom of God's sake, who shall not receive manifold more in this present time, and in the world to come life everlasting" (Luke 18:28-30).

"Peter . . . said unto Him . . . ." Peter again speaks for his fellow apostles, as well as for himself. *"Behold, we have forsaken all, and followed thee."* Peter reminded Jesus that he and the other apostles had done what the rich young ruler *refused* to do. Although there is no record that any of the twelve had any great amount of this world's goods, they *had* left everything to follow Jesus. Peter, James, and John had left their nets. Matthew had left his seat of custom where he collected taxes. *Whatever* had been counted as assets to these men, they had left their respective vocations to follow where Jesus led—and surely no one was more aware of this than the Lord Himself.

"What shall WE have therefore?" There was nothing wrong in what Peter asked. What he said was true. They had left all to walk with Jesus. Now what would be the *reward* for such sacrifice?

267

He had heard Jesus promise treasure in heaven to the young ruler if he would forsake his earthly possessions and follow Him. Since Peter and the other apostles had done exactly that, surely their reward would be as great as that promised the rich young man. But coming at that particular time and expressed in such a manner, the question could easily be understood as inspired of personal greed.

Verse 28: *"And Jesus said unto them, Verily I say unto you, That ye which have followed me, in the regeneration when the Son of man shall sit in the throne of His glory, ye also shall sit upon twelve thrones, judging the twelve tribes of Israel."*

The Greek word here rendered *"regeneration"* occurs only one other time in the New Testament. It is used in Titus 3:5 where we read of "the washing of regeneration." The meaning of the word is "a new birth, being born again." As applied to man, it denotes the great change, the new life, the new heart when one becomes a Christian. "Therefore if any man be in Christ, he is a new creature: old things are passed away; behold, all things are become new" (II Cor. 5:17).

However, as Jesus used *"regeneration"* here, it speaks primarily of the birth of a nation, the time when Israel will be restored to her homeland. Every foot of the land God promised Abraham and his descendants will be given to the nation at the appointed time. A nation—God's elect nation—will be born in a day (Isa. 66:8) and will dwell in the land of Palestine.

In the fuller sense, the regeneration of which Jesus speaks could also apply to the new birth of the entire creation. There will be new heavens and a new earth:

"The day of the Lord will come as a thief in the night; in the which the heavens shall pass away with a great noise, and the elements shall melt with fervent heat, the earth also and the works that are therein shall be burned up. Seeing then that all these things shall be dissolved, what manner of persons ought ye to be in all holy conversation and godliness, looking for and hasting unto the coming of the day of God, wherein the heavens being on fire shall be dissolved, and the elements shall melt with fervent heat? Nevertheless we, according to His promise, look for *new heavens and a new earth, wherein dwelleth righteousness.* Wherefore, beloved, seeing that ye look for such things, be diligent that ye may be found of Him in peace, without spot, and blameless" (II Pet. 3:10-14).

In Revelation 21:1-5 John the Beloved wrote: "And I saw *a new heaven and a new earth: for the first heaven and the first earth were passed away;* and there was no more sea. And I John saw the holy city, new Jerusalem, coming down from God out of heaven, prepared as a bride adorned for her husband. And I heard a great voice out of heaven saying, Behold, the tabernacle of God is with men, and He will dwell with them, and they shall be His people, and God Himself shall be with them, and be their God. And God shall wipe away all tears from their eyes; and there shall be no more death, neither sorrow, nor crying, neither shall there be any more pain: for the former things are passed away. And He that sat upon the throne said, Behold, *I make all things new.* And He said unto me, Write: for these words are true and faithful."

Then in verses 9 through 11 in that same chapter, we read: "And there came unto me one of the seven angels which had the seven vials full of the seven last plagues, and talked with me, saying, Come hither, I will shew thee the bride, the Lamb's wife. And he carried me away in the spirit to a great and high mountain, and shewed me that great city, the holy Jerusalem, descending out of heaven from God, having the glory of God: and her light was like unto a stone most precious, even like a jasper stone, clear as crystal."

Former things will pass away and *ALL things* will become new.

"When the Son of man shall sit in the throne of His glory . . . ." This speaks of the time when Jesus will return to this earth in power and great glory, the time when every eye shall see Him

and all men shall wail because of Him (Rev. 1:7).

I believe this will be a literal throne, the throne of David, and Jesus will sit on that throne in Jerusalem. In the Annunciation, the angel of God said to Mary: "And, behold, thou shalt conceive in thy womb, and bring forth a son, and shalt call His name JESUS. He shall be great, and shall be called the Son of the Highest: *and the Lord God shall give unto Him the throne of His father David: and He shall reign over the house of Jacob for ever;* and of His Kingdom there shall be no end" (Luke 1:31-33).

To date, this promise has not been fulfilled. But it will be fulfilled literally when Jesus returns to establish His Kingdom on earth, as He promised His disciples here in our present Scripture.

"*. . . ye also shall sit upon twelve thrones, judging the twelve tribes of Israel.*" A judgeship signifies authority, power, rank. In the Old Testament era the judges of Israel were men of courage, patriotism, honor, and valor. To judge denotes power of passing judgment. Honor is attached to that office. Earthly rulers have around them judges to assist and advise them. In like manner, Christ will have the apostles with Him to judge the twelve tribes of Israel. When Jesus came on the scene and said to these men, "Follow me," they left all that they had and stepped out by faith to follow the Stranger of Galilee. They will be rewarded accordingly.

271

"The twelve tribes of Israel" is the name by which the people of God were distinguished. The apostles will have a special place in the government of Israel, a government of which there shall be no end. The Prophet Isaiah declared, "Of the increase of His government and peace there shall be no end, upon the throne of David, and upon His kingdom, to order it, and to establish it with judgment and with justice from henceforth even for ever. The zeal of the Lord of hosts will perform this" (Isa. 9:7).

The Kingdom—and the King—are described in Isaiah 11:2-10:

"And the Spirit of the Lord shall rest upon Him, the spirit of wisdom and understanding, the spirit of counsel and might, the spirit of knowledge and of the fear of the Lord; and shall make Him of quick understanding in the fear of the Lord: and He shall not judge after the sight of His eyes, neither reprove after the hearing of His ears: But with righteousness shall He judge the poor, and reprove with equity for the meek of the earth: and He shall smite the earth with the rod of His mouth, and with the breath of His lips shall He slay the wicked. And righteousness shall be the girdle of His loins, and faithfulness the girdle of His reins.

"The wolf also shall dwell with the lamb, and the leopard shall lie down with the kid; and the calf and the young lion and the fatling together;

272

and a little child shall lead them. And the cow and the bear shall feed; their young ones shall lie down together: and the lion shall eat straw like the ox. And the sucking child shall play on the hole of the asp, and the weaned child shall put his hand on the cockatrice' den. They shall not hurt nor destroy in all my holy mountain: for the earth shall be full of the knowledge of the Lord, as the waters cover the sea. And in that day there shall be a root of Jesse, which shall stand for an ensign of the people; to it shall the Gentiles seek: and His rest shall be glorious."

In this Kingdom, then, when the Lord sits *"in the throne of His glory,"* all things will be glorious and the apostles will reign with Him from twelve thrones, over the twelve tribes of Israel.

The Word of God offers similar encouragement to believers today, words that should encourage our own hearts. In Romans 8:16-18 we read:

"The Spirit itself beareth witness with our spirit, that we are the children of God: and if children, then heirs; heirs of God, and joint-heirs with Christ; *if so be that we suffer with Him, that we may be also GLORIFIED together.* For I reckon that the sufferings of this present time are not worthy to be compared with *the glory which shall be REVEALED IN US."*

II Timothy 2:12 declares that if we *suffer* with Christ, we shall also *reign* with Him.

Verse 29: *"And every one that hath forsaken houses, or brethren, or sisters, or father, or mother, or wife, or children, or lands, for my name's sake, shall receive an hundredfold, and shall inherit everlasting life."*

When Jesus tabernacled among men, those who followed Him were compelled, generally speaking, to forsake home, houses, lands, even family, to follow Him as He traveled from place to place. In this present day, however, not many are required to *literally* leave home and loved ones. There are other ways to serve God devotedly. Only foreign missionaries, as a rule, leave the shores of their own land and go into far places—jungles and other remote sections of this earth. Many do this gladly for the sake of the Gospel and those who have never heard the message of salvation. To me, these are the most honored and blessed people on earth today. But even though pastors and ministers like myself are not called upon to leave home and loved ones, we are instructed to love these less than we love the Lord Jesus Christ and the Gospel. If we love any earthly thing more than we love the service of God, then we are not worthy to be called His messengers!

Those who leave all—houses, brethren, sisters, father, mother, wife, children, lands—to serve God *"shall receive AN HUNDREDFOLD, and shall inherit everlasting life."* A hundredfold means a hundred times as much. We are not to demand this literally from the Lord, but we may rest assured that for whatever we forsake or sacrifice for Jesus' sake and the Gospel, we will be rewarded abundantly. In other words, we should not say that God has promised to give us a hundred homes if we leave our home for His name's sake. The meaning is that if we forsake our earthly home for Jesus' sake, we will have a home in heaven that will far exceed any home we could hope to have on earth. The person who must forsake brothers, sisters, family, and friends to follow Jesus finds an abundance of brothers and sisters in Christ, and the soul winner, in leading people to Christ, receives joy, peace, and happiness that is a hundred times better than anything earthly relationships can give, even though the ultimate reward comes in eternity — *throughout* eternity.

You will notice in Mark's recording, already quoted, Jesus says we will receive a hundredfold of all that we have forsaken to follow Him, and then He adds, *"with PERSECUTIONS."* It matters not where we serve Jesus, at home or abroad, if we follow Him as closely as we should and consistently give out the good news of the Gospel — that Christ died for our sins according to the Scriptures — *we will be persecuted.* Jesus was persecuted, and so will we be if we follow Him as we should.

Jesus *promised* persecution in this life. In Matthew 5:10-12 He said, "Blessed are they which are persecuted for righteousness' sake: for their's is the Kingdom of Heaven. Blessed are ye, when men shall revile you, and persecute you, and shall say all manner of evil against you *falsely, FOR MY SAKE.* Rejoice, and be exceeding glad: *for great is your reward in heaven:* for so persecuted they the prophets which were before you."

Jesus also said: "If the world hate you, ye know that it hated me before it hated you. If ye were of the world, the world would love his own: but because ye are not of the world, but I have chosen you out of the world, therefore the world hateth you. Remember the word that I said unto you, *The servant is not greater than his lord. If they have persecuted me, they will also persecute you . . .*" (John 15:18-20).

Also, in II Timothy 3:12 the Word of God tells us, "Yea, and *ALL that will live godly in Christ Jesus SHALL suffer PERSECUTION.*" It does not say that if we "live godly in Christ Jesus" we *may—*or, it is *possible* that we will—suffer persecution. The statement is very plain and definitely conclusive: If we live for Christ *we WILL* be persecuted. I suppose it might be possible to be so timid about our Christianity that the world would not be too greatly aware that we are Christian; but the person who lives and testifies out-and-out for Christ is going to be persecuted by the world.

Jesus said, "*. . . In the world ye shall have*

tribulation: BUT BE OF GOOD CHEER; I HAVE OVERCOME THE WORLD" (John 16:33).

Verse 30: *"But many that are first shall be last; and the last shall be first."*

This statement is repeated in Matthew 20:16, just after Jesus gave the parable of the man who hired workers for his vineyard. At the end of the day, the employer paid an equal wage to all who had labored for him that day—a penny to those who had worked from early morning until evening, and a penny to those who had worked only from mid-morning or noon time. The early laborers expressed disappointment with their wages. They had expected to receive *more* than those who came in late. The employer replied, "Is it not lawful for me to do what I will with mine own? . . . *So the last shall be first, and the first last."*

Jesus was teaching here that He alone has the right and the ability to reward righteously. There will be no preference because of residence, prominence in position, nor, for that matter, *length of service as such.* That is, some saints who enter God's service late in life will receive a greater reward than others who entered earlier. Some are more faithful and work untiringly because of their deep devotion and love for the Lord Jesus. *We* see the outward appearance, but God sees the intent and attitude of the heart. He does not measure our reward according to the number of years we have been saved. Our reward will be determined by our faithfulness—not *how MUCH* we do, not how big a name we make, but with what degree of faithfulness and for what purpose we *performed* our service. Was it to the glory of God? or was it for personal glory?

The Apostle Paul explains this wonderfully well in I Corinthians 3:9-15:

"For we are labourers together with God: ye are God's husbandry, ye are God's building. According to the grace of God which is given unto me, as a wise masterbuilder, I have laid the foundation, and another buildeth thereon. But let every man take heed how he buildeth thereupon. For other foundation can no man lay than that is laid, which is Jesus Christ.

"Now if any man build upon this foundation gold, silver, precious stones, wood, hay, stubble; every man's work shall be made manifest: for the day shall declare it, because it shall be revealed by fire; and *the fire shall try every man's work, of what SORT it is.* If any man's work abide which he hath built thereupon, he shall receive a reward. If any man's work shall be burned, he shall suffer loss: but he himself shall be saved; yet so as by fire."

Every man's work *will be made manifest.* In that day when the Righteous Judge rewards His servants in righteousness, *every man's work will be tried by fire*—not as to quantity, but *quality,*

278

"of what SORT it is." Jesus rewards for faithful stewardship carried out in His name and to the glory of God. That is building gold, silver, and precious stones. Whatever we do that is for personal glory or for pride, or to make a name for ourselves, will be counted wood, hay, and stubble— and it will be burned.

Paul was called much later than Peter, James, John, and the rest of the twelve; but I suppose there has never been—nor ever will be—a more faithful, dedicated steward than the Apostle Paul. He served the Lord untiringly and with a singular mind until finally he sealed his testimony with his life's blood as his head was severed from his shoulders by the headsman's axe. There will be degrees of reward in heaven just as there will be degrees of punishment in hell. (Read Luke 12:47, 48.) But such rewards will not be determined by the length of service nor necessarily the *visible amount*. That which is visible to you and to me may not all be gold, silver, and precious stones. It may *resemble* those precious qualities, but when it is tried by God's fire it may turn out to be wood, hay, and stubble.

We might consider that James laid his life down for the Gospel (Acts 12:1, 2), while his brother John lived and served for many more years. But James gave *all that he had,* including his life. How much more can *anyone* give? So the Righteous Judge will reward these men in righteousness.

Our God is not stingy or cheap. Christianity has great rewards. *In Christ* we find much, much more than we let go of in this world for His name's sake. Regardless of what we give, surrender or let go, Christianity rewards more than equal compensation for all that we give up. We find peace that the world cannot give. We have joy that is unspeakable and full of glory. We have comfort in Christ that the world knows not of. Thus do we reap great rewards while we live on this earth, and when we come to depart this life the reward in eternity will be more than man's language can express. Paul said, "Eye hath not seen, nor ear heard, neither have entered into the heart of man, the things which God hath prepared for them that love Him" (I Cor. 2:9).

"The fruit of the righteous is a tree of life; and *he that winneth souls is wise*" (Prov. 11:30).

"*And they that be WISE shall shine as the brightness of the firmament; and they that turn many to righteousness as the stars FOR EVER AND EVER*" (Dan. 12:3).

Chapter XX

1. For the kingdom of heaven is like unto a man that is an householder, which went out early in the morning to hire labourers into his vineyard.

2. And when he had agreed with the labourers for a penny a day, he sent them into his vineyard.

3. And he went out about the third hour, and saw others standing idle in the marketplace,

4. And said unto them; Go ye also into the vineyard, and whatsoever is right I will give you. And they went their way.

5. Again he went out about the sixth and ninth hour, and did likewise.

6. And about the eleventh hour he went out, and found others standing idle, and saith unto them, Why stand ye here all the day idle?

7. They say unto him, Because no man hath hired us. He saith unto them, Go ye also into the vineyard; and whatsoever is right, that shall ye receive.

8. So when even was come, the lord of the vineyard saith unto his steward, Call the labourers, and give them their hire, beginning from the last unto the first.

9. And when they came that were hired about the eleventh hour, they received every man a penny.

10. But when the first came, they supposed that they should have received more; and they likewise received every man a penny.

11. And when they had received it, they murmured against the goodman of the house,

12. Saying, These last have wrought but one hour, and thou hast made them equal unto us, which have borne the burden and heat of the day.

13. But he answered one of them, and said, Friend, I do thee no wrong: didst not thou agree with me for a penny?

14. Take that thine is, and go thy way: I will give unto this last, even as unto thee.

15. Is it not lawful for me to do what I will with mine own? Is thine eye evil, because I am good?

16. So the last shall be first, and the first last: for many be called, but few chosen.

17. And Jesus going up to Jerusalem took the twelve disciples apart in the way, and said unto them,

18. Behold, we go up to Jerusalem; and the Son of man shall be betrayed unto the chief priests and unto the scribes, and they shall condemn him to death,

19. And shall deliver him to the Gentiles to mock, and to scourge, and to crucify him: and the third day he shall rise again.

20. Then came to him the mother of Zebedee's children with her sons, worshipping him, and desiring a certain thing of him.

21. And he said unto her, What wilt thou? She saith unto him, Grant that these my two sons may sit, the one on thy right hand, and the other on the left, in thy kingdom.

22. But Jesus answered and said, Ye know not what ye ask. Are ye able to drink of the cup that I shall drink of, and to be baptized with the baptism that I am baptized with? They say unto him, We are able.

23. And he saith unto them, Ye shall drink indeed of my cup, and be baptized with the baptism that I am

baptized with: but to sit on my right hand, and on my left, is not mine to give, but it shall be given to them for whom it is prepared of my Father.

24. And when the ten heard it, they were moved with indignation against the two brethren.

25. But Jesus called them unto him, and said, Ye know that the princes of the Gentiles exercise dominion over them, and they that are great exercise authority upon them.

26. But it shall not be so among you: but whosoever will be great among you, let him be your minister;

27. And whosoever will be chief among you, let him be your servant:

28. Even as the Son of man came not to be ministered unto, but to minister, and to give his life a ransom for many.

29. And as they departed from Jericho, a great multitude followed him.

30. And, behold, two blind men sitting by the way side, when they heard that Jesus passed by, cried out, saying, Have mercy on us, O Lord, thou son of David.

31. And the multitude rebuked them, because they should hold their peace: but they cried the more, saying, Have mercy on us, O Lord, thou son of David.

32. And Jesus stood still, and called them, and said, What will ye that I shall do unto you?

33. They say unto him, Lord, that our eyes may be opened.

34. So Jesus had compassion on them, and touched their eyes: and immediately their eyes received sight, and they followed him.

In Matthew chapter 13, Jesus gave seven parables by way of explaining the mysteries of the Kingdom of Heaven. He gave the parables of the Sower (vv. 1-9), the tares and the wheat (vv. 24-30), the mustard seed (vv. 31, 32), the leaven (v. 33), the hidden treasure (v. 44), the pearl of great price (vv. 45, 46), and the dragnet (vv. 47, 48). Now in this chapter we will study another parable of the Kingdom of Heaven.

The Parable of the Laborers in the Vineyard

Verse 1: *"For the Kingdom of Heaven is like unto a man that is an householder, which went out early in the morning to hire labourers into his vineyard."*

This parable of the laborers in the vineyard is found in Matthew only. It illustrates the meaning of the closing verse of the preceding chapter— that is, "Many that are first shall be last; and the last shall be first." The same statement is repeated in this chapter at the close of the parable. (See verse 16.) The preposition "for" at the beginning of verse 1 links this parable with the closing verses of chapter 19, after Peter asked what they (the twelve) would receive, having left all to follow Jesus. Since this parable has reference to rewards for labor, we could read, without damaging the Scriptures, "Rewards shall be bestowed upon faithful laborers in my Kingdom in like manner as they were bestowed by a certain householder upon *his* laborers, in such a way that the last shall be equal to the first, and the first equal to the last."

284

"The Kingdom of Heaven" signifies, literally, *"the kingdom of the heavenlies."* It refers to the rule of the heavens over the earth and speaks of the thousand-year reign of Jesus on the throne of David in Jerusalem. That period of time is commonly referred to as the *Millennium,* formed from the Latin word *mille* which means one thousand. In Revelation 20:6 John the Beloved penned these inspiring words concerning that glorious time:

"Blessed and holy is he that hath part in the first resurrection: on such the second death hath no power, but they shall be priests of God and of Christ, *and shall reign with Him A THOUSAND YEARS."*

In the model prayer, Jesus taught His disciples to pray, "Our Father which art in heaven, Hallowed be thy name. *Thy Kingdom come. Thy will be done IN EARTH, as it is in heaven"* (Matt. 6:9,10). The kingdom of the heavenlies will be right here on this earth. Jesus will sit on a literal throne in the literal city of Jerusalem, and will reign over a literal kingdom.

This is the kingdom spoken of by Daniel as *the Kingdom of the God of heaven:*

"And in the days of these kings shall *THE GOD OF HEAVEN set up a kingdom, which shall never be destroyed:* and the kingdom shall not be left to other people, but it shall break in pieces and consume all these kingdoms, *and it shall stand for ever.* Forasmuch as thou sawest that the stone was cut out of the mountain without hands, and that it brake in pieces the iron, the brass, the clay, the silver, and the gold; the great God hath made known to the king what shall come to pass hereafter: and the dream is certain, and the interpretation thereof sure" (Dan. 2:44, 45).

Then in Daniel 7:27 we read: "And the kingdom and dominion, and the greatness of the kingdom under the whole heaven, shall be given to the people of the saints of the most High, whose kingdom is *an everlasting kingdom,* and all dominions shall serve and obey Him."

The Kingdom of which Daniel speaks will be set up when the Stone "cut out of the mountain without hands" destroys the Gentile world system which will be in power on earth when Jesus returns to set up His Kingdom.

The Kingdom of Heaven is the kingdom given to David and to David's seed. God promised David:

"When thy days be fulfilled, and thou shalt sleep with thy fathers, I will set up thy seed after thee, which shall proceed out of thy bowels, and I will establish his kingdom. He shall build an house for my name, *and I will establish the throne of his kingdom FOR EVER. . . .* And thine house and thy kingdom shall be established for ever before thee: *THY THRONE shall be established FOR EVER"* (II Sam. 7:12-16 in part).

The Old Testament prophets speak of this kingdom and describe it. Also, the angel Gabriel promised Mary:

"Behold, thou shalt conceive in thy womb, and bring forth a son, and shalt call His name JESUS. He shall be great, and shall be called the Son of the Highest: and the Lord God shall give unto Him *the throne of His father David: and He shall reign over the house of Jacob FOR EVER;* and of His Kingdom there shall be no end" (Luke 1:31-33).

John the Baptist, forerunner of the Lord Jesus, announced the Kingdom "at hand":

"In those days came John the Baptist, preaching in the wilderness of Judaea, and saying, *Repent ye: for the Kingdom of Heaven is at hand*" (Matt. 3:1, 2).

Truly, the Kingdom *was* at hand for the King had come; but the Jews rejected their King and His Kingdom. They cried out to Pilate: *"Let Him be crucified. . . . His blood be on us, and on our children"* (Matt. 27:22, 25). They would not have Him to reign over them, and they crucified their King. Therefore the Kingdom was postponed, but every prophecy concerning that Kingdom will be literally fulfilled and the Kingdom of Heaven will be set up at the return of the King in glory.

The *Kingdom of Heaven* is not the Church, nor is it the Kingdom of *God*. (Please study Matthew 24:29 through Matthew 25:46, Luke 19: 12-27, and Acts 15:14-17 in connection with this.)

We *must* distinguish between the Kingdom of *Heaven* and the Kingdom of *God* if we are to rightly divide the Word of Truth. It is scripturally incorrect to say that they are one and the same.

The Kingdom of Heaven and the Kingdom of God have many things in common—and naturally so, because God is the Omnipotent One and He rules over all things. Since the Kingdom of Heaven is a sphere of the Kingdom of God, the two are *both* spoken of in *some* of the parables, while other parables speak only of the Kingdom of *Heaven.* For example, the parable of the wheat and the tares speaks of the Kingdom of Heaven, as does the parable of the net. There are no "tares" nor "bad fish" in the Kingdom of *God.*

The Kingdom of *God* is universal, including the Church, saints of the past or saints of the future—willingly submitting to the will of God. (Please study Luke 13:28, 29.) We can enter the Kingdom of God only by the miracle of the new birth. Jesus explained to Nicodemus, "Verily, verily, I say unto thee, Except a man be born again, he cannot see the Kingdom of God. . . . Except a man be born of water and of the Spirit, he cannot enter into the Kingdom of God" (John 3:3, 5). The Kingdom of *Heaven* is Messianic, mediatorial, and Davidic. It will be the earthly reign of Jesus here on earth. He will reign from the throne of David in Jerusalem and the Church, His bride, will reign with Him.

The Kingdom of *God* is *spiritual*. It comes not with outward show, it is within the hearts of believers: "The Kingdom of God cometh not with observation. . . . The Kingdom of God is *within you*" (Luke 17:20, 21). Romans 14:17 declares, "The Kingdom of God is not meat and drink; but righteousness, and peace, and joy in the Holy Ghost." The Kingdom of *Heaven* is *organic*. In the Kingdom of Heaven the people will pray, "Give us this day our daily bread." The Lord Jesus will reign until He puts all enemies under His feet, and when that has been done He will deliver the Kingdom of Heaven up to God the Father. At that time the Kingdom of Heaven will merge into the Kingdom of God, and throughout the ages of eternity the two kingdoms will be one and the same.

The Kingdom of *Heaven* will be for one thousand years under the righteous reign of Jesus. The Kingdom of *God* is *unending* and will go on throughout the endless ages of eternity:

"Then cometh the end, when He shall have delivered up the Kingdom to God, even the Father; when He shall have put down all rule and all authority and power. For He must reign, till He hath put all enemies under His feet. The last enemy that shall be destroyed is death. For He hath put all things under His feet. But when He saith all things are put under Him, it is manifest that He is excepted, which did put all things under

Him, And when all things shall be subdued unto Him, then shall the Son also Himself be subject unto Him that put all things under Him, that God may be all in all" (I Cor. 15:24-28).

"*. . . a man that is an householder*" speaks of the head of a family, or one who is in charge of family affairs. Such reference today would probably point to the father of a family.

This specific householder *"went out early in the morning to hire labourers into his vineyard."* Vineyards were common in Judaea, and in Scripture a vineyard is often used to illustrate spiritual matters. We read of the *fruit* of the vineyard, we read of the *care* of the vineyard, all with reference to the Christian's labor in "the vineyard of the Lord." Let us keep this in mind as we go more fully into the study of this particular parable.

We are not told how many workers this householder hired, but from later verses we could draw the conclusion that he hired a goodly number. So evidently this was a large vineyard and the fruit needed to be harvested quickly before it could spoil on the vine or be destroyed in some way.

Verse 2:   *"And when he had agreed with the labourers for a penny a day, he sent them into his vineyard."*

The *"penny"* mentioned here is misleading if we think of it in terms of present-day economy. To speak of a penny as pay for a day's labor would be ridiculous. But the coin which is here called *"a penny"* was the *denarius,* and in the days of Christ's earthly ministry it was a generous day's wage. According to history, it was the common daily wage of a Roman soldier. From history we also learn that a penny a day would buy the necessities of life.

Notice that these workers *"agreed"* to work for this wage *before the householder "sent them into his vineyard."*

Verse 3: *"And he went out about the third hour, and saw others standing idle in the market-place."*

"And he went out about the third hour...." The Jewish day began at sunrise and ended at sunset. This would average about twelve hours in a normal day. The *third hour* would be approximately nine o'clock in the morning.

". . . and saw others standing idle in the marketplace." If you have visited the mission fields in foreign lands you know that in many countries the marketplace is still very much in evidence. It is the place where all kinds of provisions and merchandise are sold. I visited such marketplaces in South America, in Africa, and other countries. Day by day people came to the marketplace in great numbers to buy food and other commodities. Our Scripture here indicates that laborers who were for hire gathered at the marketplace, and

farmers and other employers went there in search of workers. Therefore we are not to suppose that these laborers were *"idle"* because they were lazy and would not work. They were *ready and willing* to work if someone hired them.

Verse 4: *"And said unto them: Go ye also into the vineyard, and whatsoever is right I will give you. And they went their way."*

Please notice that the householder did not promise *these* workers a *penny* for their labor. In fact, he did not mention any specific amount to be paid them. He simply told them to go into the vineyard, and *"whatsoever is RIGHT"* was what they would be paid. They did not ask for a guarantee of a wage. They accepted the man's invitation and *"went their way"* to work in his vineyard.

I do not believe it would be abusing the Scriptures to say that this parable would have us see that if the men worked faithfully and untiringly they would be rewarded accordingly, and from the settlement set forth in later verses we conclude that these men labored as untiringly as did the first group. The wage agreed upon with the first group was definite—a penny a day; but the wage to be paid to the second group depended on the judgment of the householder in whose vineyard they worked.

Verse 5: *"Again he went out about the sixth and ninth hour, and did likewise."*

292

The householder *"went out about the sixth and ninth hour . . . ."* The Jewish day was divided into four parts. The *sixth hour* would be about twelve o'clock noon and the *ninth* hour would be about three o'clock in the afternoon. This tells us that the householder went out at noon, saw other laborers standing in the marketplace, and he hired them. Then at mid-afternoon he went back to the marketplace, saw other workers, and hired *them.*

Nothing is said about wages in this verse, but since we are told that the householder *"did likewise"*—referring back to the previous verse—we may safely assume that he also told these two groups of workers the same thing he had told the second group. They were to go work in his vineyard, and their wages would be whatsoever was *right.*

Verses 6 and 7: *"And about the eleventh hour he went out, and found others standing idle, and saith unto them, Why stand ye here all the day idle? They say unto him, Because no man hath hired us. He saith unto them, Go ye also into the vineyard; and whatsoever is right, that shall ye receive."*

"About the eleventh hour he went out . . . ." The *eleventh* hour would be about five o'clock in the afternoon, with scarcely more than one working hour of the day remaining. The householder

returned once more to the marketplace, saw other men standing about, and asked them, *"Why stand ye here ALL THE DAY idle?"* This also indicates that the hour was late in the day.

The laborers replied that they were idle because no one had hired them. The householder then said to them, *"Go ye also into the vineyard, and whatsoever is RIGHT, that shall ye receive."* Again, there is no promise of any specific amount of payment. This man had hired one group of workers early in the morning. He had hired the second group at mid-morning, the third group at noon, the fourth group at mid-afternoon, and this last group he hired approximately an hour before the working day came to a close. I stress this fact in order to point ahead to the time when the wages for this day's work would be paid.

Verse 8: *"So when even was come, the lord of the vineyard saith unto his steward, Call the labourers, and give them their hire, beginning from the last unto the first."*

"When even was come . . . ." The twelfth hour arrived and the day came to a close. It was time to pay the laborers for the day's work.

". . . the lord of the vineyard saith unto his steward . . . ." The primary definition of a steward sets up his position as one of honor. He is entrusted with the management of the household or estate of his master. He may be called upon to

294

act as superintendent over servants of the household, and to collect rents or other income, to keep the accounts, and to perform various other duties pertaining to supervising his master's affairs. A steward was required to take scrupulous care of whatever was entrusted to him, and he was to administer his responsibility faithfully as directed by his master.

Stewards were common to households in Old Testament times. It was to his steward Eliezer that Abraham gave the duty of finding a wife for Isaac. (Read Genesis 15:2 and 24:1-44. You will find there a very interesting account of Eliezer's conscientious fulfillment of that mission.)

In Christ's day, every household of means or distinction had a steward in charge. Matthew 24:45 seems to indicate that many stewards were slaves. From the parable given in Luke 12:42-48 we know that Jesus expected the disciples to act as His stewards in His absence after He returned to the heavenly Father. Certainly we know they were left in charge of the Gospel—and the same is true of Christians today. I Peter 4:10 instructs us, "As every man hath *received* the gift, even so minister the same one to another, *as GOOD STEWARDS of the manifold grace of God.*"

Also, in I Corinthians 4:1, 2 the Apostle Paul admonishes us, "Let a man so account of us, as of the ministers of Christ, and *stewards of the mysteries of God.* Moreover it is required in stewards, that a man be found *faithful.''* We are acting as stewards for the Lord Jesus Christ, and our duty to the household of God is to furnish ''meat in due season'' (Matt. 24:45)—that is, the pure Gospel of the grace of God.

''. . . Call the labourers, and give them their hire . . . .'' We may conclude that this steward was in the habit of administering responsible duties. In this instance, it involved the handling of the householder's money, and we find no record that there was any monitoring of his administration of his master's finances.

''. . . beginning from the last unto the first.'' Three instructions were given to the steward: (1) Call the laborers; (2) Give them their wages; (3) Pay the last *first,* and the first *last.* He was to pay the men *in order* from the last up to the first. Thus the men who had worked just one hour were to be paid ahead of those who had worked since mid-afternoon, noon, mid-morning, and early morn. But each was to receive his just wage.

Now if the men who were *first hired* had been *paid* first, they would have taken their wages and gone their way, not knowing what the others received, and the lesson taught by this parable would have been lost altogether. So—the men who worked only an hour were paid first, those who began work at three o'clock in the afternoon were paid next, those who entered the vineyard at noon were next, then the workers who went to work at mid-morning, and those who went into the vineyard in early morning were paid last of all. So they knew what all of the others were paid for their labor in the vineyard.

Verse 9: *"And when they came that were hired about the eleventh hour, they received every man a penny."*

"They . . . that were hired about the eleventh hour" had had no agreement as to how much they would receive in wages. The owner of the vineyard told them that they would receive justice, and they trusted him to do what was right.

". . . they received every man a penny." We have no way of knowing how the householder figured this wage as related to the laborers who had worked much longer than those who were hired at the eleventh hour. Perhaps he believed that by their attitude and attention to their duty they had actually *earned* what he paid them. Or perhaps out of appreciation for their willingness to work when he needed them he simply rewarded them by paying them for a full day's work. It really matters not what his reasoning was. He owned the vineyard, it was his money which paid the workers, and since he had made no specific commitment to this group of men he had a perfect right to pay them what he deemed to be right.

Verse 10: *"But when the first came, they sup-*

posed that they should have received more; and they likewise received every man a penny."

The laborers who were hired in early morning "*supposed that THEY should have received MORE*" than the other workers were paid. After all, they had toiled many more hours, they had worked through the discomfort of the noonday heat, and it stands to reason that they had harvested more fruit than the laborers who came in late. Therefore they thought they were entitled to more pay, greater reward. But they were paid exactly what they had been promised.

Verses 11 and 12: "*And when they had received it, they murmured against the goodman of the house, saying, These last have wrought but one hour, and thou hast made them equal unto us, which have borne the burden and heat of the day.*"

"*. . . they murmured against the goodman of the house . . . .*" These men who had worked since early morning began to complain and find fault with the householder, even though when he hired them they had *agreed* to work in his vineyard for a penny. (The word here translated "*goodman*" is the same Greek word rendered "householder" in verse 1. It does not express any higher moral quality. It simply speaks of the head of the household.)

"*These last have wrought but ONE HOUR, and thou hast made them equal to US . . . .*"

These men were paid what they had been promised and what they had agreed to accept. They had no right to expect *more*—and they might have been satisfied with their wage had they not seen the other men receive that same amount of money, even though they had worked a much shorter time.

Spiritually applied, this reflects the attitude of many Christians today. They are willing to work in the church, they may even seem *eager* to do so; but they are dissatisfied, given to grumbling and complaining, if someone else in the congregation comes into a place of equal or greater importance.

". . . *us, which have borne the burden and heat of the day.*" These laborers had worked through "the heat of the day," when the sun is hot and any work more tiring and exhausting than in any other hour of the daylight hours. By the time the workers came in at the ninth hour, the heat had begun to subside, and by the time the *eleventh* hour workers came in, the hour they worked was in the cool of the day.

Verse 13: *"But he answered one of them, and said, Friend, I do thee no wrong: didst not thou agree with me for a penny?"*

In other words, the householder said to these complaining workers: "We had a contract, you and I. We agreed that your wages would be a penny for a day's labor. You kept your part of the agreement by working all day, and I have met my part of the agreement by paying you what I agreed to pay.   The contract between us has been fulfilled and you have no right to complain or accuse me of being unfair."

Verses 14 and 15:   *"Take that thine is, and go thy way: I will give unto this last, even as unto thee.   Is it not lawful for me to do what I will with mine own?   Is thine eye evil, because I am good?"*

"Take that thine is, and go thy way . . . ." The householder considered the matter settled. He had contracted with this group of men for a day's labor in his vineyard in return for a penny— and as previously explained, that was a reasonable wage for a day's work in those days.   They had *worked* as they promised, and he had paid the *wages* he promised.   Therefore the matter was settled and there was no more to be done about it.
". . . I will give unto this last, even as unto thee.   Is it not lawful for me to do what I will with mine own?"   It was the householder's vineyard, it was his own money, he had met his full obligation to these men and they had no further claim upon him.   It was his privilege to give to the other workers what he saw fit to give.

We must bear in mind that this parable was given to teach a spiritual truth and it must be so applied.   Peter had shown a mercenary spirit when he asked Jesus what reward he and the other apostles would have in the coming Kingdom. Upon this little band of apostles would rest the sacred responsibility for spreading the Gospel and carrying on the work Jesus had begun, and they must be rid of selfish pride and personal ambition lest the cause of Christ be hindered. They must realize that *whatever* their reward, they would receive from their Master a just and righteous consideration.

"Is thine eye evil, because I am good?" The "evil eye" was a term much used by the Hebrews. It denoted a person who was envious, jealous, or malicious. In Deuteronomy 15:9 we read:

"Beware that there be not a thought in thy wicked heart, saying, The seventh year, the year of release, is at hand; *and thine eye be evil against thy poor brother,* and thou givest him nought; and he cry unto the Lord against thee, and it be sin unto thee."

Proverbs 23:6 warns, "Eat thou not the bread of *him that hath an evil eye,* neither desire thou his dainty meats."

The eyes tell much, and even today a person who is envious or filled with malice will show it in his eyes.

Verse 16: *"So the last shall be first, and the first last: for many be called, but few chosen."*

In this verse the moral or scope of this parable

is stated. Our Lord used the parable to teach His disciples that insofar as the *order of time* is concerned, many who enter the Kingdom *last* shall be *first* in order of rewards. Rewards will be given according to faithful, untiring stewardship which results from a heart of love, and not according to the number of hours, months, or years one may labor. Jesus will reward faithfully, even for a cup of cold water given in His name; but we are not to labor for Him with the thought in mind, "What will I get in return?" The labor of the Christian is a labor of love. We love Him because He first loved us. We serve Him because He laid down His life that we might have life eternal.

The natural man is forever crying out, "What do I get out of this?" But when we become spiritual, when the Spirit of God abides in our bosom, then the desire of the heart should be, "What can I do to glorify the Lord Jesus Christ who has done so much for me?" We do not then think of what we will *receive*, we praise God for what we have *already received*—the forgiveness of sins.

The apostles were the first to be called into the Lord's service in this new Kingdom, and they left all to follow Jesus. But He warned them to watch, be sober and take care, lest they fall behind those who should be called later and when the time for *rewards* comes they could be *last* instead of first.

I would like to point out here that some Bible teachers use the coin in this parable as representing *salvation* which is received alike by all believers. This could not be true, because *salvation is not EARNED.* Salvation is *by GRACE through FAITH.* It is the gift of God, not of works. The following Scriptures bear out this fact:

"For by grace are ye saved through faith; and that not of yourselves: it is the gift of God: not of works, lest any man should boast" (Eph. 2:8, 9).

"For the wages of sin is death; but the gift of God is eternal life through Jesus Christ our Lord" (Rom. 6:23).

"Not by works of righteousness which we have done, but according to His mercy He saved us, by the washing of regeneration, and renewing of the Holy Ghost" (Tit. 3:5).

Remember, this parable has to do with the Kingdom of Heaven, not with the New Testament Church. But "all Scripture is given by inspiration of God, and is profitable for doctrine, for reproof, for correction, for instruction in righteousness: that the man of God may be perfect, throughly furnished unto all good works" (II Tim. 3:16, 17). Therefore there is a definite lesson here for believers in this present time. We can look back over the years and see that God has chosen some men who became spiritual giants. Those men moved the world, while others, also chosen of God, have labored for a lifetime in small or remote fields and have not been known outside their own community or area. God chose men like Martin Luther, David Livingstone, Dwight L. Moody, and Charles Spurgeon, and He used those men to move millions for Christ. The majority of us are not used in such a spectacular, world-wide way, but we have no basis for complaint. We have no right to be envious. If we are faithful in the ministry God has given us, we will be rewarded *in full* for our faithfulness. God forbid that we should grumble and murmur because we are less outstanding than others, or because God bestows upon some believers greater influence and power, and blesses the ministry of others with greater scope than ours. We all serve the same Lord. We are "labourers together with God" (I Cor. 3:9). Therefore we must labor to the glory of His precious name.

We know there are carnal Christians in the Church today, just as there were carnal Christians in the Church during the ministry of the Apostle Paul. He dealt with this condition in the assembly at Corinth, and I think it would be well if we give heed to the inspired words he wrote to the Corinthians. I give you those words here, that you may study them, meditate upon them, and allow them to sink deep into your heart. In I Corinthians, chapter 3, Paul penned these instructions concerning carnal Christians:

"And I, brethren, could not speak unto you as unto spiritual, but as unto carnal, even as unto

304

babes in Christ. I have fed you with milk, and not with meat: for hitherto ye were not able to bear it, neither yet now are ye able. For *ye are yet carnal: for whereas there is among you envying, and strife, and divisions, are ye not carnal,* and walk as men? For while one saith, I am of Paul; and another, I am of Apollos; *are ye not carnal?*

"Who then is Paul, and who is Apollos, but ministers by whom ye believed, even as the Lord gave to every man? I have planted, Apollos watered; but God gave the increase. So then neither is he that planteth any thing, neither he that watereth; but God that giveth the increase. Now he that planteth and he that watereth are one: and every man shall receive his own reward according to his own labour. For we are labourers together with God: ye are God's husbandry, ye are God's building. According to the grace of God which is given unto me, as a wise masterbuilder, I have laid the foundation, and another buildeth thereon. But let every man take heed how he buildeth thereupon. For other foundation can no man lay than that is laid, which is Jesus Christ.

"Now if any man build upon this foundation gold, silver, precious stones, wood, hay, stubble; every man's work shall be made manifest; for the day shall declare it, because it shall be revealed by fire; and the fire shall try every man's work of what sort it is. If any man's work abide which he hath built thereupon, he shall receive a reward. If any man's work shall be burned, he shall suffer loss: but he himself shall be saved; yet so as by fire.

"Know ye not that ye are the temple of God, and that the Spirit of God dwelleth in you? If any man defile the temple of God, him shall God destroy; for the temple of God is holy, which temple ye are.

"Let no man deceive himself. If any man among you seemeth to be wise in this world, let him become a fool, that he may be wise. For the wisdom of this world is foolishness with God. For it is written, He taketh the wise in their own craftiness. And again, The Lord knoweth the thoughts of the wise, that they are vain. Therefore let no man glory in men. For all things are your's; whether Paul, or Apollos, or Cephas, or the world, or life, or death, or things present, or things to come; all are your's; and ye are Christ's; and Christ is God's" (I Cor. 3:1-23).

We come now to the last phrase in the parable of the laborers in the vineyard—*"many be called, but few chosen."* Why did Jesus end the parable with these words? I have searched the Scriptures, I have meditated in prayer, and I find only one answer to that question:

When Jesus ministered on earth, He *called* MANY who did not *follow* Him. He invited many who did not choose to serve Him. Some walked with Him as long as they had "the loaves and fishes," so to speak, but when He taught them of the true meaning of the bread of life they found His teaching hard to accept. Therefore, "many of His disciples went back, and walked no more with Him" (John 6:66). You see, it is not God's will "that any should perish, but that all should come to repentance" (II Pet. 3:9). Yet the Scripture teaches that not all who are invited respond to the invitation.

This does not mean that God calls some people, they respond to the call and come to Him, but they do not meet the required qualifications and therefore God does not save them. It is sometimes erroneously taught that these people are not "elected" and so they are not "chosen." I cannot accept such teaching. God would not call a man and then turn that man down when he comes to Jesus seeking eternal life! Such is not in keeping with the character of God. I believe the Scripture teaches that *"whosoever will"* may come to Jesus, and that He will save whosoever comes to Him in faith believing:

"WHOSOEVER shall call upon the name of the Lord SHALL BE SAVED" (Rom. 10:13).

Jesus invited, *"Come unto me, ALL ye that labour and are heavy laden, and I WILL give you rest.* Take my yoke upon you, and learn of me; for I am meek and lowly in heart: and *ye shall find rest unto your SOULS.* For my yoke is easy, and my burden is light" (Matt. 11:28-30).

Yes, *many* are called, but those who are chosen are those who hear and answer the call. Many are called who do not respond to the call, therefore they are not chosen. The following Scriptures shed light on this:

John 1:11-13: "He came unto His own, and His own received Him not. *But as many as RECEIVED Him, to them gave He power to become the sons of God, even to them that believe on His name:* which were born, not of blood, nor of the will of the flesh, nor of the will of man, but of God."

John 5:39, 40: "Search the Scriptures; for in them ye think ye have eternal life: and they are they which testify of me. *And YE WILL NOT come to me,* that ye might have life."

John 6:37: "All that the Father giveth me shall come to me; and him that cometh to me *I will IN NO WISE cast out.*"

Luke 13:34: "O Jerusalem, Jerusalem, which killest the prophets, and stonest them that are sent unto thee; *how often would I have gathered thy children together, as a hen doth gather her brood under her wings—and YE WOULD NOT.*"

Revelation 22:17: "The Spirit and the bride say, *Come.* And let him that heareth say, *Come.* And let him that is *athirst* come. *And WHOSOEVER WILL, let him take the water of life freely.*"

God calls *many,* and all who receive Him on

His terms are saved. We do not proposition God. We accept or reject Him on His own terms.

Jesus Again Foretells
His Crucifixion and Resurrection

Verses 17 and 18: *"And Jesus going up to Jeru-salem took the twelve disciples apart in the way, and said unto them, Behold, we go up to Jerusa-lem; and the Son of man shall be betrayed unto the chief priests, and unto the scribes, and they shall condemn Him to death."*

". . . *Jesus going up to Jerusalem* . . . ." This was His last journey to Jerusalem, and it was made when He traveled to the Passover. All male Jews were required to attend the feast of the Passover (Ex. 23:17). You can well imagine how crowded were the roads and trails throughout the countryside on such an occasion, as throngs of Jews traveled toward Jerusalem. Bible history tells us that they traveled in companies, and some-times an entire neighborhood would travel together. Scripture bears this out. For example, when Mary and Joseph were returning home from the feast of the Passover, they supposed that Jesus, then twelve years old, was "in the company" and they went a full day's journey from Jerusalem before they discovered He was not with them!

Our Lord knew what lay ahead of Him when He reached Jerusalem. He knew for what purpose

He had come into the world. But He was man as well as He was God, and I believe He felt a deep pressure upon Him now, knowing that every step He took carried Him that much nearer Golgotha, and every day He lived He moved one day nearer the accomplishment of what He had left the Father's bosom to do. He came to die, to lay His life down, and the fulfillment of that mission was now pressing in upon Him. Luke tells us, "He took unto Him the twelve, and said unto them, Behold, we go up to Jerusalem, and *all things that are written by the prophets concerning the Son of man shall be accomplished"* (Luke 18:31).

"Jesus . . . took the twelve disciples apart in the way . . . ." As I have already mentioned, the roads would have been thronged with people journeying to Jerusalem for the feast of the Passover, and since Jesus had instructions for the twelve alone, He took them aside in order to talk with them privately.

Mark 10:32 tells us, "And they were in the way going up to Jerusalem; and Jesus went before them: and they were amazed; and as they followed, they were afraid. And He took again the twelve, and began to tell them what things should happen unto Him."

The disciples were "amazed" no doubt at the boldness of Jesus and by His calmness and determination as He moved on toward the Holy City regardless of the threats on His life. It is small wonder that "they were *afraid*," because even though they did not fully understand all that Jesus had told them, they realized that real danger lay ahead, and I do not doubt that a strange foreboding filled their hearts.

However, they followed Jesus as He took them aside and said to them, *"Behold, we go up to Jerusalem; and the Son of man shall be betrayed . . . ."* The journey of His utmost grief was now beginning and the end was hastening on. He announced His coming betrayal in the presence of the one who would betray Him. I wonder if Judas felt any conviction or remorse when he heard the Lord's announcement?

". . . unto the chief priests and unto the scribes . . . ." Jesus had no more cruel foe than these men of the Sanhedrin. Throughout His public ministry they had opposed Him, and they had gone to no end of trouble in their efforts to trap and ensnare Him. And now He was on His way to the city where the religious leaders would at last be able to do what they had for so long been trying to do.

". . . and they shall condemn Him to death." Here, for the third time, Jesus foretells His death. (He previously mentioned that subject in Matthew 16:21 and 17:22, 23.) We find the same account in Mark 10:32-34 and in Luke 18:31-34.

Yes, they condemned Him to death! He was

arrested in the Garden of Gethsemane, where Judas betrayed Him with a hypocritical kiss. He was then taken before unscrupulous, ungodly men to stand trial—a trial that was both illegal and farcical. There was no justice in it. He was arrested on false charges. False witnesses were hired to testify against Him as He stood before the chief priests and other members of the Sanhedrin, the "Supreme Court" of the Jews. They had already reached a verdict before Jesus was even brought to trial. Even though He was innocent, the spotless Lamb of God, they meant to convict Him and nail Him to a cross. The sentence to be passed upon Him was determined before He was arrested.

Verse 19: *"And shall deliver Him to the Gentiles to mock, and to scourge, and to crucify Him: and the third day He shall rise again."*

The Jews arrested Jesus and tried Him before their ruling body, but they no longer had the power to execute Him. They therefore had to *"deliver Him to the Gentiles"* for execution. He was condemned to death by the Jews, but He was actually executed by Roman soldiers.

". . . to mock and to scourge . . . ." How intimately Jesus knew the details of the experiences that faced Him and through which He must pass before He faced the scene of the crucifixion! He was mocked and He was cruelly scourged, just as

312

He said He would be. We will study this in detail when we reach that part of our study.

"... *and to crucify Him* ...." Crucifixion was a Roman mode of execution, and it was so horrible that Roman law forbade the crucifixion of any Roman citizen. The Jews put people to death by *stoning*. (See Exodus 19:13, Leviticus 20:27, Luke 20:6, Acts 7:58 and 14:5.)

Jesus knew what manner of death He would die. He traced the line of action from the moment here when He spoke with His disciples, on until He was nailed to the cross. He omitted none of the shameful details—and everything He prophesied was fulfilled:

He was betrayed by Judas (Matt. 26:14-16, 47-50).

He was delivered to the chief priests and the scribes (Matt. 26:57).

They did deliver Him to the Gentiles (the Romans) to be put to death (Matt. 26:66; 27:2).

But in spite of all that Jesus told the twelve about His coming death and resurrection, *"they understood none of these things:* and this saying was hid from them, neither knew they the things which were spoken" (Luke 18:34). These things Jesus told them could not be true, they could not come to pass literally, they reasoned. He was the Messiah, and the things He told them were utterly contrary to all of their ideas of what the Messiah would be and the work He would do. They were convinced that He was *the promised*

Messiah, but such a death as He spelled out to them was so inconsistent with their conception of the Messiah who would come to Israel that they evidently came to the conclusion that He was speaking figuratively, not literally. They did not understand that this was the purpose for which He had left the glories of heaven and come to earth—to die for the sins of the world. He had come, not to be ministered unto, but to minister, and to give His life a ransom for sinners. In John 10:17, 18 He declared, "Therefore doth my Father love me, because I lay down my life, that I might take it again. No man taketh it from me, but I lay it down of myself. I have power to lay it down, and I have power to take it again. This commandment have I received of my Father."

The heart, the bloodstream, and the life of the Gospel message is the death of Jesus on Calvary and His resurrection from the tomb. Had He not died, there would be no Gospel to preach. Paul defines the Gospel in his first letter to the church at Corinth. He wrote:

"Moreover, brethren, I declare unto you the Gospel which I preached unto you, which also ye have received, and wherein ye stand; by which also ye are saved, if ye keep in memory what I preached unto you, unless ye have believed in vain. For I delivered unto you first of all that which I also received, how that *Christ died for our sins according to the Scriptures; and that*

314

He was buried, and that He rose again the third day according to the Scriptures: and that He was seen of Cephas, then of the twelve: after that, He was seen of above five hundred brethren at once: of whom the greater part remain unto this present, but some are fallen asleep.

"After that, He was seen of James; then of all the apostles. And last of all He was seen of me also, as of one born out of due time. For I am the least of the apostles, that am not meet to be called an apostle, because I persecuted the church of God. But by the grace of God I am what I am: and His grace which was bestowed upon me was not in vain; but I laboured more abundantly than they all: yet not I, but the grace of God which was with me. Therefore whether it were I or they, so we preach, and so ye believed" (I Cor. 15:1-11).

According to the Apostle Paul, called and ordained of God as minister to the Gentiles and to whom God revealed the mystery of the New Testament Church, *the Gospel is the death, burial, and resurrection of the Lord Jesus Christ "ACCORDING TO THE SCRIPTURES"*—not according to religion, not according to denominations, but *according to the SCRIPTURES.*

". . . and the third day He shall RISE AGAIN." Here was the silver lining to the dark cloud of the crucifixion. This statement should have brought joy to overflow the hearts of the disciples. The

315

Lord Jesus *spoke much* about His death. *We* should talk much about His death. Preachers should *preach* about it, teachers should *teach* about it, and believers should *talk* about it. It should be the theme of our message to a sin-cursed world. *But we must not stop there.* Christ *rose from the grave—and because HE lives, WE live!*

The liberals and modernists today tell us to think of the *life* of Jesus rather than His death. They tell us we should talk about His wonderful *miracles* instead of His horrible death on the cross. But the Word of God tells us to *"preach Christ crucified."* Therefore, *as long as I live* I will preach the death, burial, and resurrection of Jesus. That is the heart and soul of the Gospel, and *without* His death, burial, and resurrection we would have no Gospel to preach.

Yes, we preach Christ crucified, risen, and redeeming, and I say with the Apostle Paul, "God forbid that I should glory, save in the cross of our Lord Jesus Christ, by whom the world is crucified unto me, and I unto the world" (Gal. 6:14). Take the cross out of the Bible and you destroy that Holy Book.

The Ambitious Request
of the Mother of James and John

Verse 20: *"Then came to Him the mother of Zebedee's children with her sons, worshipping Him, and desiring a certain thing of Him."*

316

Again we see that while Jesus was thinking of His death on Calvary, His followers were thinking of their own honor and glory. Poor, poor *human nature!* and we are all human, not one excepted. This mother spoke what others in the group felt. Her mother's heart wanted to see her two sons in positions of honor in the Kingdom which she believed would shortly be set up. (In verse 24 we see that the other disciples were ambitious also. They were "moved with indignation" against James and John. It seems reasonable that with the self-seeking attitude already seen in the group, some of them may have been hoping for the same positions James and John desired.)

The mother approached Jesus in humility and reverence, *"worshipping Him and desiring a CERTAIN THING of Him."* Her request was unnamed in this verse and therefore could mean *anything.*

Verse 21: *"And He said unto her, What wilt thou? She saith unto Him, Grant that these my two sons may sit, the one on thy right hand, and the other on the left, in thy Kingdom."*

Jesus did not say He would grant the request. He knew what was in her heart, but even so, He asked her, *"What wilt thou?"* A point to notice here: Know what you promise before you promise *anything.* This woman had great faith in the Lord's victory and the fact that He would occupy a throne. She regarded His reign as fixed and certain. She believed it so strongly that she was putting in an advance application for her two sons to sit in His courts, one on His right hand and the other on His left.

This mother not only demonstrated a mother's *love.* She also demonstrated a mother's *pride.* She said *"these MY two sons."* To *me* there is no other boy quite like *MY boys.* To a mother, there is no other boy quite like her own son. No love, except the love of Jesus, is quite as strong as a mother's love. We cannot discount the selfishness of this woman's ambition for her sons, but we dare not censure her. We need rather to ask ourselves how much deep concern and interest *we* have in the success of our own boys and girls where their relationship with Christ is concerned.

The mother of James and John had no reference to the Kingdom of Heaven (the Millennium) as we know it. She was thinking of the Kingdom which she thought was about to be set up on earth at that time. She did not understand that the cross would precede the crown. She did not see this Dispensation of Grace during which the Church would be formed, after which the Kingdom of Heaven on earth would come. Like the disciples and others, she was expecting a temporal kingdom of great power and glory. They believed that the Messiah would conquer the Romans and the known world at that time, and reign over it. She had a mental picture of Jesus on the throne and, on either side of the throne, seats to be occupied by those who would reign with Him in power. Therefore she asked that her two sons might sit, one on the Lord's right hand and the other on His left in the Kingdom.

You see, according to the Old Testament, to sit at the right hand or the left hand of a king was a token of confidence and trust. The right and left hand positions were the highest honors a king could grant to one of his subjects or officers of his court. In I Kings 2:19 we are told that King Solomon prepared a seat for his mother at his right hand. In Psalm 110:1 David wrote, "The LORD said unto my Lord, Sit thou at my right hand, until I make thine enemies thy footstool." Today, Jesus Himself sits "on the right hand of the Majesty on high" (Heb. 1:3).

Verse 22: *"But Jesus answered and said, Ye know not what ye ask. Are ye able to drink of the cup that I shall drink of, and to be baptized with the baptism that I am baptized with? They say unto Him, We are able."*

"Ye know not what ye ask." In the mother's ambition for her sons she saw only the honor, glory, and happiness they might attain from such positions as she coveted for them. She knew nothing of the other consequences involved in her request. She never imagined that her sons would face suffering, trials, and finally *death*. We know

James was martyred by Herod (Acts 12:2), and John was exiled to Patmos where God gave him *The Revelation.* The Bible does not tell us how that beloved disciple finally passed from this life into the presence of God, but when this mother requested seats for him and for his brother James on the right hand and the left hand of the King, she was asking for them not only a position of honor and glory, but also a position of danger— suffering, persecution, and martyrdom. The King was crucified and His apostles were martyred.

"Are ye able to drink of the cup that I shall drink of . . . ?" To *drink the cup*, in Scriptures, usually signifies suffering, afflictions, persecution, and even death. (Please study Matthew 26:39, Psalms 73:10 and 75:8 in connection with the cup.) The cup to which Jesus referred is mentioned again in John 18:11: "Then said Jesus unto Peter, Put up thy sword into the sheath: *the cup which my Father hath given me, shall I not drink it?"*

Matthew 26:36-39 speaks of the cup in describing the agony of Jesus in the Garden of Gethsemane: "Then cometh Jesus with them unto a place called Gethsemane, and saith unto the disciples, Sit ye here, while I go and pray yonder. And He took with Him Peter and the two sons of Zebedee, and began to be sorrowful and very heavy. Then saith He unto them, My soul is exceeding sorrowful, even unto death: tarry ye here, and watch with me.

320

"And He went a little farther, and fell on His face, and prayed, saying, *O my Father, if it be POSSIBLE, let this CUP pass from me: nevertheless not as I will, but as thou wilt.*"

Mark 14:32-36 tells of the cup: "And they came to a place which was named Gethsemane: and He saith to His disciples, Sit ye here, while I shall pray. And He taketh with Him Peter and James and John, and began to be sore amazed, and to be very heavy; and saith unto them, My soul is exceeding sorrowful unto death: tarry ye here, and watch. And He went forward a little, and fell on the ground, and prayed that, if it were possible, the hour might pass from Him. And He said, *Abba, Father, all things are possible unto thee; take away this cup from me: nevertheless not what I will, but what thou wilt.*"

Luke also speaks of this cup, and tells of the perspiration that fell from the brow of Jesus:

"And He came out, and went, as He was wont, to the Mount of Olives; and His disciples also followed Him. And when He was at the place, He said unto them, Pray that ye enter not into temptation. And He was withdrawn from them about a stone's cast, and kneeled down, and prayed, saying, *Father, if thou be willing, remove this cup from me: nevertheless not my will, but thine, be done.*

"And there appeared an angel unto Him from heaven, strengthening Him. And being in an agony

He prayed more earnestly: *and His sweat was as it were GREAT DROPS OF BLOOD falling down to the ground.* And when He rose up from prayer, and was come to His disciples, He found them sleeping for sorrow, and said unto them, Why sleep ye? rise and pray, lest ye enter into temptation" (Luke 22:39-46).

Luke was a physician, and as a doctor he would naturally observe blood before an ordinary person would be aware of it. But there are no words in man's language that could adequately describe this horrible cup which Jesus drank for you and for me!

". . . *and to be baptized with the baptism that I am baptized with?*" This undoubtedly signifies the same thing as the cup signifies. Jesus was asking James and John if they were able to endure the pain, the heartbreaks and disappointment with which He was faced and which He must endure. Were they able to bear the sorrows that would cover them like a flood? Would they endure when they were sunk beneath calamities or plunged into the depths of despair and persecution? (Please read Psalms 59:1,2; 124:2-5; Isaiah 43:2; and Lamentations 3:54.)

"They say unto Him, We are able." Just as the mother of these young men did not realize the import of what she asked, so *they, in reply,* did not know what they answered! I see no lack of love for the Lord in these two. There can be no

doubt of their love, even though at this time that love was tinged with personal ambition. They were willing to follow Him anywhere He led—or so they thought, having no idea of what it would mean to them to follow Him all the way.

Verse 23: *"And He saith unto them, Ye shall drink indeed of my cup, and be baptized with the baptism that I am baptized with: but to sit on my right hand, and on my left, is not mine to give, but it shall be given to them for whom it is prepared of my Father."*

"Ye shall drink indeed of my cup . . . ." No one but Jesus could drink the fulness of that cup, no one but He could drain the last bitter dregs. But insofar as it is possible for man to partake of the sufferings of Jesus, these two brothers did indeed partake of His afflictions, His persecutions, and even of His death. Those who walk with Him must suffer with Him. As I have previously stated, James was slain by Herod (Acts 12:2). John, the beloved disciple who leaned his head on the breast of Jesus when they were reclining at the Last Supper, was exiled to the Isle of Patmos for his testimony. We are not told what death he died, but he spent the evening years of his life on a small island—ten miles long by six miles across, barren, rocky, one of the places to which Rome banished her exiles. We know from his own testimony that John was a companion

of others in tribulation and suffering (Rev. 1:9).

"*. . . but to sit on my right hand, and on my left, is not mine to give, but it shall be given to them for whom it is prepared of my Father.*" As we study the life of Christ we see how thoroughly the Lord Jesus took a humble, lowly place for our sakes. In this laying aside of authority He gives silent rebuke to man's self-seeking for glory, honor, and fame. It is true that all things were created *by* Christ and *for* Christ (Col. 1:16), and all are His to give; but as Mediator He came not to do His own will, but the will of God the Father who sent Him. He would and could give rewards to those who follow Him, but only to such as should be *entitled* to His rewards *according to the purpose of God*. He could not bestow honors out of the course of things as planned and willed by the heavenly Father. Therefore the places of honor being sought by James and John were not His to give—*EXCEPT to those for whom such places are prepared by God the Father.* Those positions of honor will be occupied by persons who have earned that position by means of obedience and faithful stewardship. Everything about the Kingdom over which Jesus will be King is divinely arranged. Nothing is left to chance or fate. Even Jesus, King of kings and Lord of lords, will not interfere with the divine appointment concerning His Kingdom on earth and His reign as King. Therefore He did not deny that these brothers, these sons of Zebedee, would have a place in His Kingdom—but neither did He foretell their degree of glory.

Verse 24: *"And when the ten heard it, they were moved with indignation against the two brethren."*

The twelve apostles were present, and the other ten heard the request made by the mother of James and John, and they also heard the reply the brothers made to the questions Jesus asked them. It did not matter to them that Jesus had refused the request. They were offended at the presumption of James and John, offended at their ambition and their bid to be exalted above others. It is evident that on more than one occasion Jesus had preferred Peter, James, and John over the other disciples, but it is nowhere suggested that the others resented that preference. However, when these two sought precedence for themselves, the other disciples were *"moved with indignation against the two brethren."*

Verse 25: *"But Jesus called them unto Him, and said, Ye know that the princes of the Gentiles exercise dominion over them, and they that are great exercise authority upon them."*

The Son of God was making His last journey to Jerusalem. His earthly ministry was drawing to a close. He had not much time left with these men, and He moved daily in the shadow of the cross. He was burdened and heavy of heart, and the responsibility that rested upon Him was of a magnitude such as defied human conception. Even if the disciples had thoroughly understood and sympathized with Him, no finite mind could have grasped the depth or scope of Calvary from the Saviour's viewpoint.

But the disciples *did not* understand. Furthermore, their little band was divided by jealousy, envy, and personal ambition. It was in the hands of these weak, selfish, and unperceptive men that Jesus would soon leave the stewardship of the Gospel and the full weight of carrying on the work He had begun. Yet note, if you will, the divine patience and longsuffering with which He *"called them unto Him"* to continue His teaching of humility and service!

"The princes of the Gentiles" speaks of the Gentile rulers—kings and princes—who governed the great Gentile kingdoms. They ruled with authority—*by FORCE if need be.*

". . . and they that are great exercise authority upon them." So-called "great" men are often presumptuous and overbearing, using their authority with a heavy hand. They are many times so filled with a sense of power, so deluded with their own importance, that they command—and expect—unquestioned obedience from those whom they command. They are authoritative, but not necessarily

considerate of those over whom they have authority.

Verse 26: *"But it shall not be so among you: but whosoever will be great among you, let him be your minister."*

"But it shall not be so among you . . . ." To be a disciple of Jesus was a high and honorable calling, and certainly to follow Him made the disciples partakers of His Kingdom. But His Kingdom was not to be like *earthly* kingdoms. These men must learn that the rule in the Kingdom of Heaven would be administered in love, compassion, and righteousness, not by pomp and grandeur. The dignity of His Kingdom would be in humble service. There would be no *"lords"* over God's heritage (I Pet. 5:3).

". . . but whosoever will be GREAT among you, let him be your minister." Whosoever serves most will be greatest in the Kingdom of Heaven. The one who is most humble and lowly in service to others will be most honored in the Kingdom of Heaven. In this day and hour, when we look around us and see the "nobles" of this earth, men in high places in religion contending for the highest office, the most power and honor, we need to hear the gentle voice of Jesus saying to us, *"It shall not be so among you. If you would be great in my Kingdom, lay aside all pomp and pretense and serve others in humbleness of heart."*

Beloved, as born again believers, sons of God, we must quit longing for and seeking out power, influence, and praise of men. If we hope to be great in the Kingdom of Heaven, our greatness must be attained by humble service and by ministering to the brethren.

Verse 27: *"And whosoever will be chief among you, let him be your servant."*

The Apostle Paul wrote to the Galatian believers: "Brethren, ye have been called unto liberty; only use not liberty for an occasion to the flesh, but by love *serve one another"* (Gal. 5:13). And in I Corinthians 9:19 he said, "Though I be free from all men, *yet have I made myself servant unto all,* that I might gain the more." The way *"up"* with Christ is *"down."* To be *"chief"* in the service of the Lord, one must become a *servant,* submitting entirely to Jesus. It is necessary to realize in the heart the unworthiness of oneself and the absolute worthiness of the Saviour.

Verse 28: *"Even as the Son of man came not to be ministered unto, but to minister, and to give His life a ransom for many."*

"Even as the Son of man came . . . ." Very early in His ministry Jesus made it clear that He had come into the world in a humble way, and that He was without earthly possessions. In Matthew 8:20 He declared: "The foxes have holes,

and the birds of the air have nests; but the Son of man hath not where to lay His head." He came to *give,* not to receive, and He is here pointing to Himself as an example set before the disciples who were yearning for prominence as set by worldly standards. He was inviting them to check *His own life* since He had come into His public ministry.

He who had the form of God "made Himself of no reputation" and came down to this earth in "the form of a servant" (Phil. 2:6, 7). Paul reminds us, "For ye know the grace of our Lord Jesus Christ, that, *though He was rich, yet for your sakes He became poor, that ye through His poverty might be rich*" (II Cor. 8:9). He did not come with pomp and pride. He came as a Babe in a manger, born in a stable and reared in a carpenter's shop. He never performed a miracle in order to provide for His own needs. His miracles were always for others. He lived humbly, rendering good to others, always first in sufferings and self-denial. He did not come into the world to be served, but to serve others, *"not to be ministered unto, but to minister."*

On one occasion, Jesus stepped into the place of a lowly servant, perhaps the lowliest servant in any household:

"Now before the feast of the passover, when Jesus knew that His hour was come that He should depart out of this world unto the Father, having loved His own which were in the world, He loved them unto the end. And supper being ended, the devil having now put into the heart of Judas Iscariot, Simon's son, to betray Him; Jesus knowing that the Father had given all things into His hands, and that He was come from God, and went to God; *He riseth from supper, and laid aside His garments; and took a towel, and girded Himself. After that He poureth water into a bason, and began to wash the disciples' feet, and to wipe them with the towel wherewith He was girded. . . .*

"So after He had washed their feet, and had taken His garments, and was set down again, He said unto them, Know ye what I have done to you? Ye call me Master and Lord: and ye say well; for so I am. If I then, your Lord and Master, have washed your feet; ye also ought to wash one another's feet. For I have given you an example, that ye should do as I have done to you.

"Verily, verily, I say unto you, The servant is not greater than his lord; neither he that is sent greater than he that sent him. If ye know these things, happy are ye if ye do them" (John 13:1-17 in part).

"*. . . and to give His life a RANSOM for many.*" This is a phrase of the highest moment, a phrase that expresses what the Saviour had not previously expressed so clearly to the disciples. He had repeatedly spoken of His approaching death (Matt. 16:21; 17:23; 20:19). Now He makes it known that His death would be different from any death in past or future—that is, His death would be redeeming and vicarious. This was the design and plan of His coming into the world in a body of humiliation. This remarkable statement was no doubt quite amazing to the disciples, amazing beyond their comprehension, until later when the Holy Spirit brought the words of Jesus to their remembrance, as He promised: "The Comforter, which is the Holy Ghost, whom the Father will send in my name, He shall teach you all things, and *bring all things to your remembrance, whatsoever I have said unto you*" (John 14:26).

The Greek word translated *"ransom"* is *lutron.* The Greek verb *luo* means "to loose, release, or set free, as to set free a prisoner." The same word is used in Acts 22:30 when the Apostle Paul, a prisoner in Jerusalem, was *"loosed* from his bands." The words translated "redeem" and "redemption" in the New Testament are also formed from the Greek word *lutron.*

The Greek word here translated *"for"* means *instead of.* This involves substitution, and substitution demands a vicarious death. So the Lord Jesus announced that He was giving His life as a ransom to redeem, set free, release, and loose men from captivity, from the slavery and power of sin, spiritual death, and damnation. He would pay

the ransom for all who would accept His substitutionary sacrifice, He would die *in our stead.*

In Mark 14:24—and many times in the epistles of
Paul—we find the Greek preposition *huber* ("for"),
with reference to the death of the Lord Jesus for
us. The word means "in behalf of...for the benefit of," and derivatively, *"instead of."* I Timothy
2:5, 6 explains: "For there is one God, and one
Mediator between God and men, the Man Christ
Jesus; *who gave Himself a ransom for all,* to be
testified in due time."

What Jesus actually said to His disciples on
this occasion was that He had come to give Himself a substitutionary ransom *for all.* In other
words, *"for MANY"* in our present verse does not
conflict with the *"for ALL"* in Paul's statement
to Timothy. The atoning death of the Lord Jesus
Christ made it compatible with the divine justice
of Almighty God that *ALL should be saved IF
they would accept salvation on the ground* of the
substitutionary ransom paid by Jesus in full. In
that sense, Jesus gave Himself *"a ransom for
ALL."* He tasted death *"for EVERY man"* (Heb.
2:9). He is "the propitiation for our sins: and
not for our's only, but also for *the sins of the
whole world"* (I John 2:2).

But the death of Jesus was not divinely designed to secure the salvation of *every* person,
even against their will. And so in the sense
of specific results Jesus came "to give His life

a ransom for MANY." His vicarious, substitutionary death was *SUFFICIENT for all,* and it was
*effectual for MANY—*as many as *received* Him
(John 1:12).

I pray you will not jump to any conclusions
after reading what I have just said—namely, that
the vicarious death of Jesus was not expected to
secure salvation for every person on earth. Since
God was omniscient, He knew that not all would
accept the death of Jesus by faith; but that does
not make it true that He did not *want* them to
accept the salvation He provided! Jesus died for
ALL, but in God's omniscience He knew when
He designed, perfected, and offered salvation, that
not all would be saved. In His omniscience, He
knew man even before man was created.

We should be extremely thankful for the Lord
Jesus and for His love; but we must never forget
that it was God the Father who "so loved the
world, that He gave His only begotten Son, that
whosoever believeth in Him should not perish, but
have everlasting life" (John 3:16).

"In this was manifested the love of God toward
us, because that God sent His only begotten Son
into the world, that we might live through Him.
Herein is love, not that we loved God, but that
He loved us, and sent His Son to be the propitiation for our sins" (I John 4:9, 10).

"Forasmuch as ye know that ye were not redeemed with corruptible things, as silver and gold,

from your vain conversation received by tradition from your fathers; but with the precious blood of Christ, as of a lamb without blemish and without spot" (I Pet. 1:18, 19).

In Hebrews chapter 10 we read: "Having therefore, brethren, boldness to enter into the holiest *by the blood of Jesus, by a new and living way, which He hath consecrated for us, through the veil, that is to say, HIS FLESH*; and having an high priest over the house of God; let us draw near with a true heart in full assurance of faith, having our hearts sprinkled from an evil conscience, and our bodies washed with pure water" (Heb. 10:19-22).

Then in Isaiah chapter 53 we read of the vicarious atonement of the Lord Jesus Christ:

"Who hath believed our report? and to whom is the arm of the Lord revealed? For He shall grow up before Him as a tender plant, and as a root out of a dry ground: He hath no form nor comeliness; and when we shall see Him, there is no beauty that we should desire Him.

"He is despised and rejected of men; a Man of sorrows, and acquainted with grief: and we hid as it were our faces from Him; He was despised, and we esteemed Him not. Surely *He hath borne our griefs, and carried our sorrows:* yet we did esteem Him stricken, smitten of God, and afflicted. But *He was wounded for our transgressions, He was bruised for our iniquities: the chastisement*

*of our peace was upon Him; and with His stripes
we are healed.*

"All we like sheep have gone astray; we have
turned every one to his own way; and *the Lord
hath laid on Him the iniquity of us all.* He was
oppressed, and He was afflicted, yet He opened
not His mouth: He is brought as a lamb to the
slaughter, and as a sheep before her shearers is
dumb, so He openeth not His mouth.

"He was taken from prison and from judgment:
and who shall declare His generation? for He was
cut off out of the land of the living: for the
transgression of my people was He stricken. And
He made His grave with the wicked, and with
the rich in His death; because He had done no
violence, neither was any deceit in His mouth.
Yet it pleased the Lord to bruise Him; He hath
put Him to grief: when thou shalt make His soul
an offering for sin, He shall see His seed, He shall
prolong His days, and the pleasure of the Lord
shall prosper in His hand. He shall see of the
travail of His soul, and shall be satisfied: by His
knowledge shall my righteous Servant justify many;
for *He shall bear their iniquities.*

"Therefore will I divide Him a portion with
the great, and He shall divide the spoil with the
strong; because He hath poured out His soul unto
death: and He was numbered with the transgressors; and *He bare the sin of many,* and made
intercession for the transgressors."

Finally, in Revelation 1:5, John the Beloved speaks of "Jesus Christ, who is the faithful witness, and the first begotten of the dead, and the prince of the kings of the earth. . . . *Him that loved us, and washed us from our sins in His own blood.*"

At the institution of the Lord's Supper, as He passed the cup, Jesus announced: "This is my blood of the new testament, which is shed for many for the remission of sins" (Matt. 26:28). Through the Saviour's death and His shed blood we have "remission" of sins, and *remission* means more than remitting or cancelling a penalty. It means the *letting loose* from the sins which *brought* the penalty. That was the end Jesus had in view in going to the cross and laying His life down for us. The penalty of sin is death. He came to bear that penalty in our stead.

The death of Jesus on the cross as the vicarious offering for sin stands alone—*the one basis and procuring cause* of redemption from the damnation and eternal death sin brings. His blood was shed for the remission of sin, and it is *His blood alone* that brings remission.

The account of the Lord's Supper is given four times in the New Testament: Matthew 26:26-29, Mark 14:22-25, Luke 22:17-20, and I Corinthians 11:23-26. In all four accounts the blood of Jesus is definitely mentioned, emphasizing the vital fact that Christ laid His life down and shed His blood for the remission of sin. No one should doubt this cardinal doctrine of Christianity, which is made so impressive in the Scriptures. Apart from the shedding of blood there is no remission (Heb. 9:22). We are redeemed through the precious blood of Jesus and not by corruptible things.

Jesus alone finished redemption, and *He finished it ALONE.* No one helped Him, and nothing can be added to what He finished. No one can do over again what He finished when He gave up the ghost on Calvary—and thank God, no one *needs* to do it over again! It is done, finished, accomplished, and what God Almighty provided by means of the death of Jesus cannot be improved upon, needs nothing added. It is as perfect and as complete as God Himself.

Jesus said to His disciples, *"Follow ME."* This teaches me that the spirit in which Christ lived and died here on this earth should be *our* spirit today in living for Christ and, if it should become necessary, *dying* for Him. We are sons of God now (I John 3:2), and as sons of God we are to be identified with Him in all things, especially in His complete renunciation of sin and His complete devotion to God. But even though we live a life so devoted to God that we imitate Christ in all that we do or say, and such devotion to God should lead us to martyrdom and literal crucifixion, our death could not add anything to that which Christ Himself has finished and made perfect through His shed blood.

Only the Lord Jesus could look to the heavenly Father and say, "I have glorified thee on the earth: I have finished the work which thou gavest me to do" (John 17:4). If you will read the intercessory prayer of Jesus (recorded in John chapter 17), you will find that He used the personal pronoun "I" thirty-one times. I declare unto you that no one but the Lamb of God, God in flesh, could make the marvelous statements He made in this prayer. He is the center, soul, bloodstream, and life of all that we have in redemption and the hope of an eternal inheritance with Him in heaven. All mortals, regardless of how spiritual they may be, must say with Paul, *"By the GRACE OF GOD I am what I am"* (I Cor. 15:10).

The suffering, death, and sacrifice of Jesus should check all religious ambition and jealousy in the hearts of the saints of God. If we will turn our eyes upon the suffering Saviour, the awareness of His suffering will cure us of worldly striving and will remove all religious jealousy and envy from our hearts. God give us grace to be faithful servants until He calls us unto Himself.

The Healing of Two Blind Men

Verse 29: *"And as they departed from Jericho, a great multitude followed Him."*

"And as they departed from Jericho . . . ." Jericho at that time was a large and busy city located

approximately eight miles west of the Jordan river and nineteen miles northeast from Jerusalem. It was near the city of Jericho that the Israelites crossed the Jordan when they entered the land of Canaan (Josh. 3:16). In fact, Jericho was the first city taken by Joshua, and he destroyed it to its very foundations. (The record of the miracle of that destruction is found in Joshua chapter 6.) He not only *destroyed* the city, he also pronounced a *curse* on whosoever should rebuild it (Josh. 6:20-26). That curse was literally fulfilled five hundred years later, in the days of Ahab (I Kings 16:34). Jericho later became the location of the school of the prophets (II Kings 2:5).

It was near the city of Jericho that Elisha performed the miracle of changing the bitter water into water that was sweet and wholesome:

"And the men of the city said unto Elisha, Behold, I pray thee, the situation of this city is pleasant, as my lord seeth: but the water is naught, and the ground barren. And he said, Bring me a new cruse, and put salt therein. And they brought it to him.

"And he went forth unto the spring of the waters, and cast the salt in there, and said, Thus saith the LORD, I have healed these waters; there shall not be from thence any more death or barren land. So the waters were healed unto this day, according to the saying of Elisha which he spake" (II Kings 2:19-22).

In size, Jericho was second only to the city of Jerusalem. It was known as the city of palm trees because there were so many beautiful palms in that vicinity. Even today a few palms remain. It was at Jericho that King Herod died with a most terrible and foul disease. Today Jericho is a small village inhabited by only a small group. It is nothing like it was in the days when Jesus tabernacled among men.

The Jericho road which runs between Jerusalem and Jericho is called "the wilderness of Jericho." Modern travelers declare that it is the most dangerous road in all of Palestine. The parable of the good Samaritan (Luke 10:30-37) speaks of the man who "went down from Jerusalem to Jericho and fell among thieves" on the way. Many have been robbed, stripped of their earthly belongings, on the Jericho road. Jesus was going to Jerusalem from the east side of Jordan, and His journey would naturally lead Him through the city of Jericho.

"... *a great multitude followed Him.*" Luke 19:1 tells us that Jesus *entered and passed through* Jericho. To me, this suggests that He did not remain there very long. He entered—but He passed through the city to the other side traveling on toward Jerusalem.

Verse 30: "*And, behold, two blind men sitting by the way side, when they heard that Jesus passed by, cried out, saying, Have mercy on us, O Lord, thou son of David."*

We find an account of this healing in Mark 10:46-52, and a similar one in Luke 18:35-43. It has been suggested that a discrepancy exists here between the accounts given by Mark, Luke, and Matthew. These three narratives *supplement* each other, but there is no contradiction. We may not fully understand all about what occurred, but the Holy Spirit gave these words to Matthew, Mark, and Luke, and they penned them down. Therefore there can be no discrepancy or error here.

Matthew and Mark refer to a miracle of healing as Jesus *left—"departed from"—*the city of Jericho on His way to Jerusalem. Mark 10:46 says, ". . . as He *went out of Jericho* with His disciples and a great number of people, blind Bartimaeus, the son of Timaeus, sat by the highway side begging." Bartimaeus, seemingly of the same impulsive nature as Peter, was outspoken and active. He was one of the two, and he cried out, *"O Lord, thou son of David."* The other blind man did not speak and we read nothing about him after his eyes were opened, other than that he followed Jesus (v. 34).

Luke 18:35 speaks of a miracle which occurred *before Jesus entered* the city of Jericho—*"as He was come nigh unto* Jericho." We must remember that if all Jesus said and did had been written down, "even the world itself could not contain the books that should be written" (John 21:25).

We do not know how many blind men Jesus healed during His ministry on earth—it could have been hundreds—that were not written down. Therefore it is not disturbing to me to read the accounts recorded in these Gospels even though they do not identically correspond.

It is true that Mark's account mentions *only ONE* blind man, but I would point out that he does not say that there were *no more* than one. There could have been two—or several. He mentioned *one* because that one (Bartimaeus) was very outspoken. If Mark had clearly declared that there was *only one* blind man healed, there would be a contradiction in the accounts. But there is no contradiction.

"Have mercy on us, O Lord, thou son of David." This was the name by which the promised Messiah was to be known. The first verse of Matthew's Gospel reads: "The book of the generation of *Jesus Christ, the son of David,* the son of Abraham." He was to be a direct descendant of David, as the prophets prophesied, and the promises to Israel were to come through the son of David:

"The Lord hath sworn in truth unto David; He will not turn from it: Of the fruit of thy body will I set upon thy throne. If thy children will keep my covenant and my testimony that I shall teach them, their children shall also sit upon thy throne for evermore" (Psalm 132:11, 12).

342

Verse 31: *"And the multitude rebuked them, because they should hold their peace: but they cried the more, saying, Have mercy on us, O Lord, thou son of David."*

"The multitude rebuked them . . . ." The multitude wanted to hear what Jesus was saying but the cries of the blind men were so loud they drowned out the voice of the Saviour. The crowd therefore rebuked them and commanded them to *"hold their peace."* But the rebuke did not silence them. It only caused them to cry out the louder, saying, *"Have mercy on us, O Lord, thou son of David!"*

Mark 10:49, 50 tells us, of Bartimaeus, "Jesus stood still, and commanded him to be called. And they call the blind man, saying unto him, Be of good comfort, rise; He calleth thee. *And he, casting away his garment, rose, and came to Jesus."* The garment Bartimaeus cast aside was his outer garment, a kind of cape thrown loosely about him. It was a cumbersome garment, and blind Bartimaeus was in a hurry to get to Jesus. He had never seen the Lord, but he had heard Him. Faith comes by hearing, and hearing by the Word of God. Every word Jesus spoke was the Word of God. The blind man heard the words of Jesus, he had faith in Jesus, and in faith he hurried to Him.

Verse 32: *"And Jesus stood still, and called*

them, and said, What will ye that I shall do unto you?"

"Jesus stood still . . . ." Jesus always has time to hear the cry of a needy soul. The voice of sincere prayer from poor, lost souls will cause the Son of God to "stand still" and hear the plea of that prayer. He is equally able to supply the need of His born again ones.

". . . and called them, and said, What will ye that I shall do unto you?" This meant that whatever the need, Jesus was able to supply that need. They should make their requests known—although, because He was God in flesh, Jesus already knew what that request would be.

Verse 33: *"They say unto Him, Lord, that our eyes may be opened."*

The Lord's question was not hard for the blind men to answer. They did not need time to think it over and decide what they desired. More than all else, they wanted physical sight. They answered immediately, *"Lord, that our EYES may be opened!"*

Many times when sinners hear the call of Jesus and are convicted of sin, they put off answering the call. They want to think about it. Like Felix when Paul reasoned with him, they wait for a more "convenient season" (Acts 24:25). The devil always tempts sinners to put off salvation; but these blind men did not ask for more time, they

344

did not say, "Let us discuss it awhile." They did not even say, "Lord, *IF you are able* . . . ." They put no frills on their prayer, they used no moving language to dress it up. They spoke seven words, and those seven words brought their eyesight. The deep desire of their hearts clothed itself in simple, earnest language, and that is the way Jesus wants us to approach Him in our need.

Verse 34: *"So Jesus had compassion on them, and touched their eyes: and immediately their eyes received sight, and they followed Him."*

"Jesus had compassion on them . . . ." In the darkness of their blindness, deprived of the beauties around them, these men missed so much, and because of their lack of eyesight they lived in poverty. Their pitiable condition touched the heart of Jesus and He was moved with compassion, *"and touched their eyes."* How tender must have been the Saviour's touch! (In Mark 10:52, concerning Bartimaeus, we read, "Jesus said unto him, *"Go thy way; thy faith hath made thee whole."*)

". . . and IMMEDIATELY their eyes received sight . . . ." Only a touch from Jesus and blinded eyes were given sight. The touch of Jesus is powerful, yet tender and loving. Only a touch from Him and lepers were cleansed and made perfect. Only a touch from Him and a dead boy was given life. The touch of Jesus can not only put life in a body that has died, but His touch

345

can make alive a dead spirit that is destined to die eternally in the lake of fire.

The two blind men received their sight *"and they followed Him."* We prove that we have been delivered from the darkness of sin by following Jesus. We do not follow Him *in order to BE saved,* we follow Him *because we ARE saved.* We do not change *the habits of life in order to BE saved,* we change the habits of life *because we ARE saved.* Jesus is the Light of the world, and when He came "the people which sat in darkness saw great light; and to them which sat in the region and shadow of death light is sprung up" (Matt. 4:16).

Jesus said, *"I am the LIGHT OF THE WORLD:* he that followeth me shall not walk in darkness, but shall have the light of life" (John 8:12).

Jesus also said, *"Ye shall know the TRUTH, and the truth shall make you FREE. . . .* If the Son therefore shall make you free, ye shall be free indeed" (John 8:32, 36).

Jesus sets men free from darkness and death, He gives them light and life everlasting. If you have never called on Him to open your blinded eyes in order that you may see your need of a Saviour and cry out to Him for salvation and forgiveness, you are still in sin and in spiritual darkness — and it is the desire of the devil to keep you there! He knows that if you ever see the blackness of sin and your need to be *freed* from

346

that sin, you will call on Jesus and He will deliver you from darkness, destruction, and eternal death.

Paul declared this great truth: "If our Gospel be hid, it is hid to them that are lost: in whom the god of this world (Satan) hath blinded the minds of them which believe not, lest the light of the glorious Gospel of Christ, who is the image of God, should shine unto them" (II Cor. 4:3, 4).

The idea of real, true sacrifice and service takes hold upon us extremely slowly. Among church people and professed Christians there is much talk of consecration, much talk of self-denial; but the contrast between reality and sham is sharp and evident. May the God of love and the Christ of compassionate tenderness help us to learn the secret of the Lord Jesus—that is, that the only way to true power and true greatness is the way of humble service and sacrifice, the way of the cross. May we hear and answer His call, "Take up thy cross and follow me."